CRITICAL CONVERSATIONS ABOUT PLAGIARISM

LENSES ON COMPOSITION STUDIES
Series Editors, Sheryl I. Fontaine and Steve Westbrook

Lenses on Composition Studies offers authors the unique opportunity to write for advanced undergraduate and beginning graduate students who are new to the discipline of Composition Studies. While the series aims to maintain the rigor and depth of contemporary composition scholarship, it seeks to offer this particular group of students an introduction to key disciplinary issues in accessible prose that does not assume prior advanced knowledge of scholars and theoretical debates. The series provides instructors of advanced undergraduate or beginning graduate students texts that are both appropriate and inviting for this fresh but professionally directed audience.

OTHER BOOKS IN THE SERIES
Bibliographic Research in Composition Studies, by Vicki Byard (2009)

Critical Conversations About Plagiarism

Edited by
Michael Donnelly, Rebecca Ingalls,
Tracy Ann Morse, Joanna Castner Post,
and Anne Meade Stockdell-Giesler

Parlor Press
Anderson, South Carolina
www.parlorpress.com

Parlor Press LLC, Anderson, South Carolina, USA

S A N: 2 5 4 - 8 8 7 9

Library of Congress Cataloging-in-Publication Data

Critical conversations about plagiarism / edited by Michael Donnelly... [et al.].
     p. cm. -- (Lenses on composition studies)
  Includes bibliographical references and index.
  ISBN 978-1-60235-348-0 (pbk. : alk. paper) -- ISBN 978-1-60235-349-7 (hardcover : alk. paper) -- ISBN 978-1-60235-350-3 (adobe ebook) -- ISBN 978-1-60235-351-0 (epub)
  1. Plagiarism. 2. Imitation in literature. 3. Authorship--Study and teaching. I. Donnelly, Michael, 1968-
  PN167.C75 2012
  808.02'5--dc23
                                    2012030779

1 2 3 4 5

Cover design by David Blakesley.
Printed on acid-free paper.

Parlor Press, LLC is an independent publisher of scholarly and trade titles in print and multimedia formats. This book is available in paper, cloth and eBook formats from Parlor Press on the World Wide Web at http://www.parlorpress.com or through online and brick-and-mortar bookstores. For submission information or to find out about Parlor Press publications, write to Parlor Press, 3015 Brackenberry Drive, Anderson, South Carolina, 29621, or email editor@parlorpress.com.

Contents

Preface

As a field, composition studies acknowledges that writing is a complicated process; indeed, one might say its existence as a field of study is predicated upon that fundamental belief. Yet, discussions about plagiarism for students tend to remain flat and simplistic and often reinscribe a traditional, antagonistic divide between students and teachers. In *Guiding Students from Cheating and Plagiarism to Honesty and Integrity: Strategies for Change*, for example, a book intended to help teachers and students discuss issues of academic integrity and create more honest school climates, David Callahan describes academic culture as a "culture of cheating" that must be dismantled (xvi). This view, in which students are assumed to be criminals and their teachers are the police, is, we feel, counterproductive to the goals of higher education in general and of writing instruction in particular. In contrast, we believe that as teachers and scholars we must do more than simplistically define plagiarism and exhort students to "do honest work." We must engage them in an intellectual and critical discussion of a multivalent issue.

There has been groundbreaking work on plagiarism by a variety of scholars, from a variety of quarters (LaFollette; Robin; Woodmansee and Jaszi). The majority of critical scholarship has, unsurprisingly, emanated from English Studies. Some of this work appropriately falls under the category of literary history (Kewes; Macfarlane; Mazzeo; Randall), but the most significant body of work has been in or attached to composition studies (Buranen and Roy; Haviland and Mullin; Howard, "New"; Howard, *Standing*; Howard and Robillard; Vicinus and Eisner). Despite this growing body of work, the general approach to discussing plagiarism *with students* continues to focus on avoiding plagiarism rather than engaging in critical discussion of the issues (Fox, Johns and Keller; Francis; Gaines; Harris, *Plagiarism*; Harris, *Using*; Lathrop and Foss, *Guiding*; Lathrop and Foss, *Student*;

Lipson; Menager-Beeley and Paulos; Rozycki and Clabaugh; Stern). As Lise Buranen and Alice M. Roy explain in their scholarly collection:

> [. . .] in textbooks and in university publications about academic integrity, plagiarism is often treated as a monolithic, uncomplicated concept or event, whose meaning is simply taken for granted. The assumption seems to be that we all know what we mean when we talk about it: it just is. In academia, in the sciences, and in writing handbooks and classroom instruction, the main emphasis is on prevention and punishment. (xvii)

Critical discussion of the issues surrounding plagiarism is increasingly important in a world of rapidly developing technologies and changing attitudes toward language and literacy. Yet the significant scholarly work in this area, like Buranen and Roy's, tends to assume an audience of other academics, scholars, and teachers and is not intended for nor accessible to those who are actually at the center of the issue, namely, our students.

We envision this book serving an audience of advanced undergraduates and beginning graduate students interested in specific discussions related to composition studies. Our essay chapters, written by teacher-scholars in composition studies, literacy studies, and literature, are written to engage advanced students in thoughtful, theoretical inquiry that is guided by pedagogical scaffolding in the form of reading response questions, thematic points for writing and discussion, and collaborative exercises. With this combination of theoretical challenge and practical application, our text lends itself to filling a critical gap in classroom reading and discussion as well as in graduate teaching assistant training.

With this idea of conversation across approaches in mind, the authors in this collection represent a variety of positions within the academic world: fiction writer, graduate student, literary theorist, director of a writing center, middle school teacher, social psychologist, English professor. All of them are teachers, most of them in English studies at the university level. They bring to bear their different experiences with teaching and with encountering and addressing plagiarism. Their diverse experiences and approaches offer a gateway into conversations among and between teachers and students.

Moreover, we believe our collection may also serve first-year students. With so many how-to/how-not-to texts out there, we understand the potential of our collection for use in programs that want to address issues of academic integrity within their freshmen seminar programs. We think some of the essays in this collection would help first-year students think about plagiarism in new, relevant ways.

Critical Conversations about Plagiarism fills a student need in the current literature: nuanced, critical, scholarly discussions of plagiarism that are accessible to them. In so doing, we invite students *and* teachers into a conversation about a range of issues raised by plagiarism.

WORKS CITED

Buranen, Lise, and Alice M. Roy, eds. *Perspectives on Plagiarism and Intellectual Property in a Postmodern World*. Albany, NY: SUNY P, 1999. Print.

Callahan, David. Preface. *Guiding Students from Cheating and Plagiarism to Honesty and Integrity: Strategies for Change*. Ed. Ann Lathrop and Kathleen Foss. Westport, CT: Libraries Unlimited, 2005. xv–xvi. Print.

Fox, Tom, Julia Mary Johns, and Sara Keller. *Cite It Right: The SourceAid Guide to Citation, Research, and Avoiding Plagiarism*. Osterville, MA: SourceAid, 2007. Print.

Francis, Barbara. *Other People's Words: What Plagiarism Is and How to Avoid It*. Berkeley Heights, NJ: Enslow Publishers, 2005. Print.

Gaines, Ann. *Don't Steal Copyrighted Stuff!: Avoiding Plagiarism and Illegal Internet Downloading*. Berkeley Heights, NJ: Enslow Publishers, 2007. Print.

Harris, Robert A. *The Plagiarism Handbook: Strategies for Preventing, Detecting, and Dealing With Plagiarism*. Glendale, CA: Pyrczak Publishing, 2001. Print.

—. *Using Sources Effectively: Strengthening Your Writing and Avoiding Plagiarism*. Glendale, CA: Pyrczak Publishing, 2004. Print.

Haviland, Carol Peterson, and Joan A. Mullin, eds. *Who Owns This Text? Plagiarism, Authorship, and Disciplinary Cultures*. Boulder: UP of Colorado, 2005. Print.

Howard, Rebecca Moore. "The New Abolitionism Comes to Plagiarism." *Perspectives on Plagiarism and Intellectual Property in a Postmodern World*. Ed. Lise Buranen and Alice M. Roy. Albany, NY: SUNY P, 1999. 87–95. Print.

—. *Standing in the Shadow of Giants: Plagiarists, Authors, Collaborators*. Norwood, NJ: Ablex Publishing, 1999. Print.

Howard, Rebecca Moore, and Amy Robillard, eds. *Pluralizing Plagiarism: Ideas, Contexts, Pedagogies*. Portsmouth, NH: Boynton/Cook, 2008. Print.

Kewes, Pauline, ed. *Plagiarism in Early Modern England*. Longman, NY: Palgrave Macmillan, 2003. Print.

LaFollette, Marcel C. *Stealing Into Print: Fraud, Plagiarism, and Misconduct in Scientific Publishing*. Berkeley: U of California P, 1996. Print.

Lathrop, Ann, and Kathleen Foss, eds. *Guiding Students from Cheating and Plagiarism to Honesty and Integrity: Strategies for Change*. Westport, CT: Libraries Unlimited, 2005. Print.

Lathrop, Ann, and Kathleen Foss. *Student Cheating and Plagiarism in the Internet Era: A Wake-Up Call*. Westport, CT: Libraries Unlimited, 2000. Print.

Lipson, Charles. *Doing Honest Work in College: How to Prepare Citations, Avoid Plagiarism, and Achieve Real Academic Success*. Chicago: U of Chicago P, 2004. Print.

Macfarlane, Robert. *Original Copy: Plagiarism and Originality in Nineteenth-Century Literature*. New York, NY: Oxford UP, 2007. Print.

Mazzeo, Tilar J. *Plagiarism and Literary Property in the Romantic Period*. Philadelphia: U of Pennsylvania P, 2006. Print.

Menager-Beeley, Rosemarie, and Lyn Paulos. *Understanding Plagiarism: A Student Guide to Writing Your Own Work*. Boston, MA: Houghton Mifflin, 2005. Print.

Randall, Marilyn. *Pragmatic Plagiarism: Authorship, Profit, and Power*. Toronto: U of Toronto P, 2001. Print.

Robin, Ron. *Scandals and Scoundrels: Seven Cases That Shook the Academy*. Berkeley: U of California P, 2004. Print.

Rozycki, Edward G., and Gary K. Clabaugh. *The Plagiarism Book—A Student's Manual*. Oreland, PA: Newfoundations, 1999. Print.

Stern, Linda. *What Every Student Should Know About Avoiding Plagiarism*. New York, NY: Pearson Longman, 2007. Print.

Vicinus, Martha, and Caroline Eisner, eds. *Originality, Imitation, and Plagiarism: Teaching Writing in the Digital Age*. Ann Arbor: U of Michigan P, 2008.

Woodmansee, Martha, and Peter Jaszi, eds. *The Construction of Authorship: Textual Appropriation in Law and Literature*. Durham, NC: Duke UP, 1993. Print.

Introduction

Plagiarism is a hot topic these days on college and university campuses. In response to what they see as a raging epidemic, many colleges and universities have written or rewritten "Honor Codes"; others have turned to plagiarism detection software, which compares student writing to a database of other writing, usually including other student work and anything available on the Internet; and some schools have begun to use or require texts like Charles Lipson's *Doing Honest Work in College: How to Prepare Citations, Avoid Plagiarism, and Achieve Real Academic Success*. In their book *Student Cheating and Plagiarism in the Internet Era: A Wake-Up Call* Ann Lathrop and Kathleen Foss assert that it's agreed upon by academics that (1) cheating is rampant, made easy by new electronic technologies, and (2) plagiarism is a deliberate, malicious attempt on the part of students to get by with doing less. One solution they offer is character education, including the teaching of ethics (5). All of these efforts, and others, are intended to curb "rampant plagiarism," or what author David Callahan calls a "culture of cheating" (xvi) on campus.

Whether there really is an "epidemic" of cheating is still open to debate. At least one study claims that "serious cheating on tests [. . .] increased from 39 percent [of students] in 1963 to 64 percent in 1993," but "serious cheating on written work remained stable [. . .] at 65 percent in 1963 and 66 percent in 1993" (McCabe, Trevino, and Butterfield, qtd. in Blum 2). What such a study doesn't do well is distinguish between schools or types of schools, or between subjects, or kinds of assignments. Nor does it consider plagiarism as anything other than a form of cheating. It also relies on students' self-reporting—and as the same authors suggest elsewhere, and one author shows in this volume, students may not consider certain acts as "cheating," even though their teachers might view the same practices as plagiarism.

How did we get here? Concern about academic integrity is an old story, of course. Indeed, the fear of cheating in general has plagued education for decades. Longwood University, for example, has had an Honor Code in place since 1910. The code was re-ratified in 1930 and includes the Twelve Points of the Honor Code (virtues that define honor), the Honor Pledge, the Academic Pledge, and the Honor Creed. Longwood's website boasts: "As one of the most respected traditions at Longwood University, the Honor System promotes an atmosphere of trust, where students are presumed honorable unless their actions prove them otherwise" ("The Honor Code"). In a matriculation tradition, first-year students traditionally attend an Honor Code signing ceremony where they read and sign a promise to adhere to the Honor Code. Elsewhere, The College of William & Mary's honor code proudly boasts a history that goes back to 1736; new students are "administered" the honor code by other students ("Honor Code & Councils").

Obviously, an honor code would not be deemed necessary were there no fear of plagiarism; thus, it is important to consider the history of plagiarism on campus and what impact the recent perception of its massive growth has had on the composition classroom. In writing specifically, plagiarism has been on the radar of teachers and students for quite some time. In his 1944 *College English* article "Let's Teach Composition!" Edward Hamilton, in a partial defense of college students' inability to engage outside ideas without being taught how, criticizes the instructor who does not offer students enough training in research:

> Never having been trained to search out assumptions, interpretations, or conclusions in the essays contained in their anthology, [the students] turn in papers that are reminiscent of Literary Digest articles—mere chains of quotations joined by platitudinous links that reveal their incomprehension rather than represent their efforts to be unbiased. It is not surprising, furthermore, that almost every paper contains instances of innocent plagiarism. (160)

Only fifteen years later, however, in a 1959 issue of *College Composition and Communication*, Leo Hamalian turns the blame on the students themselves as he bemoans the problem of plagiarism in the composition classroom, and cites an Ohio State University survey that found that two thirds of students surveyed "said they would cheat if they had the chance" (50). His position sounds oddly familiar to today's academics who complain about the effort involved in catching cheaters and in the prevalence of plagiarism: "teachers whom the author queried [. . .] admitted that plagiarism was fast becoming the collegiate counterpart of juvenile delinquency" (50). According to Hamalian, it is a student's lack of time management, inability to engage a topic that is irrelevant to him or her, or the fact that he or she is "disturbed emotionally" (52) that leads to his or her cheating in composition, and Hamalian makes a case to his teacherly readers that "plagiarism can be controlled by the methods" he puts forth in the article. Sound familiar? This cat-and-mouse dynamic between teachers and their cheating students is not new.

Despite these early forays into the subject, plagiarism has been slow to emerge as a major concern in composition studies; yet, the issue cuts to the core of writing pedagogy and theory. Despite decades of process pedagogy(s), discussion of plagiarism remains locked in a product-oriented paradigm; but what is plagiarism if not a question of process? Traditional views would see it simply as avoiding or circumventing the writing process, but a more complicated view shows that writing processes—reading, analyzing, understanding, synthesizing, and integrating the writing of others—always touch upon and often overlap with the notion of plagiarism. Indeed, these are basic concepts of theories of writing as a social process.

Aside from this fundamental relationship between composition theory and plagiarism, there are other important reasons plagiarism is, or should be, a central concern of composition studies—practical, institutional, and cultural (i.e., technological) reasons. On a practical level, plagiarism at least seems virtually ubiquitous across composition courses and programs. This is so much the case that almost every first-year rhetoric and research guide has something to say on the subject. Moreover, because, obviously, students are typically expected to write a great deal more in writing courses, and class size is relatively small, teachers of writing are more likely to encounter plagiarism, intentional and unintentional, and/or to recognize it; they are also best positioned to recognize and take advantage of teachable moments. However, why limit discussions to those few, scattered, and idiosyncratic moments? Why not, instead, create opportunities to teach about the murky territory of plagiarism in advance?

There are, likewise, important institutional reasons for composition studies to claim plagiarism. When Deans of Students, Provosts, and Offices of Judicial Affairs constitute and reconstitute "plagiarism" in simple, uncritical ways and in so many different ways across (and sometimes within) institutions, the issue can become seriously confused. Further, these myriad constructions of plagiarism shape student-teacher relationships in ways that are beyond our control, unless the issue is foregrounded in explicit, complex ways. While the field rightfully resists the notion that first-year composition be a "dumping ground" for whatever doesn't fit neatly into the curriculum elsewhere, compositionists must also ask, "If we don't take charge of this issue, who will?"

Institutional concerns are particularly true with the advent of plagiarism detection software, which raises our next important set of reasons for plagiarism to be a central concern of composition studies: the cultural or, in this case, the technological. Developing technologies, one might say, have forced composition studies' hand on the issue of plagiarism. As Charles Moran argued in 1993, and Cynthia Selfe in 1999, developing technologies have fundamentally altered both writing processes and, therefore, the teaching of composition. We should not underestimate the role technology has played in the recent development of the cultural issue of plagiarism. Despite longstanding "honor" traditions, anti-plagiarism policy statements, and professors' many seemingly ironclad anti-plagiarism strategies, plagiarism as an issue has had an especially powerful effect on the field of composition and rhetoric in the years since computer technology and the Internet were introduced. It is both a growing topic of scholarly discussion—philosophically, politically, and academically—and a marketable one. As plagiarism has become perceived as an epidemic and a scourge upon academic ethics, it has consequently become a big business, and technology seems to be playing a major role. In fact, we can use technology itself to show us just how much more culturally visible plagiarism has become: A simple Google Scholar citation search for "plagiarism" in the publication title field yields 139 citations from the years 1950 to 1980, and 4,280 citations for the years 1981 to 2012.

The assumption, supported by a lot of anecdotal evidence, seems to be that the explosion of the Internet over the last 15–20 years has caused a massive increase in plagiarism. The argument is that it's now easier to cheat—to cut and paste material from a website, or to download a paper from an online paper mill—and so students are doing it more than they ever have. Resisting this claim, Donald L. McCabe and Jason M. Stephens make an argument that the Internet is not the cause of increases in plagiarism but is rather "just a conduit, offering a more expedient means of engaging in a behavior that one is already doing." In other words, the cheaters were going to cheat anyway, and now they have the convenience of technology and the Internet to help them. A second technological consideration is the rise of plagiarism detection services (PDSs) such as *Turnitin*. Services like *Turnitin* require a subscription fee, and universities invest in subscriptions and then urge, if not require, students and faculty to use the services. PDS software's emergence and popularity on college campuses has a significant impact on composition studies, in scholarly conversations, in teachers' practice, and in students' perceptions about writing (see Donnelly, et. al.).

These technological facets of the plagiarism issue bear heavily on scholarly discourse in the field of composition studies. As with many issues relating to writing pedagogy, there is much debate; in the case of plagiarism, however, ethics in teaching are often called into question, which is serious business in composition and rhetoric. PDSs take on a celebration and criticism of their own, and they become the springboard for passionate discussions about best practices in teaching. In his attempts to carefully analyze *Turnitin*, Bill Marsh points out

> that while recoding plagiarism detection as pre-emptive education, *Turnitin.com* still makes its money by pulling unoriginal work out of a sea of so-called originals. In short, *Turnitin.com* profits by battling those instances where learning goes wrong but nonetheless must dress its combative strategy in the uniform of pre-emptive educational reform. ("*Turnitin.com*" 435)

While his words don't overtly criticize the instructors who use *Turnitin*'s services, the embedded message in his analysis is that those educators who use it as an anti-plagiarism tool may be contributing to *Turnitin*'s duplicity, which indirectly challenges their ethics as teachers. On the high school English front, however, Thomas Atkins and Gene Nelson turn to *Turnitin* as a source of ethics *enculturation*:

> If students are allowed to use others' words and ideas as their own, they deny themselves the opportunity to develop writing fluency and critical thinking

> skills. This service is not designed to be punitive; it
> is meant to be preventive. The main goal of *TurnI-*
> *tIn.com* is to help students maintain their ethics and
> academic integrity, while learning the skills that will
> help them communicate effectively. (101)

With so many scholars in composition studies trying to investigate the
values and writing relationships that students bring with them to postsecondary education, the words of Atkins and Nelson become critical to the conversation on plagiarism in college composition. Yet the
conversation becomes even more complicated by the pointed criticism
of Rebecca Moore Howard, who has studied and written extensively
on the issue, and who does not hesitate to write candidly about how
she believes PDSs erode the identity of students and the ethos of the
teacher:

> Type in your credit card number, paste in a student's
> paper, press a button, and voila! Plagiarist caught or
> writer exonerated; anxiety assuaged. Catching plagia-
> rists is just as easy and requires just as little thinking
> as does the plagiarizing. [. . .] Plagiarism-detecting
> software also helps teachers describe the issue solely
> in terms of individual students' ethics, thereby avoid-
> ing the difficult task of constructing pedagogy that
> engages students in the topic and the learning pro-
> cess and that persuades them not just that they will
> be punished for plagiarizing but that they will able
> to and glad to do their own writing. In place of the
> pedagogy that joins teachers and students in the ed-
> ucational enterprise, plagiarism-detecting software
> offers a machine that will separate them [. . .]. ("Un-
> derstanding" 8, 11–12)

In reading these voices, it's not difficult to hear the tensions. After
all, at the heart of this conversation about plagiarism is the teaching
of writing; and at the heart of teaching writing are the teachers' and
students' goals toward clear, well-supported, ethical, authentic communication. Plagiarism seems to undermine those goals, and much of
the scholarship in the field of composition and rhetoric on plagiarism
reveals the rescue mission that teacher-scholars on all sides of the issue
have undertaken.

Likewise, the looming issues of plagiarism influence the relationships between teachers and students as they impact the environment of
the composition classroom. Expanded honor codes, plagiarism policies
on syllabi, and the use of PDSs can create an "atmosphere of mistrust"
that Sean Zwagerman argues "over time, settles in as normal and in-
visible, [where] statistical justification for acts of vigilance become
unnecessary" (678). If composition instructors take for granted that
students will cheat if given the chance, the fundamental tenets of composition pedagogy are compromised. At risk is that the atmosphere of
the composition classroom can become infected with the fear of getting caught cheating (or wrongly being accused), as well as teachers'
dread of the tiresome and upsetting process of catching and prosecut-
ing cheaters. The normalization of this atmosphere cannot leave the
composition classroom unaffected.

As for plagiarism's marketability, the mere presence of such a large
volume of publications—many of them books designed for classroom
use—indicates that there is money to be made off of plagiarism, or off
of attempts to prevent it. This question of "marketing" and "management" ideologies in a traditionally more theoretical academic environment can be problematic. How can students explore the more abstract
complexities of authorship, ethos, and writerly voice under these conditions? Is the "business" of plagiarism and the politics of its construction interfering with pedagogy and inquiry?

One of the problems with all of the discussion around plagiarism is
that it assumes that the term "plagiarism" is easily defined and obvious
to all. We hope this book will illustrate how this belief is far from true,
and how thinking through the various conceptions of "plagiarism" is
critical in understanding its origins, manifestations, and prevention.
A second and related problem is that classroom and institutional discussions and policies about plagiarism often conflate intentional and
unintentional plagiarism. One strain of the books written about plagiarism—like Lathrop and Foss's *Guiding Students from Cheating and
Plagiarism to Honesty and Integrity: Strategies for Change*—assumes
that the issue is a question of cheating versus being honest—again, an
issue only about students' ethics. A second strain, one more typically
directed at students, views plagiarism as a kind of trap for unwary students; Linda Stern's *What Every Student Should Know About Avoiding
Plagiarism* is just one example of a number of books that refer specifically to "avoiding" plagiarism, as if it's lurking out there, waiting to

ensnare you if you're not careful. These two strains reveal a broad spectrum of plagiarism definition that calls students' agency into question: Plagiarism can be about the questionable values that students possess, and it can be about their ignorance altogether.

Both sides of the spectrum, of course, have some merit to them. Some students will cheat, but we see no reason to assume most students are cheaters. Many students lack the necessary knowledge about documentation, of course, and students often plagiarize without intending to; however, the set of conventions governing academic writing is complex and sometimes confusing. Learning to navigate those conventions successfully is a long, arduous process, and not something one does by learning a simple list of rules; understanding plagiarism is more than just learning how to cite properly—and the stakes are high. Academic institutions in the United States, and elsewhere, place a high value on particular notions of creativity, originality, and authorship. Adherence to that value constitutes, in the academy's view, integrity, but those notions of creativity, originality, and authorship are hardly universal. They vary among cultures—and not just cultures according to nationality, race, or ethnicity but also social class, region, religion, and other social groups to which people belong. Students entering academia bring with them a variety of cultural values that sometimes differ from the values of academic institutions. As new members of the academic community, students are in the process of learning a new set of values, and of negotiating between those values and the values they have brought with them. This socialization plays a significant role in students' literacy learning, and it is a necessary—but unexamined—part of the conversation that should take place between students and teachers about plagiarism.

Plagiarizing, of course, regardless of intention, is not a problem isolated to composition studies, but because teaching academic writing conventions has historically been perceived as the purview of English departments generally and first-year composition teachers specifically, this issue has been the subject matter of many scholarly articles and books within that discipline. Because plagiarism, as opposed to "mere" cheating on an exam, generally involves passing off someone else's text as one's own, English and Writing departments (and the first-year writing divisions specifically) in higher education have been relied upon to teach students about plagiarism—its definitions, how to avoid it, and the repercussions of it. While course policies with broad

statements about plagiarism have expanded syllabi, and classroom lessons incorporate the subject, there is no quick fix that will universally
solve the problem of plagiarism. Teachers of writing and scholars in
composition studies have begun to recognize and discuss the complexity of the issues surrounding plagiarism in a third strain of books,
such as Rebecca Moore Howard and Amy Robillard's *Pluralizing Plagiarism: Identities, Contexts, Pedagogies*. Yet, such books are written
by scholars for other scholars. Intentionally or unintentionally, they
tend to exclude students from the conversation about student writing.
Books written for students, however, continue to emphasize simplistic
definitions of plagiarism, to exhort students to "do their own work,"
and to focus on "cheating" or "avoiding" plagiarism.

   That's where this book comes in. As editors of this volume, we reject
from the outset the notion that students are fundamentally cheaters.
As both teachers of writing and composition scholars, we understand
that students plagiarize—intentionally and unintentionally—for a
wide variety of reasons. In fact, we are uneasy even with the simple
distinction between intentional and unintentional plagiarism because
the issue itself is so fraught with philosophical, political, and cultural
elements that need to be taken into account before we can even begin
to judge an act as "on purpose" or "by mistake." We likewise have
rejected simplistic definitions and all-purpose guides for avoiding plagiarism. Because we are more interested in *teaching* students than in
catching cheaters, we believe students and teachers together need to
discuss the very notion of plagiarism, in a variety of cultural contexts.
In other words, we want to invite students into the academic conversation about plagiarism. Only in this way, can we achieve true education
and help students improve as writers.

   We assume, then, that most of you reading this book are undergraduate students (probably in an advanced writing course), or graduate students (who may or may not be new teachers yourselves), or
teachers of those courses and/or graduate students. We have encouraged the authors collected here to address both students and teachers
as their primary audience, but their essays are specifically, and intentionally, academic. As a student, then, you are likely to encounter concepts with which you are familiar, but in new and more complex ways,
as well as concepts with which you are less familiar. This is, as we view
it, the nature of higher education. Some of the essays here will explore
differing perceptions of plagiarism—between students and teachers,

between writing and music, between different cultures. Some will draw connections or distinctions between popular culture—artists like Kanye West and shows like *South Park*—and academic culture. Others still are based on more traditional forms of academic research. None of them offers The Answer. Instead, our hope is that you—students and teachers—will engage in deep, serious discussion about the complexity of "plagiarism" and the variety of issues it raises.

You will also find that this collection is enriched with some selections from interdisciplinary studies, literature, and technical communication scholars as well as a middle school teacher. The border of composition studies touches and interacts with writing practices in every discipline, certainly. Writing-across-the-curriculum and writing-in-the-disciplines initiatives, for example, are built through interdisciplinary collaborations and held in esteem by teachers across campuses. Literature and technical communication, though, are connected to composition even more closely in our focus on reading and writing, albeit from different perspectives. Scholars from these sister disciplines contributed pieces we felt were essential to presenting the issues surrounding plagiarism in their fullness. Composition studies intersects middle and high school writing pedagogy as well; concurrent credit courses are common now in every state, calling on universities and middle and high schools to share theories and practices with one another. Thus, the voice from middle school was important to providing a more complete picture of a far-reaching and complicated issue. In short, the present collection benefits from conversations about plagiarism occurring in the disciplines most closely connected to those in composition scholarship.

Part I. Definitions of Plagiarism: Distinctions, Laws, and Rules

We begin this volume, as any good critical study should, with a discussion of definitions. Simplistic definitions of plagiarism, we believe, have done more harm than good. Thus the essays collected in Section I look at plagiarism from a variety of perspectives that expose and examine some of the gray areas in and between definitions. Phillip Marzluf has developed a set of specific, hypothetical cases of "plagiarism" and asked both students and teachers to identify those that are, in fact, plagiarism. The results of his study illustrate not only that students and teachers often disagree about what constitutes plagiarism but also that teachers sometimes disagree among themselves. Students and teachers alike can use this study to begin their own discussion of what does or does not count as plagiarism and why. Moreover, this study should inspire larger questions about what difference these classroom definitions might make to the field in general: If the composition classroom becomes the laboratory for how we conceptualize plagiarism, how do these locally changing definitions shape how scholars in the field talk to one another and promote national statements on the issue?

The most important point, we argue, is not that any particular act does (or does not) constitute plagiarism, though there are greater and lesser degrees of consensus on different scenarios; rather, there are clearly differing definitions in play, and moreover, no one definition is equally germane to all possible scenarios. One way to more fruitfully explore these competing definitions is to compare notions of plagiarism to other, related concepts, as Jessica Reyman (Chapter 2) and Esra Mirze Santesso (Chapter 3) do. In asking, "Is All Copying Theft?" Reyman untangles the terms "copyright infringement" and "plagiarism." In so doing, she offers a part of the plagiarism discussion that is fairly new to composition pedagogy, which has taken for granted that students would learn to engage research in their writing development: the rights and responsibilities of students using outside sources. What are they? What is at stake? While she acknowledges the many ways writers may cheat, she argues against the tendency to quickly condemn all acts of copying as plagiarism and supports a concept of "allowable copying," which she believes to be inherent in successful academic work in the digital age. Situating a similar sort of discussion in the literature classroom, in Chapter 3 Santesso teases out the differences in meaning among concepts of plagiarism, borrowing, imitating, reworking, and reinterpreting, arguing that we must understand these differences or run the risk of oversimplified understandings of literature and confusion over the value of intellectual collaborations and artistic dialogue.

These discussions of the definitions and meanings of plagiarism demonstrate, as Paul Parker argues in Chapter 4, that avoiding plagiarism is not merely adherence to a set of technical rules but rather a complicated process involving the development of critical, "authorial judgment." It is assumed in composition pedagogy that writers must learn to navigate a complex set of texts, distinguish between the ideas of others and their own, and determine the extent to which attribution is necessary in a particular set of circumstances. It's a tall order, and few students develop a meta-awareness of how the synthesis of these skills should "look" in a text. Sure, students may read academic texts for their content; but how often do they examine the mechanical construction of those texts as researched documents? Examining the linguistics of source integration in a series of specific texts, Parker shows how academic authors construct meaning as they make informed citation decisions in their analyses.

PART II. TEXTS, TECHNOLOGIES, AND SURVEILLANCE

Competing definitions and conflicting contexts are especially significant in the digital age in which we live, work, and write, and the changes in digital technologies is at the heart of much discussion in composition studies. Thus in Part II we turn to discussions of a variety of media, which bring with them a whole new set of concepts, including creative collage, sampling, remixing, and media piracy. In Chapter 5, for example, Richard Schur explores the work of artists DJ Danger Mouse and Kanye West as a way to celebrate the collaborative culture and "ethical code" of hip hop, and to illustrate the ways academia perceives similar standards for authenticity and documentation. Schur argues that such examples of sampling in popular culture can help us better understand the creativity and integrity involved in utilizing outside sources.

Likewise, taking a progressive stance in the field to resist the traditional notion of writing as the work of an author operating inside of a bubble of unique ideas, Martine Courant Rife and Dànielle Nicole DeVoss argue in Chapter 6 that composing should instead be perceived and taught as "remixing." This term recognizes the innovation of technology, which encourages authors to construct new meaning by assembling pieces that are often derived from others' work. This concept of "writing-as-remix," the authors argue, should inspire us to embrace and complicate the conversation around an "ethic of Fair Use."

These essays discuss some of the ways the digital age has raised the stakes. In some ways, it seems, it is easier to plagiarize; in other ways, it is also both harder and easier to spot and identify. What some scholars and cultural critics view as a "culture of cheating" (Callahan xvi) has created an academic culture of suspicion and surveillance, as demonstrated by the development (and increasing popularity) of plagiarism detection software. Such a climate, in which the focus is on policing plagiarism rather than teaching and supporting students as they learn conventions of attribution and citation, is counterproductive. In Chapter 7, Deborah Harris-Moore draws from Michel Foucault's *Discipline and Punish* to highlight the ways plagiarism detection software can be used by administrators and teachers to abuse their power over students. It is important to consider here the complexities of teacher authority and power in the composition classroom, especially in contrast to other classroom settings. How should we define the culture of the composition classroom? What effect does an adversarial relationship between teacher and student have on that culture?

In a similar vein, but for different reasons, Sean Zwagerman argues in Chapter 8 that enforcing anti-plagiarism policies through surveillance and punishment creates hostile divisions between students and teachers and even between those students who do plagiarize and those who don't. These divisions can have negative effects particularly in the composition classroom, which relies on a collaborative, cooperative environment between teacher and student. Zwagerman explains that both students and teachers are sometimes oversensitive to evaluation; students sometimes plagiarize to avoid bad evaluation, and teachers sometimes deal with such plagiarism unproductively, also to avoid negative teaching evaluations. Zwagerman believes plagiarism policies reliant on surveillance and punishment exacerbate these divisions, and he calls for more collaborative policies that might heal unproductive rifts.

Part III. Authorship and Ownership: Cultural and Cross-Cultural Perspectives

Ultimately, plagiarism is a cultural concept. In a digital, multicultural, and global context, then, cultural and cross-cultural perspectives on authorship and ownership merit exploration. Thus, we begin the final section with Bridget M. Marshall's "Who Cares About Plagiarism? Cheating and Consequences in the Pop Culture Classroom," an examination of portrayals of plagiarism and cheating in American popular culture. Using specific examples from television, literature, and film, such as *Harry Potter* and *South Park*, and comparing/contrasting these with examples of other media, Marshall reveals the mixed messages sent by pop culture about what constitutes "cheating." Indeed, students and teachers live in a daily barrage of media references from pop culture, and these references help shape not only the content of our compositions but also our relationships to those texts. Marshall's chapter offers us a meeting place and an entryway into deeper discussions about the power and responsibility of popular culture in depicting and defining plagiarism.

Marshall's essay also provides a useful contrast to the discussions of authorship, ownership, and "cheating" that follow. Because first-year composition often offers students their only (or at least primary) instruction on the ethics of ownership in academic culture, composition teachers are routinely expected to behave as gatekeepers, stemming the flow of dishonesty and confusion about plagiarism; as gatekeepers these instructors are expected to not only be aware of cultural differences in their first-year students but also to understand these differences sufficiently to provide clear instruction for preventing any kind of "cheating" in college. In Chapter 10, Rachel Knaizer highlights the overlapping and often conflicting cultural understandings of plagiarism that exist in any one classroom, and shows how those overlaps can confuse students about the nature of plagiarism, especially as students don't get their information about plagiarism solely from teachers but also from one another. She explains that writers from different countries are especially at risk for being misidentified as plagiarists due to their cultures' different understandings of language and ownership.

Lise Buranen, in Chapter 11, discusses how various cultures define concepts related to plagiarism and the ownership of language. Based on the results of her own qualitative study, Buranen argues that much of the literature about cross-cultural understandings of plagiarism has resulted in oversimplified maxims for the classroom. Such maxims put all students at risk of believing they don't understand the rules simply through some fault of their own rather than as a result of complex influences embedded in their individual cultures. Anne-Marie Pederson likewise complicates ideas about plagiarism in Chapter 12 by explaining some of the cultural contexts that contribute to misunderstandings about what constitutes plagiarism and why some people do plagiarize. She explains how Western ideas about property ownership tie to common ideas about plagiarism, and then explains how material conditions and educational experiences facilitate the practice of plagiarism in some cases.

All of these ideas—cross-cultural, popular, academic—provide fertile ground for discussion and, taken together, they present contrasts that are important to examine. Rather than offer a simplistic definition and a guide to avoiding plagiarism, this volume is intended to help students and teachers alike think critically about the very concept itself, and to participate in serious intellectual inquiry and discussion. It is the contention of the editors of this collection that all of us be aware of and understand in a deep way the controversies about plagiarism that writers continually negotiate. All writers, for example, must confront the "problem" that we all owe an enormous debt to those who have come before us, and to our contemporaries, for feeding and shaping our own ideas. All writers struggle to understand what plagiarism really is. Are all ideas plagiarized? Is there really such a thing as true originality? How do we deal with information overload versus our responsibility to document the writers and thinkers already published? *Critical Conversations About Plagiarism* opens these questions for a collaborative exploration of their meaning and implications in our increasingly complex academic lives.

WORKS CITED

Atkins, Thomas, and Gene Nelson. "Plagiarism and the Internet: Turning the Tables." *English Journal* 90 (4): 101–104. Print.

Blum, Susan D. *My Word!: Plagiarism and College Culture*. Ithaca, NY: Cornell UP, 2009. Print.

Callahan, David. Preface. *Guiding Students from Cheating and Plagiarism to Honesty and Integrity: Strategies for Change*. Ed. Ann Lathrop and Kathleen Foss. Westport, CT: Libraries Unlimited, 2005. xv–xvi. Print.

Donnelly, Michael, Rebecca Ingalls, Tracy Ann Morse, Joanna Castner, and Anne Meade Stockdell-Giesler. "(Mis)Trusting Technology that Polices Integrity: A Critical Assessment of *Turnitin.com*." *inventio* 8:1 (Fall 2006). Web. 14 January 2010.

Hamalian, Leo. "Plagiarism: Suggestions for its Cure and Prevention." *College Composition and Communication* 10.1 (1959): 50–53. Print.

Hamilton, Edward. "Let's Teach Composition!" *College English* 6.3 (December 1944): 159–164.

"Honor Code & Councils." *WM.edu*. The College of William and Mary. n.d. Web. 14 January 2010.

"The Honor Code at Longwood University." *Longwood.edu*. Longwood University. n.d. Web. 14 January 2010.

Howard, Rebecca Moore, and Amy Robillard, eds. *Pluralizing Plagiarism: Ideas, Contexts, Pedagogies.* Portsmouth, NH: Boynton/Cook, 2008. Print.

Lathrop, Ann, and Kathleen Foss, eds. *Guiding Students from Cheating and Plagiarism to Honesty and Integrity: Strategies for Change.* Westport, CT: Libraries Unlimited, 2005. Print.

Lathrop, Ann, and Kathleen Foss. *Student Cheating and Plagiarism in the Internet Era: A Wake-Up Call.* Westport, CT: Libraries Unlimited, 2000. Print.

Lipson, Charles. *Doing Honest Work in College: How to Prepare Citations, Avoid Plagiarism, and Achieve Real Academic Success.* Chicago, IL: U of Chicago P, 2004. Print.

Marsh, Bill. "*Turnitin.com* and the Scriptural Enterprise of Plagiarism Detection." *Computers and Composition* 21 (2004): 427–438. Print.

McCabe, Donald L., Linda Klebe Trevino, and Kenneth D. Butterfield. "Cheating in Academic Institutions: A Decade of Research." *Ethics & Behavior* 11.3 (2001): 219–232. Print.

McCabe, Donald L., and Jason M. Stephens. "'Epidemic' as Opportunity: Internet Plagiarism as a Lever for Cultural Change." *Teachers College Record* (30 November 2006). Web. 14 January 2010.

Moran, Charles. "The Winds, and the Costs, of Change." *Computers and Composition* 9.2 (April 1993): 35–44. Print.

Selfe, Cynthia. "Technology and Literacy: A Story about the Perils of Not Paying Attention." *College Composition and Communication* 50.3 (1999): 411–36. Print.

Stern, Linda. *What Every Student Should Know About Avoiding Plagiarism.* New York: Pearson Longman, 2007. Print.

Zwagerman, Sean. "The Scarlet P: Plagiarism, Panopticism, and the Rhetoric of Academic Integrity." *College Composition and Communication* 59.4 (2008): 676–710. Print.

Critical Conversations About Plagiarism

Part I
Definitions of Plagiarism:
Distinctions, Laws, and Rules

In most discussions, the definition of plagiarism is assumed to be ob-vious to all. Most composition textbooks, especially those that deal with research writing, contain sections on plagiarism and appropriate citation of sources. Virtually every writing "handbook," a staple of the first-year writing course, does the same. In most cases, these texts of-fer a simple one- or two-sentence definition, as if plagiarism is really a simple matter—agreed upon by all—and easily avoided by the use of proper citation. Few offer more in terms of critical discussion or even indicate that there is disagreement over what plagiarism is.

The fact is—there is no one simple definition of plagiarism that works clearly and effectively for all cases. Consider, for example, the following definitions provided by three different writing handbooks:

- "Plagiarism is understood to be a writer's deliberate misrep-resentation of another's writing or ideas as his or her own" (Blakesley and Hoogeveen 358).
- Researchers who fail to acknowledge their sources—either in-tentionally or unintentionally—commit plagiarism. Buying a term paper from an online paper mill or "borrowing" a friend's completed assignment are obvious forms of plagiarism. But plagiarism also includes paraphrasing or summarizing mate-rial without properly citing its source. (Maimon, Peritz, and Yancey 265)
- "Plagiarism is defined as the unauthorized or misleading use of the language and text of another author" (Hult and Huckin 142).

Each of these definitions is, basically, as good as any other, but notice the differences in the territory they do and do not cover. One specifi-

cally states that plagiarism is the "*deliberate* misrepresentation of another's writing or ideas" (emphasis added), while the next says "either
intentionally or unintentionally," and the third makes no reference
at all to the writer's intent. Further, the second identifies the failure
to cite sources as the defining feature; yet, one might acknowledge a
source and still misrepresent "another's writing or ideas as his or her
own"; conversely, one might not "misrepresent" another's writing, yet
fail to properly cite the source. The third definition is murkier still.
What does "unauthorized" use mean? Do I need the author's permission to cite her work? What does "misleading" mean here? This definition also specifies use of only the "language and text," while the first
definition specifies "writing or *ideas*" (emphasis added), and the second includes ideas only when they are expressed through paraphrasing
and summarizing.

The issue is among those that are so troublesome and so central
to the teaching of writing that the Council of Writing Program Administrators, the national organization of those who oversee various
types of writing programs and writing centers, was compelled in 2003
to issue a Statement on Best Practices with regard to "Defining and
Avoiding Plagiarism." While the statement acknowledges that "[i]n instructional settings, plagiarism is a multifaceted and ethically complex
problem," it then goes on to provide a simple, one-sentence definition:
"In an instructional setting, plagiarism occurs when a writer deliber-
ately uses someone else's language, ideas, or other original (not common knowledge) material without acknowledging its source." Since
then, scholars in composition studies have begun to explore more fully,
rather than assume, conflicting definitions and their relationship to
the processes of learning to write, as well as to a number of critical,
related concepts like originality, identity, authorship, ownership, and
context. Martha Vicinus and Caroline Eisner's *Originality, Imitation,
and Plagiarism: Teaching Writing in the Digital Age*; Rebecca Moore
Howard and Amy Robillard's *Pluralizing Plagiarism: Identities, Contexts, Pedagogies*; Carol Peterson Haviland and Joan A. Mullin's *Who
Owns This Text?: Plagiarism, Authorship, and Disciplinary Cultures*—
these and others have called simplistic definitions of plagiarism into
question and complicated our understanding of the issues. Like them,
the authors collected here in Part I do not assume a single, fixed definition of plagiarism. Instead, they consider the issue of definition by
examining how perceptions of plagiarism often differ; how the con-

cept of plagiarism relates to other concepts like copyright law, on the one hand, and artistic or creative "borrowing," on the other; and how notions of plagiarism are tangled up in the process of learning to write in academic contexts.

Plagiarism is a complicated concept, one that has much to do with cultural notions of authorship and the ownership of both language and ideas, and it functions in a variety of sometimes contradictory and often mysterious ways. It is not something that can be avoided simply, the way one might avoid speeding by keeping an eye on the speedometer. Understanding plagiarism is, therefore, a complex process—one that requires deep, critical thinking and discussion about writing, about developing one's own ideas while responding to and incorporating the ideas of others.

WORKS CITED

Blakesley, David, and Jeffrey L. Hoogeveen. *The Thomson Handbook: Preview Edition*. Boston, MA: Thomson Wadsworth, 2007. Print.

Council of Writing Program Administrators. "Defining and Avoiding Plagiarism: The WPA Statement on Best Practices." January 2003. Web. 1 February 2010.

Haviland, Carol Peterson, and Joan A. Mullin, eds. *Who Owns This Text?: Plagiarism, Authorship, and Disciplinary Cultures*. Logan: Utah State UP, 2008. Print.

Howard, Rebecca Moore, and Amy Robillard, eds. *Pluralizing Plagiarism: Ideas, Contexts, Pedagogies*. Portsmouth, NH: Boynton/Cook, 2008. Print.

Hult, Christine A., and Thomas N. Huckin. *The Brief New Century Handbook*. 2nd ed. New York: Pearson Longman, 2004. Print.

Maimon, Elaine P., Janice H. Peritz, and Kathleen Blake Yancey. *A Writer's Resource: A Handbook for Writing and Research*. 2nd ed. Boston, MA: McGraw-Hill, 2007. Print.

Vicinus, Martha, and Caroline Eisner, eds. *Originality, Imitation, and Plagiarism: Teaching Writing in the Digital Age*. Ann Arbor: U of Michigan P, 2008. Print.

1 Examining Teachers' and Students' Attitudes towards Plagiarism

Phillip Marzluf

Before You Read: *In the following essay, Phillip Marzluf claims that students and teachers have "different assumptions about such concepts as originality, common knowledge, and collaboration." How would you define someone's work as plagiarized? Take a few minutes to articulate a definition of plagiarism in writing. Among many factors to consider, you might think about whether the writer meant to do it, and how much of another's source a writer used as his or her own.*

As the director of a writing program at a public university, I work with teachers who possess a wide range of attitudes towards plagiarism, ranging from nonchalance to hostility, and who rely upon varying definitions of plagiarism. As a writing teacher, I often work with students who appear mystified, scared, or downright cynical about what constitutes plagiarism and academic misconduct. Their confusion is easy to understand, given the conflicting definitions and suggestions they receive from class to class and from high school to college and university levels. In order to more fully explore the sometimes mystifying range of ideas surrounding plagiarism, for both students and teachers, I designed the "Attitudes towards Plagiarism" questionnaire, which prompts users to classify and rate ten scenarios describing possible plagiarism or academic misconduct cases. By asking us to reflect on our definitions of plagiarism, the "Attitudes towards Plagiarism" questionnaire encourages dialogue between teachers and students, allowing us to compare our assumptions about responsible research, the ownership of writing, collaboration, and the incorporation of outside sources.

In this brief study[1] I examine how teachers and students classify the scenarios in the "Attitudes towards Plagiarism" questionnaire and, for the cases they regard as plagiarism, how seriously they consider them. In the fall of 2006, forty-four instructors, professors, and librarians who worked with first- and second-year students in a wide range of disciplines at a public Midwestern university completed an online version of the questionnaire, which also elicited written comments. In addition to their participation, 138 students from nine second-year writing courses completed a paper version of the questionnaire. For the student participants, either an experienced graduate teaching assistant or I conducted a brief feedback session and discussed their responses.[2] Below, I first describe the questionnaire, providing the ten scenarios and defining the four variables that constitute them. Then, I summarize the study results and conclude with a few observations about how the questionnaire can contribute to teachers' and students' discussions.

The Questionnaire

While developing the ten scenarios for the "Attitudes towards Plagiarism" questionnaire, I kept in mind the various definitions of plagiarism (Howard 475), the reasons researchers have identified for why students plagiarize (e.g., Ashworth, Bannister, and Thorne 202; Love and Simmons 544; Roig 979), and the practices of collaboration and peer editing. The questionnaire asks teachers and students to read ten scenarios of possible acts of plagiarism, to judge whether these acts should be considered plagiarism, and then to determine the severity of each case. These judgments are made according to the following five-point scale:

1. Not plagiarism.

2. Although this scenario represents an act of plagiarism or academic misconduct, it is not serious. This act is incidental or possibly unintentional. The student does not deserve severe punishment.

3. This act is slightly more serious. There is more of a possibility that it was intentional. The student might deserve punishment.

4. This act is more serious. It is clearly intentional. The student definitely deserves punishment.

5. This is the most serious act of plagiarism or academic misconduct. This act calls for severe consequences.

The ten scenarios are listed below. In parentheses before each scenario appears the title by which we refer to it in this essay.

#1 (Friend's Paper Scenario) Kathy is having difficulty finding ideas for her take-home history exam. After discussing her problems with a friend, she finds out that her friend had to write on a similar question the previous semester. Using a draft of her friend's paper, which only got a "C," Kathy rewrites it to make it sound more like her. Also, she completely changes her introduction. In the body of the paper, she includes a few new points.

#2 (Conclusion Scenario) John hates writing conclusions. Thus, instead of summarizing the paper himself, he reads his paper aloud to his friend and then asks her to briefly sum up the paper. John writes down exactly what she says. After making a couple of grammatical changes, he includes this at the end of his paper.

#3 (Vietnam Scenario) Sandra, who is writing about the Vietnam War, has collected ten newspaper articles that mention an important battle. As she writes her description of this battle, she makes sure to include proper citations whenever she uses direct quotations from the articles. However, she doesn't cite the sources for names, dates, statistics, and geographical places. In her opinion, these are just basic historical facts.

#4 (Faulty Paraphrase Scenario) In *The Concise Columbia Encyclopedia*, Michael looks up a definition on "occupational disease" and finds the following:

> Occupational disease: an illness resulting from the conditions or environment of employment. Some time usually elapses between exposure to the cause and development of the symptoms of an occupational disease. Among the causes of such diseases are toxic chemicals, such as benzene and dioxin.

In a report for his business communications class, Michael includes this definition by writing:

> Occupational disease is an illness resulting from job-related conditions. Usually, there is an elapse of time between exposure to the cause and development of the symptoms of this disease. Toxic chemicals, like benzene and dioxin, are common causes (*The Concise Columbia Encyclopedia*).

#5 (Sight Gag Scenario) Margaret, in her paper that summarizes different techniques in film comedy, reads this definition about a "sight gag" in Noel Carroll's "Notes on the Sight Gag" (from Andrew S. Horton's *Comedy/Cinema/Theory*, page 26).

> The sight gag is a form of visual humor in which amusement is generated by the play of alternative interpretations projected by the image or image series. Sight gags existed in theater prior to their cinematic refinement, and sight gags, although they are regarded as the hallmark of the silent comedy, can occur in films that are neither silent nor comic.

Margaret, however, thinks this definition is too complicated. She rewrites it as:

> The sight gag, which is a common feature in many types of film, has been around since the days of theater. It involves a visual image that makes you laugh, especially when this image has many different meanings.

Since she has changed the definition so much, she feels that she doesn't need to cite the source.

#6 (Shakespeare Scenario) The assignment in Cody's drama class asks students to write a three-page interpretation of a Shakespearean play. Glancing through a book about Shakespeare, *Elizabethan Playwrights*, Cody finds an analysis of *The Tempest* that he likes. Cody then extends the analysis to write his paper on Shakespeare's *King Lear*. Although he cites the Shakespeare anthology he is using, he doesn't indicate his use of *Elizabethan Playwrights*.

#7 (Mother Scenario) In her opinion, Lindsay feels that she has a lot to say, but, at the same time, feels that she can never find the right words to express her thoughts. All her sentences are always the same length and start in the same way. Her mother, fortunately, is a retired high school English teacher. She reworks Lindsay's papers until they sound more academic. "She only touches the grammar, and stuff like words and punctuation," Lindsay says. "The ideas are mine. That's the important part."

#8 (Collaboration Scenario) In Frank's writing class, group editing is emphasized. And, since Frank's usual partners, Erica and Keith, are recognized as the best students in class, he thinks it is in his best interest to rewrite the final drafts of his papers by including the exact words and sentence structures they suggest. This is especially easy since the instructor tells his students to write, in a different color ink, directly on the rough drafts of their partners.

#9 (Salinger Scenario) Lynn's favorite book in high school was *The Catcher in the Rye*. She liked the smart-alecky tone of the book and how the main character's thoughts are depicted with mild swears and informal phrases. The first sentence of this book, for example, reads, "If you really want to hear about it, the first thing you'll probably want to know is where I was born [. . .] and all that David Copperfield kind of crap." In her first paper for Expository Writing I, a description of a real experience from her past, Lynn tried to imitate the tone of *The Catcher in the Rye*. Yet, though she wanted to make herself sound like the main character from that book, she was careful to only directly use single words or short, two-to-three-word phrases.

#10 (Downloading Scenario) Ashley, a Chemistry major, finds out that her final Expository Writing I paper is due on the following day. Since there is no time left to do research and plan her topic—and since she still has to study for her organic chemistry exam—she can think of only one solution to her problem: Ashley jumps on the Internet, finds the www.collegepapers.com site, and, after paying $42.50, downloads what is advertised as the "perfect paper."

The scenarios consist of the four variables that appear most often in my discussions about plagiarism with teachers and students: the writer's level of intentionality, the degree of appropriation, the borrowing of ideas and/or expression, and the status of the source. I hypothesize that though teachers and students make judgments based upon these variables, disagreements may arise in regards to which variables should be emphasized as well as how they should be interpreted. I describe these variables briefly below.

INTENTIONALITY AND APPROPRIATION

These two variables are grouped together because the intention of plagiarizers, their conscious desires to deceive their teachers, may directly relate to appropriation, the amount of the source text they use. The Downloading Scenario (#10), for example, indicates an obvious case of academic fraud: The student purchases an online essay and willfully submits it as her own writing; she has, therefore, acted with clear intentions and appropriated the source text completely. Not surprisingly, teachers react strongly to acts in which students are consciously attempting to deceive them, and I thus surmised that teachers would mark these types of scenarios severely.

IDEAS AND EXPRESSIONS

These variables are implicit in American copyright law, which separates the ideas of texts from their specific forms of expression. This separation protects the interests of authors by making their particular expressions a property they own; on the other hand, by allowing the public limited access to the ideas of authors, copyright laws insure that society in general can benefit from exploring, extending, and distributing these ideas (Spigelman 246). In her research, Candace Spigelman explores how students working collaboratively in writing groups negotiate these complicated concepts of textual ownership. When students are confronted with the possibility that their ideas and expressions can be separated, Spigelman finds that they apply different ways of thinking about how textual ownership is decided, about when they can claim a text is their own, and about whether ownership can be based upon the origins of expression or that of ideas (247–48). Similar to one of Spigelman's study participants (248–49), the writer in the Mother Scenario (#7) responds to these questions by indicating that ideas, not surface expression, are what make a text authentically hers.

STATUS OF THE SOURCE

This variable refers to the type of source text that the writer has used. Writers may, as in the Friend's Paper Scenario (#1), appropriate texts from their friends or, as in the Shakespeare Scenario (#6), borrow ideas from a published text on Shakespearean criticism. This consideration of the status of the source—in other words, the difference in power and status between writers and the types of texts they use—may influence how students and teachers determine the severity of the plagiaristic act. Teachers, in particular, will have to examine the differences, if any do exist, of students who borrow from credible, published texts from those who borrow from the texts of their peers.

Many of the scenarios reveal the assumptions and complex judgments that go into making determinations about plagiarism. Because most of the scenarios do represent the problematic gray area of identifying plagiarism, the variables quickly become messy and overlap with each other. For instance, Cody, the student in the Shakespeare Scenario (#6), can be regarded as acting with a high degree of intentionality (though the scenario does not provide us with a clear description of his desires), as appropriating ideas, and as borrowing from a high status source text. Furthermore, the scenarios rarely provide all of the necessary information in order for teachers and students to make definitive decisions about the writers' intentions and about what rules of plagiarism and academic misconduct were already established in these hypothetical classrooms.

STUDY RESULTS AND DISCUSSION

Overall, the questionnaire results indicate that teachers are more likely to judge the scenarios as acts of plagiarism. A larger percentage of teachers than students rate seven scenarios as plagiarism, although only four of these are statistically significant. Table 1 below lists these results. For each scenario, a higher percentage suggests more agreement that it represents plagiarism.

Table 1: Percentages of Plagiarism Ratings

Scenario	Teachers (%)	Students (%)
1*	100	94
2	93	85
3	64	73
4*	52	26
5*	91	70
6	88	93
7*	86	65
8	75	81
9	55	48
10	100	99

*Differences are statistically significant (p=.005).

Teachers are also more likely to rate cases of plagiarism more severely, though the differences between the teachers and students are less pronounced. Only two of these scenarios, the Friend's Paper (#1) and Mother (#7) scenarios, are statistically significant, which can be accounted for by the fact that a larger percentage of students do not regard these cases as plagiarism. Table 2 lists the questionnaire averages for teachers and students. An average closer to 1 indicates that the scenario is either not classified as plagiarism or is marked as a less serious case; an average closer to 5 indicates that the scenario is regarded as a more serious offense.

Table 2: Comparison of Levels of Severity

Scenario	Teachers	Students	Scenario	Teachers	Students
1*	3.7	3.3	6	3.0	3.2
2	3.1	2.8	7*	2.7	2.2
3	1.8	2.0	8	2.3	2.6
4	1.7	1.5	9	1.8	1.8
5	2.3	2.3	10	5.0	4.9

*Differences are statistically significant (p=.005).

Below, I discuss the questionnaire results according to three categories, the scenarios that show the most agreement between teachers and students, the scenarios that show the most disparity, and the scenarios that show the most variance among teachers.

SCENARIOS SHOWING MOST AGREEMENT

Although teachers show a tendency to rate the scenarios as more serious and more likely to represent plagiarism, the results do suggest that teachers and students base their judgments upon a similar set of values. The results indicated in Table 2 confirm a strong consensus between teachers and students. It is also interesting to note that a larger percentage of students rate three scenarios as acts of plagiarism and score them more severely, yet the differences are slight and are not statistically significant. It is encouraging, though not surprising, for example, that the response to the Downloading Scenario (#10) is nearly unanimous. This case represents the most clear-cut example of a writer who intends to deceive her teacher and who completely appropriates the outside source. Furthermore, for a scenario such as the Friend's Paper Scenario (#1), even though it shows statistical significance for both comparisons, the difference is weak. A vast majority of students (94%) agrees with the 100% of instructors who rate this scenario as plagiarism, and students, similar to teachers, rate this scenario as the second most serious act of plagiarism. A small group of students, however, interpret this writer's attempts to rewrite her friend's essay exam and "make it sound more like herself" as a suitable strategy for appropriation.

SCENARIOS SHOWING MOST DISPARITY

The four statistically significant scenarios, the Friend's Paper (#1), the Faulty Paraphrase (#4), the Sight Gag (#5), and the Mother (#7) scenarios, are interesting because they represent the most disparity between how teachers and students respond. These differences suggest how subtle interpretations of the variables, especially intentionality and ideas/expression, play a role in determining these judgments.

For example, the Mother Scenario (#7) suggests that students may privilege the writer's ownership of ideas. In my discussions with student groups about this scenario, several students—though not all—have claimed that this writer is being responsible, in that she is seeking out editing help from a legitimate source, her mother, the same thing that all expert writers do. Although a statistically significant number of teachers deviate from this judgment, the responses to the online questionnaire hint that some teachers agree with these students' less text-specific approach to defining plagiarism. One teacher claims that several of the scenarios illustrate students asking for advice on content or on editing, which is "exactly the kind of collaboration that workers will participate in in many job situations." This teacher acknowledges the difficulty of judging these cases of collaboration, in that they describe exactly what writers do in real professional situations.

Finally, the two scenarios exemplifying examples of citation and paraphrasing, the Faulty Plagiarism (#4) and the Sight Gag (#5) scenarios, also reveal wide divergences of judgments between teachers and students. The fact that 74% of students, as opposed to 48% of teachers, determine the Faulty Plagiarism Scenario (#4) as not a case of plagiarism may suggest that students are willing to overlook the writer's borrowing of exact phrases and sentence structure as long as he has clearly marked his intention *not* to deceive the instructor, which he does by citing his encyclopedia source. This writer, therefore, may be signaling he is working in good faith. Of course, the responses to the Sight Gag Scenario (#5), in which the writer adequately paraphrases the source but does not cite it, reverses this logic. In this case, only 30% of students judge this scenario not to be plagiarism, indicating that, for a majority of students, the writer's failure to identify the source of her definition makes them suspicious about her intentions. As one of the comments on the online questionnaire demonstrates, some teachers respond emphatically to attempts to rationalize writers' actions in these two scenarios. The teacher writes, "Intentionally lifting a word, phrase or sentence from a source without enclosing these words in quotation marks and citing them is ALWAYS [*sic*] plagiarism, only slightly less egregious than buying a paper from a term paper site." Yet, the student responses may be hinting that interpretations of this adverb, "intentionally," make these cases difficult to define.

SCENARIOS SHOWING MOST VARIANCE

Despite several scenarios that show strong agreement, the teacher responses demonstrate that there is little unanimity and consistency among how they judge the more complicated, less obvious scenarios. In fact, in three of the scenarios—the Vietnam (#3), Faulty Paraphrasing (#4), and Salinger (#9) scenarios—there is a statistically significant difference between teachers who determine them to be cases of plagiarism as opposed to teachers who do not. Additionally, an analysis of the correlations across all the scenarios suggests a lack of consistency for how teachers score one scenario as compared with another.

These data do not necessarily suggest that teachers are randomly making decisions on what should be considered plagiarism. Instead, these findings may indicate, especially given the variance evident in the Faulty Paraphrasing Scenario (#4), that a great deal of anxiety currently exists about how to label and judge writers who may be just learning how to incorporate outside sources. Consequently, of the 52% of teachers who indicate that the Faulty Paraphrasing Scenario (#4) depicts an act of plagiarism, 83% of these teachers mark it as the least serious type. The differences among teachers may reflect definitional, not pedagogical, confusion. The Collaboration Scenario (#8) also suggests a great deal of teacher variance, as 25% of teachers judge it to be "not plagiarism," 30% as "plagiarism, not serious," 34% as "plagiarism, more serious," and 11% as either a "very serious" or an "extremely serious" case of plagiarism. Though a great deal of this variance is undoubtedly based upon different interpretations of the scenario, it is alarming that a case of peer collaboration provokes such a wide range of responses.[3] Quite possibly, it is the teachers' interpretations of the writer's intentions to deceive and to completely appropriate his peers' suggestions that influence this decision.

CONCLUSION: THE USES OF THE QUESTIONNAIRE

The "Attitudes towards Plagiarism" questionnaire can facilitate conversations about the definitions of plagiarism and about how we—both teachers and students—hold different assumptions about such concepts as originality, common knowledge, and collaboration. It is also important for us to become aware that the definitions of plagiarism are messy and that, before we rely wholeheartedly upon textbook definitions, we should reflect upon the complex factors that make up our writing, research, and collaborative strategies.

In my experiences with using the questionnaire in teacher training as well as introductory writing classrooms, I discuss the following types of questions after teachers and students have rated the scenarios:

- Which scenario was the easiest one for you to respond to? Which one was the most obvious case of plagiarism? Why?
- Which of the scenarios troubles you? Why?

- Which case of plagiarism did you find to be the most unintentional?
- What do the cases you marked as plagiarism tell you to watch out for?
- How did you decide the severity level for each scenario you marked as plagiarism? What should teachers bear in mind when making decisions about punishment?
- In high school and in your college classes, what have you been told about plagiarism? How consistent has this advice been?
- What fears or concerns do you have about your own research and use of sources?

These types of questions, and the discussions they provoke, allow us to reflect on our responsibilities as researchers and writers. They can reveal the larger purposes behind citation rules and conventional formalities: Instead of seeing these aspects of writing as final obstacles to be hurdled before handing in a paper, teachers and students can consider research, the integration of sources, and collaboration as important elements throughout their drafting.

I have found the questionnaire helpful for teachers to understand the citation "logic" of their students and for students, meanwhile, to grapple with the judgments their teachers make. For example, students, I have discovered, focus a great deal of their attention on the variable of intentionality. While discussing the Salinger Scenario (#9), two student groups defended this writer's use of the sarcastic voice of *The Catcher in the Rye*, arguing that this scenario did not represent plagiarism because the writer did not deceive the instructor and sampled a well-known text only to enhance a "sense of character." It is also interesting to listen to student groups defend the scenarios, such as the Faulty Paraphrasing (#4) and Sight Gag (#5) scenarios, that indicate wide disparity between teachers and students. In my experience, students have not focused on the writers' inability to paraphrase or on their lack of knowledge of citation conventions but upon the fact that these two writers were only attempting to incorporate definitions— not, that is, more important substantive ideas. According to this logic, "mere" definitions are not that important to cite; after all, who possesses intellectual ownership of a definition? The Vietnam Scenario (#3), similarly, highlights these issues of public knowledge, the status of facts, and their accessibility. Again, students have asked, who owns historical facts, such as names or dates? Alternatively, as one student-group implied, does the accessibility of these facts—whether it could be reasonably inferred that the general public had common knowledge of these facts—dictate whether they should be cited?

The questionnaire can also indicate how judgments about plagiarism differ among educational levels, disciplines, and institutions. I often ask students whether the plagiarism advice they receive from their teachers is consistent or if there were any differences in how their high school teachers, as compared with their college professors, talked about plagiarism. Not surprisingly, I have received several different responses. One student, for example, claimed he did not bother to read the university honor code because what constituted plagiarism had already been thoroughly dealt with in his high school. On the other hand, students indicated that plagiarism appeared more complicated at the college and university levels and that their high school teachers did not handle plagiarism cases too seriously. Regardless, the questionnaire may help students and teachers become more proactive in clarifying one of the main concerns in the scenarios—what constitutes the boundary between teacher-sanctioned collaboration and improper collaboration. For example, I have talked with students who expressed concern about how, in their geology, physics, or engineering labs, they could be accused of plagiarism simply because their final lab reports looked so similar to the reports of the peers with whom they had conducted experiments and discussed results.

As this brief study suggests, there are many uses of the "Attitudes towards Plagiarism" questionnaire, the most important of which I believe is to promote dialogue between teachers and students about such issues as collaboration, paraphrasing, and ownership of ideas. Because these scenarios may not address specific institutional concerns or technological innovations, I encourage teachers and students to create and talk about their own scenarios. In the online questionnaire, for example, two participants suggested that I should include a scenario that described a recent change in their institution's honor code, one which classified work or research conducted in one class, yet submitted to another, as academic misconduct. These types of scenarios can contribute to how we perceive plagiarism and its consequences for writing and the teaching of writing.

Notes

1. I thank Elise Barker, Jerrod Bohn, Ron Downey, and Emily Merrifield for their contributions.

2. This study was a replication of an earlier pilot study I conducted at a different institution. Amy Martin has also used a modified version of the "Attitudes towards Plagiarism" questionnaire to test the fitness of The Council of Writing Program Administrators' statement on plagiarism and to examine how faculty in the humanities, sciences, and social sciences respond to the scenarios differently.

3. Other studies that have deployed the "Attitudes towards Plagiarism" questionnaire demonstrate the variance of the Collaboration Scenario (#8). In the pilot study, 55% of the instructors considered this scenario as plagiarism. In Martin's study, 81% of humanities instructors considered it plagiarism, whereas 100% of science instructors defined it as plagiarism (69).

Works Cited

Ashworth, Peter, Philip Bannister, and Pauline Thorne. "Guilty in Whose Eyes? University Students' Perceptions of Cheating and Plagiarism in Academic Work and Assessment." *Studies in Higher Education* 22.2 (1997): 187–203. Print.

Howard, Rebecca Moore. "Sexuality, Textuality: The Cultural Work of Plagiarism." *College English* 62 (2000): 473–91. Print.

Love, Patrick, and Janice Simmons. "Factors Influencing Cheating and Plagiarism among Graduate Students in a College of Education." *College Student Journal* 32 (1998): 539–49. Print.

Martin, Amy. "Plagiarism and Collaboration: Suggestions for 'Defining and Avoiding Plagiarism: The WPA Statement on Best Practices.'" *Writing Program Administration* 28.3 (2005): 57–71. Print.

Roig, Miguel. "When College Students' Attempts at Paraphrasing Become Instances of Potential Plagiarism." *Psychological Reports* 84 (1999): 973–82. Print.

Spigelman, Candace. "Habits of Mind: Historical Configurations of Textual Ownership in Peer Writing Groups." *College Composition and Communication* 49 (1998): 234–55. Print.

Questions for Discussion

1. Discuss with peers and your instructor(s) the "concepts of originality, common knowledge, and collaboration" that Phillip Marzluf discusses. Working in groups, talk about what you think each of those

concepts means to you, and compare it to the definitions in Marzluf's essay. How do your definitions compare to or contrast with those of your instructor? Why?

2. Marzluf writes, "The scenarios consist of the four variables that appear most often in my discussions about plagiarism with teachers and students: the writer's level of intentionality, the degree of appropriation, the borrowing of ideas and/or expression, and the status of the source." Now that you have read his chapter, go back to the definition of plagiarism that you wrote before you read the chapter. How would you rank the variables Marzluf discusses in terms of their importance in determining whether something is plagiarized? How does your ranking change your definition of what constitutes plagiarism?

2 Plagiarism vs. Copyright Law: Is All Copying Theft?

Jessica Reyman

Before You Read: What images or emotions are conjured when you hear the phrases "plagiarism" and "allowable copying"? Consider what it means to "own" an idea.

SCENARIO 1

A student uses a template when creating a formal report for class. She has seen this method used for composing in her internship, where she writes letters, reports, and other documents for a company. She finds a model of a formal report on the Internet that closely matches the model she found in her textbook, and uses it as a template. She copies the headings and formatting, and even some of the sentence structures from various sections. She pastes her own content into the report. Is this stealing?

SCENARIO 2

A student is creating a website for his writing class. While he is confident in his ability to write the content for the site, he does not have the time or resources to learn advanced Web design and coding skills before the assignment is due. In order to submit a professional-looking website, he copies some source code from an existing website and pastes it into his own source code. The student has written all of the content for the website on his own, but the architecture, structure, organization, and user interface of the site is mostly derived from the source code he has copied from an existing website. Is this stealing?

SCENARIO 3

A student submits a research paper that summarizes and reports on information she has found in journals, books, websites, and blogs. In the paper, she cites many sources, but one website is particularly useful. From this source, she cites liberally, even copying and pasting whole paragraphs of text that support her points. She provides attribution in each instance, for both paraphrases and direct quotations from the source. Is this stealing?

Many students fear they may be "stealing" or committing intellectual property "theft" whenever they make use of any existing material in their writing. They have been warned against such uses by several sources. Instructors and university administrators tell them they must follow plagiarism policies or they will be expelled from school. In the news, they see their peers venture into the professional world and face public criticism for plagiarism. Consider the 2003 scandal surrounding Jayson Blair, a recent college graduate who was employed as a staff writer for the *New York Times*, who allegedly plagiarized an article from another newspaper; and, the 2006 accusations against undergraduate student Kaavya Viswanathan for allegedly plagiarizing passages for her novel, *How Opal Mehta Got Kissed, Got Wild, and Got a Life*. Warnings against copyright infringement claims are also prevalent, as students are inundated by the messages from media companies and campus officials alike, who counsel them on the dangers of pirating music and movies from the Internet. Some universities have even aided the entertainment industry in pursuing legal action against individual students caught illegally downloading files, resulting in costly settlements. These stories and others have infiltrated conversations on many college campuses, warning students against copying with a seemingly simple message: "Don't steal."

However, the message is not that simple. Students often hold misconceptions about what constitutes theft of intellectual property. Such misconceptions have the potential to lead students to unwittingly commit a legal and/or ethical offense by assuming that all copying is acceptable, a great concern for college instructors and administrators.

Alternatively, they can lead to students not using the material in question for fear of punishment, another serious problem that can frustrate students' writing efforts and lessen the value of their work. Students will want to better understand the nuances inherent in defining what constitutes plagiarism and copyright infringement so that they can make more informed choices about when and how to use external sources. As a starting point, this chapter seeks to complicate the message of "don't steal" in two ways. First, I show that what intellectual theft refers to is actually two separate offenses: copyright infringement and plagiarism. While the concepts are intertwined in popular discourse as constituting "stealing," the label conflates and oversimplifies two distinct and complex offenses. Campus administrators, instructors, and students often misunderstand the relationship between plagiarism and copyright law. Many think plagiarism is wrong because it is illegal, and many believe attribution affects cases of copyright infringement. These misunderstandings, among others, can confuse conversations about student writers' ethical and legal responsibilities when using sources. After defining key differences between the two concepts, I then show how much of what is regarded as stealing might actually fall within the range of what is considered allowable copying. For instance, do the tasks of downloading papers from an online paper mill, and cutting, pasting, and reusing excerpts of text with attribution demand equal treatment under plagiarism policies and under the law? Is either acceptable practice? In the second part of this chapter, I argue for a distinction between allowable copying and theft that acknowledges the gray areas that exist between original composition, copyright infringement, plagiarism, copying, and reusing text.

Plagiarism vs. Copyright Infringement

In order to complicate the notion of intellectual theft, it is first important to make clear distinctions between the institutional concept of plagiarism and the legal concept of copyright infringement. The two concepts are two distinct offenses that student writers face, both in their current academic settings and in their future professional contexts. As defined in the *Council Chronicle*, a publication for the National Council of Teachers of English (NCTE):

> Plagiarism is using someone else's idea (usually a written idea) without giving proper credit for the idea,

a failure to cite adequately. ("Plagiarism and Copyright")

[and]

Copyright infringement is using someone else's creative idea, which can include a song, a video, a movie clip, a piece of visual art, a photograph, and other creative works, without authorization or compensation, if compensation is appropriate. ("Plagiarism and Copyright")

Using this definition as a starting point, there are several distinctions that I'll parse so that we can better understand the differences between the two: the offense of copying ideas vs. copying the expression of those ideas, the practice of attribution, and institutional vs. legal ramifications.

Copying Ideas vs. Expression

The first and most fundamental distinction to be made between plagiarism and copyright is what type of copying constitutes each activity. Plagiarizing a text and committing copyright infringement of that same work may not result from the same behavior. This disparity arises because plagiarism policies and copyright law protect different things. Plagiarism policies are designed to protect the academic integrity of the classroom and the university; they attempt to prevent cheating. Copyright law, on the other hand, is designed to protect the exclusive rights of authors to seek rewards from copying, distributing, and performing works they've created; it attempts, primarily, to protect a vibrant and dynamic economic market of creative production.

Definitions of plagiarism are specific to individual academic institutions and sometimes to departments or units within a given institution. Here is the definition of plagiarism at my institution, Northern Illinois University, which I believe is typical of many definitions: "Students are guilty of plagiarism, intentional or not, if they copy material from books, magazines, or other sources without identifying and acknowledging those sources or if they paraphrase ideas from such sources without acknowledging them" (*Undergraduate Catalog* 49).

We can see from this definition that plagiarism refers to both copying of exact text ("material from books, magazines, or other sources") in addition to using the ideas contained within those sources ("paraphrasing ideas"), even if they are rewritten in a student's own words. Copying both ideas and the expression of ideas without acknowledging a source are violations of plagiarism policies.

Copyright law does not protect this same type of activity. Copyright provides the creators of original works of authorship with the exclusive rights to copy, distribute, and perform their works, among other privileges. Such protection, however, only applies to the "expression" of ideas, not the ideas themselves. In order for a work to be protected by copyright, it needs to be "fixed in a tangible medium of expression." Therefore, many types of works are protected by copyright as soon as they become fixed in a tangible form—such as an essay, a book, a website, a motion picture, a song, or an architectural work, among others. At the same time, ideas themselves are not copyrightable. For instance, while a particular motion picture (*Pretty Woman*) is copyrighted, the idea for a common plot theme contained within it ("rags to riches") is not. Think of all of the other movies that have used this same plotline before and since the release of *Pretty Woman*, each lawfully doing so due to the fact the copyright law does not protect ideas.

INSTITUTIONAL VS. LEGAL OFFENSES

Another important distinction to be made between plagiarism and copyright infringement is that the two offenses are enforced by different governing bodies. As the NCTE points out, "Schools enforce plagiarism. The courts enforce copyright infringement" ("Plagiarism and Copyright"). While plagiarism is an academic offense, punishable within the school or university setting, copyright infringement is a legal offense, punishable under the United States legal system.

Punishment for plagiarism runs the gamut from a verbal reprimand, to earning a failing grade on an assignment, to failing a class, to being expelled from an institution. Punishment is often assigned at the discretion of the individual instructor or administrative body (such as an academic integrity committee) at a given school or university; it is not dictated by the legal system. As an example, the plagiarism policy at my institution says that "Students guilty of, or assisting others in, either cheating or plagiarism on an assignment, quiz, or examination may receive a grade of F for the course involved and may be suspended or dismissed from the university" (*Undergraduate Catalog* 49). The wording "*may* receive a grade of F" and "*may* be suspended or dismissed" (emphasis added) shows there is a variety of levels of punishment for students caught committing plagiarism.

Copyright infringement claims, because they are supported by federal law, are enforced according to a single definition under the legal system. Punishment for committing copyright infringement includes fines and, because it is a federal offense, even the possibility of a prison sentence. The legal system decides what activity is infringing and what constitutes a fair punishment for the crime. To decide whether a particular use is infringing or not, the courts often rely on what is called the Fair Use Doctrine of U.S. Copyright Law. The Fair Use Doctrine in copyright law specifies that "purposes such as criticism, comment, news reporting, teaching (including multiple copies for classroom use), scholarship, or research" are all instances in which otherwise infringing activity would not be subject to penalty. The Fair Use clause is used within the legal system to evaluate each use according to this four-point test:

> In determining whether the use made of a work in any particular case is a Fair Use, the factors to be considered shall include:
>
> 1. The purpose and character of the use, including whether such use is of a commercial nature or is for nonprofit educational purposes;
>
> 2. The nature of the copyrighted work;
>
> 3. The amount and substantiality of the portion used in relation to the copyrighted work as a whole;
>
> 4. The effect of the use upon the potential market for or value of the copyrighted work. (U.S. Copyright Law)

It is not within the scope of this essay to offer a lengthy commentary on the Fair Use clause and its applicability for students and educators. Suffice it to say, the effect of this four-factor balancing act has been considerable uncertainty and confusion over whether certain uses are infringing or not. In order to understand whether a particular use is a Fair Use, creators must carefully weigh each factor against all other factors for each particular use in each instance. Nevertheless, the Fair Use Doctrine remains perhaps the most important and wide-reaching exemption from copyright protection for students and instructors, whose use of others' copyrighted works is often for the purposes of criticism, commentary, teaching, or research. It is this important exemption that the legal system relies on most heavily to determine whether the copying required by the common activities of students and instructors is lawful or not.

ATTRIBUTION OF SOURCES

The third and last distinction I'll make between plagiarism and copyright infringement is the role of attribution, or citing sources. Many students and instructors alike believe that as long as writers cite their sources, they are free and clear of any accusations of intellectual theft. While attribution is important for avoiding plagiarism claims, copyright infringement does not directly relate to the presence or lack of attribution when copying a work. This distinction is based on the differences between the types of harm resulting from each offense. In acts of plagiarism, the harm is related to academic integrity. Plagiarism is considered cheating: if grades and degrees are awarded according to individual effort and ability, then plagiarism is a dishonest representation of this effort and ability and, thus, an offense against the academic integrity of the institution. Because plagiarism is an ethical violation rather than a legal violation, attribution plays a key role. To avoid claims of cheating, a student is required to cite sources to demonstrate that she or he is not intending to present as her or his own work that which she or he has not produced. Attribution provides an ethical means through which to distinguish a student's work from another's in an assignment submitted for a grade.

Copyright infringement, on the other hand, serves to protect the rights of an author to a reward for her or his work and incentive for creating future works. Copyright infringement claims are usually brought under the legal system when an act of copying has caused some sort of loss of monetary value in the work. If a person writes a book, but another person copies parts of it, markets it, and sells it, even when giving attribution to the original author, the new work will compete in the same market as the first book and negatively affect its sales. This is not to say that writers may feel free to copy a copyrighted work if it is for a nonprofit purpose. Some nonprofit uses also have an adverse effect on the value of intellectual and creative works. Therefore, in the case of copyright infringement, even if attribution for a source is given, copying, using, and/or distributing another's copyrighted work may prevent an author from receiving reward for their work. While attribution will assist with plagiarism charges, in itself it does not negate copyright infringement claims.

MISCONCEPTIONS ABOUT COPYRIGHT INFRINGEMENT AND PLAGIARISM

Given these key distinctions between plagiarism and copyright law, we can begin to complicate the seemingly simple message perpetuated in popular discourse often circulated on college campuses, "don't steal." We have seen that not all copying is treated equally; that is, different types of copying for different purposes yield different consequences. Based on the discussion above, we know that some copying may constitute plagiarism but not copyright infringement, and vice versa. We might further complicate the relationship between plagiarism and copyright infringement by considering the ways popular misconceptions of intellectual theft are often in conflict with the common composing activities of recycling and reusing materials that student writers engage in, such as those presented in the scenarios at the opening of this chapter. It is important to recognize that there are other "gray areas" that exist between what is considered intellectual theft under plagiarism policies and the law, and the range of composing activities that require the copying and reuse of existing materials.

Is All Copying Theft?

Often in writing classes, the act of copying is equated with intellectual theft, which is contrasted with the notion of originality of words and ideas. What makes this dichotomy between theft and originality problematic is that an autonomous, proprietary model for textual ownership conflicts with what we understand about actual composing processes. As Rebecca Moore Howard points out in *Standing in the Shadows of Giants: Plagiarists, Authors, Collaborators*, student writers move toward membership of a discourse community by using other writers' texts and drawing from multiple voices. For instance, when learning to write a research paper, students are often asked to prepare notes or create paraphrases, summaries, and direct quotations of existing literature on a topic, and then later arrange them within the structure of their own main points or arguments. This work is often done digitally, by copying and pasting source material into a file that eventually becomes reused and revised and built upon, resulting in a polished research essay. In this process, we can see that the distinctions between copied texts and students' own words can become less obvious, and the dichotomy between theft and originality can become blurred. Writers relying on this process do not create new works from nothing, in isolation, but rather they borrow, build on, and interact with other texts with which they have come into contact. This act of writing is fundamentally collaborative with other texts, relying on reuse and integration of existing works.

In fact, we copy works without plagiarizing or committing copyright infringement all the time. There are many examples of ways writers copy and reuse materials that do not constitute an unethical act of intellectual "theft." For instance, consider the following activities in which writers copy others' works:

- Using models or templates when writing within a new genre or completing an assignment (i.e., using the design, layout, categories, and format, but plugging in one's own content);
- Summarizing or paraphrasing ideas from texts into notes when preparing to write a research paper; and
- Incorporating ideas from a peer, writing tutor, or other influential source when revising a piece of writing.

While these activities obviously require some level of copying, they are also common activities engaged in by writers as we perform the activities required of us in the classroom. Therefore, rather than understanding that "all copying is theft," we might instead understand that "some copying is allowable." The task for instructors and students is to think critically and carefully about under what circumstances and for what purposes the copying occurs.

This is not to say that some copying is not unethical or not allowable in certain contexts. There is a tension that exists between borrowing too much from an existing source and building on a source to offer something new: Copying and passing something off as your own can be an ethical and legal violation, but copying something with the intention of adding value, or because it is part of a natural composing process, may not. For instance, a writer might choose to create a parody of an existing work of art, perhaps a parody of a beauty advice column from *Cosmopolitan* magazine that provides social commentary on media-imposed standards for beauty inflicted on women. This act of copying would likely be an ethical and lawful form of copying, contributing to the advancement of knowledge on issues of gender and the media. However, downloading a copy of a research paper on media portrayals of standards of beauty and turning it in for class credit is an obvious ethical (and likely legal) violation, offering no added value in the creation of a new work. The point here is that there are gray areas that exist between different forms of copying: Some forms of copying are beneficial and others detrimental to the promotion of learning.

Does the Internet Contribute to Plagiarism?

Seeking to further complicate the conflation of all types of copying as intellectual "theft," it is also useful to think about a common belief that the Internet itself contributes to intellectual theft. Writing online often involves collaborating with other writers or cutting, pasting, and reusing text, all of which may be at odds with common understandings of plagiarism policies and/or copyright law. It is not uncommon to hear on our campuses and in our classrooms that the Internet makes plagiarism easier, or that cutting and pasting material from the Internet should be avoided altogether. In these statements and others like them, the Internet itself is credited for undesirable outcomes: the facilitation of legal and ethical infractions. Rather than viewing the use of writing technologies as facilitating common modes of composing, these perspectives posit writing electronically as *causing* certain offenses. The common activities of student writers—copying and pasting excerpts from online texts when conducting research, finding templates and models from other sources, relying on existing discussions to inform and guide their own writing—are each facilitated by Internet technologies. However, these same technologies are often presented as inherently dangerous, as causing a rise in cases of plagiarism or making copyright infringement more prevalent. We should be particularly careful about assuming this negative approach to the relationship between technology and writing. Instead of "blaming" technology for unethical or unlawful practices, we might instead view technologies as facilitators, through their copy, paste, and distribution functionalities, of the strategies fundamental to contemporary composing practices.

The misconceptions about copying in composing processes presented here are only two among many. Broadly speaking, the approaches to plagiarism and copyright infringement in writing classrooms and on college campuses often appear to have a common goal of exposing intellectual thieves, with the ultimate intention of denouncing and punishing them. Students who commit ethical infractions by cheating certainly deserve punishment within the academic setting, and students who knowingly commit copyright infringement are certainly liable under the law. Unfortunately, contemporary approaches to the two offenses do not offer effective strategies for addressing the range of activities that student writers engage in that might be allowable copying. Too often, a student writer engaging in any of a wide range of activities may be unfairly accused of either plagiarism (at the academic level) or copyright infringement (at the legal level) while performing the processes inherent to composing in a digital age.

CONCLUSION: TOWARD AN UNDERSTANDING
OF ALLOWABLE COPYING

In light of public discourse surrounding recent offenses of plagiarism and copyright infringement, the writing activities that many students encounter might be unfairly characterized as illegal and/or in violation of plagiarism policies. If we, as students and instructors of writing, seek to better understand the dangers of the label "stealing" as applied equally to all copying, we need to more openly acknowledge the range of acceptable copying and reuse of intellectual property that is inherent in many composing practices. With the aim of distinguishing between acceptable copying and theft, it's useful to make explicit those types of composing that occur within the gray areas that exist between original composition, copyright infringement, plagiarism, copying, and reusing text. To do so, let's return to the three scenarios presented at the opening of this chapter. Based on the content of this chapter, each might be considered as copyright infringement, plagiarism, both, or neither.

In *Scenario #1*, where the student relies on a model for a formal report, this student is behaving in a manner consistent with common workplace practices (for more on the discrepancies that exist between professional writing practices and plagiarism, see Logie; Reyman). Recall that this student uses the formatting and structure of the report, but plugs in her own content. In determining whether this copying is acceptable or not, we will need to consider the circumstances of the particular situation. It is essential to know whether the student has provided attribution for use of this template. If not, this copying may very well constitute plagiarism, particularly if a requirement for the assignment were to create a professional layout and design for a report. Without attributing the source of the model, the student could be accused of misrepresenting the design and layout as her own. On the other hand, if the assignment did not ask the student to demonstrate design skills, then the student may meet instructor expectations by following a stock format for a particular type of report (such as the IMRAD format for scientific reports). This type of copying would most likely not be considered copyright infringement. Because a model for a report likely constitutes an idea, rather than an original expression of an idea, it would not likely constitute a legal offense.

Scenario #2 involves the copying of lengthy passages of text into a research report, with correct attributions of all passages. Attribution counters accusations of plagiarism, even though the essay may not offer as much of the student's voice or thoughts as the instructor would like, but the act of attributing to its source a copied passage does not necessarily allay all claims of copyright infringement if this essay were published or distributed outside of the classroom. In this case, the student would need to consider the four factors of Fair Use to determine whether this copying is lawful. While it is for a nonprofit, educational purpose, the student would also need to consider the other three factors—the amount of use, the nature of the work, and the potential effect on the market for the original work—to determine whether or not this is an example of allowable copying. The length of the passages the student has copied could weigh against Fair Use when considering the four factors.

Finally, in *Scenario #3* we see the copying of HTML code for a website. Again, considering the context for the use is essential. Since the instructor may expect students to demonstrate that they understand the principles of good Web design by creating their own architecture, navigational structure, and page design elements for a website, then this copying would likely be considered plagiarism. Attribution of the source of the code may serve to counter such accusations. At the same time, plagiarism would not be an issue if the instructor explicitly recommended that students use an existing website template to present original content. Further, because some HTML code is protected by copyright and presumably, the websites are available to the public, the student would need to consider carefully whether the copying might also be an infringement of copyright. She would need to consider whether her copying of the code might be considered Fair Use according to an analysis of the four factors.

In closing, I want to stress again that, of course, cheating is a serious infraction. When a student copies a written work and turns it in with the intention of presenting the work as an assignment she or he has written, she or he has behaved unethically and perhaps illegally. At the same time, this chapter asks writers and writing instructors to complicate the seemingly simple message of "don't steal." Problematizing this message can occur on two fronts: First, we can consider the distinctions between the two offenses of plagiarism and copyright infringement that are often conflated in public and academic discourse, and, second, we can recognize the range of types of allowable copying that commonly occur in contemporary composing processes but are often misunderstood as intellectual theft.

WORKS CITED

Howard, Rebecca Moore. *Standing in the Shadows of Giants: Plagiarists, Authors, Collaborators*. Stamford, CT: Ablex, 1999. Print.

Logie, John. "Cut and Paste: Remixing Composition Pedagogy for Online Workspaces." *Internet-Based Workplace Communications: Industry and Academic Applications*. Ed. Kirk St. Amant and Pavel Zemliansky. Hershey, PA: Information Science Publishing, 2005. 299–316. Print.

—"Plagiarism and Copyright—What Are the Differences?" *Council Chronicle*. National Council for Teachers of English. November 2005. Web. 20 October 2006.

Reyman, Jessica. "Rethinking Plagiarism for Technical Communication." *Technical Communication* 55.1 (2008): 61–67. Print.

Undergraduate Catalog: 2006-2007. Northern Illinois University. NIU Bulletin Series. 35 (2): May 2005. Print.

U.S. Copyright Law. Title 17, Chapter 1, Section 101. U.S. Copyright Office. Web. 20 October 2006.

QUESTIONS FOR DISCUSSION

1. While plagiarism is discussed widely in secondary and postsecondary education, concepts like Fair Use and intellectual property are not. Why do you think this is so? Has your understanding of these terms, and those terms you analyzed in the "Before You Read" section, changed after you read this essay? How are these terms relevant to you now?

2. Jessica Reyman writes: "Therefore, rather than understanding that 'all copying is theft,' we might instead understand that 'some copying is allowable.'" In what ways does her disentanglement of the definitions of plagiarism and copyright law surprise you and/or change the ways in which you view "plagiarism" and "allowable copying"? Think back to Phillip Marzluf's chapter: Do Reyman's definitions change your ranking and rationale for Marzluf's ten scenarios? Why or why not? In which cases do you believe the students are engaging in "allowable copying"?

3 Art and the Question of Borrowing: Approaches to Plagiarism in Literature Courses

Esra Mirze Santesso

Before You Read*: Many of today's movies are remakes or reinterpreta-tions of older movies or books, sometimes even classic books, like William Shakespeare's* Romeo and Juliet *or Jane Austin's* Emma. *Do you consider this "borrowing" or "stealing"? In what sense are such movies "original"?*

"Immature poets imitate; mature poets steal." T. S. Eliot's famous claim demonstrates the complicated nature of literary inspiration: Authorial borrowing is not only condoned, but even celebrated, often as a way of paying homage, or reviving ideas. Indeed, earlier literature often treats originality as vaguely improper: Consider the Renaissance emphasis on "Imitation" or the eighteenth-century notion that the proper subject of poetry, to use Alexander Pope's phrase, was "What oft was thought." There has been much discussion in the academy—in the United States and abroad—about how and where artists get their inspiration, and how much of that inspiration feeds into their works. In *The Polemic of Stealing* (*Çalinti Polemikleri*), Mahmut Çetin looks at the artistic process in literature, film, and criticism arguing that the act of creation rests often on the ability to find stimulation in earlier works. Giving specific examples of identical passages, Çetin substantiates his accusations of direct plagiarism in popular texts. The line between borrowing—that is, the recycling of an idea in a parodic manner—and stealing often naturally blurs. This blurring raises ques-tions about possible cases of plagiarism and copyright violations in the professional world, creating negative outcomes both morally and legally. In the light of these discussions, the challenge is to understand how and why literary borrowing is often permissible, while plagiarism is not. This chapter addresses the ambiguous relationship between literary borrowing, on the one hand, and plagiarism on the other; the discussion will reveal that these terms are often conflated gratuitously, and that the desire to reduce plagiarism cases in the classroom has led to disengagement with questions about artistic borrowing. By distinguishing between plagiarism (an ethical issue based on the failure to give due credit to the sources adopted in a paper), and borrowing (an acceptable form of inspiration leading to the reinterpretation of an earlier work), I attempt to explore both terms in a critical manner.

Often, the discussion on plagiarism between instructors and students of literature is not a discussion at all but rather a quick mention in the syllabus. In "Plagiarism: The Worm of Reason," Augustus M. Kolich argues that there is a tendency to overlook plagiarism as a problem in the classroom since such discussion is seen by some as an admission of the instructor's failings:

> [I]f students plagiarize, either the teacher has failed to "engage" them in a proper system of learning, or they are psychopaths who cannot be helped. Any successful writing program, and by extension, any successful teacher who teaches in that program need not bother with precautions against plagiarism or with lengthy discussions of its causes and effects. The problem is best ignored. (141)

Yet, unless there is an effort to make plagiarism a continuous and genuinely intellectual conversation during the semester, it is unrealistic to assume students will pay serious attention to it. With a strict list of do's and don'ts, plagiarism becomes a venial sin, the equivalent of jaywalking, a mindless rule that seems unimportant and inconsequential.

One specific problem faced in the literature classroom is the lack of consensus on the definition of plagiarism. Nebulous definitions, however, need not necessarily be an obstacle; on the contrary, they provide an opportunity to stimulate a philosophical conversation about artistic rights and practices. Despite (or perhaps because of) the complications provided by a literary consideration of plagiarism, I maintain that it is possible, and indeed imperative, to invite students and teachers to work together on viable definitions of plagiarism without discouraging student writers from borrowing from previous works. In this way, we can better appreciate the value of art as a dialogic process, a process through which different "voices" come alive, while becoming better informed about the moral issues related to stealing. We can treat this challenge as a teaching and learning moment in the literature classroom. By doing so, it is possible to move away from formulaic discussions of plagiarism as just another unexamined and "unfair" rule, and refocus our energies on an academic debate, one which we all must engage with intellectually.

An immediate obstacle in classroom discussions of plagiarism is the risk of demonizing intellectual collaborations and artistic dialogue. Christina Eira observes that

> in the rapid increase of the focus on the threat of plagiarism, it appears that the academic community has lost track of the implications of intertextuality, as a necessary aspect of the creation and communication of meaning. Reincorporating these established understandings of intertextuality [. . .] will offer a balancing function in our attempts to make sense of plagiarism issues.

What Eira expresses here is a caution against textual purity, the illusion that all writing could and should be original. It is impossible to think about literature as something created in a vacuum. Different forms of engagement with texts should prompt different results; it is important for writers to understand and identify both acceptable and unacceptable conventions of writing in different contexts. By separating issues of plagiarism, which describes the dishonest practice of refereeing someone else's work without proper citations, from borrowing, an attempt at reinterpreting older ideas to generate a new experience beyond the original intent, we can engage in fruitful conversation in the classroom. One way to demonstrate this is to show, for example, Marcel Duchamp's parody of the *Mona Lisa* in his work titled *elle a chaud au cul* ("she's got a hot ass") created in 1919. While Duchamp is clearly making a reference to an earlier work, his recreation cannot be perceived as stealing, but as an effort to insert his own creative self into an intellectual frame to question and reevaluate a work that has great influence in the art world. Or, one might turn to music: Pearl Jam's "Yellow Ledbetter" starts with a guitar solo inspired by the opening melody of Jimi Hendrix's "Little Wing." Such borrowings must be viewed as the natural by-product of a continuous dialogue with previous works of art.

Let me demonstrate how this perspective feeds into the literature courses I teach. Last semester I taught an upper division class of Contemporary World Literature which specifically focused on the art of borrowing. This course allowed me as an instructor to rethink how one might respond differently to the idea of recycling intellectual property without the threat of plagiarism. I arranged my course into several subdivisions connected by a consideration of globalization and its impact on literary production. The first subsection specifically addressed the notion of intertextuality, a concept we approached via Bakhtinian dialogism, which presupposes communication as a multilayered act: "everything means, is understood, as a part of a greater whole—there is a constant interaction between meanings, all of which have potential for conditioning others" (Bakhtin 426). Dialogism describes communication as a multifaceted practice, which complicates the relation between the sender (person uttering the word) and the receiver (person who interprets the meaning of the word). According to Mikhail Bakhtin, each word uttered has a complex history, and the interpretation of that history is what ultimately determines the effectiveness of communication. Deciphering a message, then, requires a collaborative effort between the sender and receiver, who attach a particular meaning to each word in light of its history. This idea is very much linked with the notion of intertextuality, a term that is useful in distinguishing between borrowing and stealing. Intertextuality can be defined simply as making deliberate allusions to an earlier work while interpreting another. The act of borrowing remains at the heart of intertextuality. Julia Kristeva explains:

> The word's status is thus defined horizontally (the word in the text belongs to both writing subject and addressee) as well as vertically (the word in the text is oriented towards an anterior or synchronic literary corpus) [. . .] each word (text) is an intersection of words (texts) where at least one other word (text) can be read [. . .] any text is constructed as a mosaic of quotations; any text is the absorption and transformation of another. (37)

Here, Kristeva discusses the interpretation of a text as a synchronic act; that is, one which requires an awareness of linguistic history. By alluding to earlier texts, the author complicates the reader's experience, and allows him/her to engage indirectly with an outside text that remains an integral part of the primary story. In other words, allusions demonstrate the intricate correlation between the past and the present, between experience and innovation. This notion is useful for understanding how writers around the globe engage in dialogue with one another, transcending time and space.

To demonstrate this point in my own class, I turned to literature and focused our attention on Orhan Pamuk's *My Name is Red* and Naguip Mahfouz's *Arabian Nights and Days*. Both of these novels stand in relation to other oral and written works. Pamuk's novel, for example, follows a dispute between Ottoman miniaturists, a division between those determined to honor tradition by imitating it and those who are seeking more progressive ways of representing the world on their canvases. The miniaturists who wish to continue to imitate earlier illustrations do not perceive this as stealing, but as replicating the perfection of the old masters. In their reproductions, they avoid introducing innovations and recycle the same classic subject matter inspired by ancient oral tales. Artists view their efforts as a way of complementing the stories; therefore, their ability to represent the symbolic meaning of the tale without the interference of personal style is highly esteemed. A master miniaturist in the novel reveals, "Where there is true art and genuine virtuosity the artist can paint an incomparable masterpiece without leaving even a trace of his identity" (19). Pamuk, therefore, creates sympathy for a medium in which originality is condemned and collectivity is celebrated, which presents a contrast with the modern celebration of originality and creativity. That world is clearly defined by the principles of collaboration and intertextuality while the contemporary world emphasizes unambiguous individual creation and ownership; and Pamuk himself, I always point out, makes this point by quoting traditional Persian stories about creation. In this light, the way the author employs intertextuality in his own writing can be seen as raising the question of how to pay homage to earlier artists.

Similarly, Mahfouz's *Arabian Nights and Days* can be read not only as a sequel to *The Thousand and One Nights* but also as a work that raises questions about textual reproduction. The book begins with Shahrazad's marriage to Shahryar, the infamous sultan who, after being cuckolded by his wife, decides to take a new wife each night only to murder her the next day. He finally meets his match with Shahrazad, who manages to survive due to her storytelling skills. Shahryar falls first to the spell of these stories, and then to the spell of the storyteller, and takes her as his final wife. Mahfouz's novel begins at this moment, where the original one ends. By choosing this particular literary moment, Mahfouz recycles a widely popular tale and reinvents an ending for the characters. In this way, he intricately weds tradition with modernity: The addition of a psychological dimension to the flat characters, and the writer's treatment of the existential crisis experienced by the protagonists are his way of reimagining what he borrows. Like Pamuk, Mahfouz also invokes popular oral tales from Arabic tradition (Aladdin, Sinbad, and Ali Baba, etc.), as well as engaging with Islamic wisdom literature inspired by the *hadiths* of the prophet Mohammed along with fantastic characters such as genies and angels mentioned in the Koran. These motifs intensify the primary story, which is ultimately a query about the nature of storytelling, of the complicated relationship between telling and retelling, originality and familiarity. In a way, Mahfouz's revisitation of the town originally described in *One Thousand and One Nights* summarizes the Nobel Prize winner's attitude toward the creation of the novel genre itself as a collaborative act between the East and the West as he argues:

> We Arab writers did borrow the modern concept of the short story and the novel from the West, but by now they have been internalized in our own literature. Many translations came our way during the forties and fifties; we took their style to be simply the way stories were written. We used the Western style to express our own themes and stories. But don't forget that our heritage includes such works as *Ayyam al-Arab*, which contains many stories—among them "Antar" and "Qays and Leila"—and of course *The Thousand and One Nights*. (El Shabrawy)

Mahfouz's argument that literature represents a complex mixture of "borrowing," "internalization" and "heritage" offers a jumping-off point for classroom discussions of how writing works.

The second subsection of my Contemporary World Literature course focused mainly on postcolonial rewritings: Jean Rhys's reworking of Charlotte Bronte's *Jane Eyre* in *Wide Sargasso Sea* and J. M. Coetzee's reinterpretation of Daniel Defoe's *Robinson Crusoe* in *Foe* recount familiar stories while constantly working against the assumptions of the reader. These works build on their predecessors; however, they also manipulate familiar story lines as a way of challenging the legitimacy of the original versions. By shifting between background and foreground stories, they present alternative accounts of the two highly canonized works. The motive here, then, is not to reproduce a literary experience but to create an entirely new insight into the meaning of the works, often by giving marginal characters a voice. Bertha (the madwoman in the attic in *Jane Eyre*) gains visibility in *Wide Sargasso Sea* as Antoinette, a repressed colonial woman from Jamaica. Similarly in *Foe*, Mary Barton presents her own side of the story as a shipwrecked woman sharing Crusoe's island. Through her narrative, she challenges the patriarchal authorial voice of the novel. By choosing a female character as his protagonist, Coetzee addresses the marginalization of women and questions the relationship between truth and fabrication, and how they are often intertwined in literary narratives. The rewritings of these widely known tales remain both interdependent and independent. They are, in essence, as original as the works with which they are engaged.

To further my points about intertextuality and rewriting, I turned to a different medium and played Madonna's "Music," immediately followed by Sertab Erener's rendition of the same song (featured in Fatih Akin's 2005 documentary *Crossing the Bridge: The Sound of Istanbul*). Even though Erener sings the same melody and lyrics, the arrangement of the music with Eastern rhythms and instruments generates an entirely new experience for the listener. This, I suggested, was a rewriting of the song—familiar material reinterpreted in a way that replaces the listener's original experience. I followed this with an example of intertextuality. I played Fazil Say's interpretation of Gershwin with the New York Philharmonic under Kurt Masur. During the song, "I Got Plenty O'Nuttin'," there is a brief solo by a clarinet player whose improvisation borrows from "Summer Time." This, I thought, was a clear demonstration of how intertextuality worked—a momentary reference to a familiar melody in passing, meant to enrich the larger composition in which it is located.

I thought wrong. A student raised her hand and said: "I don't think this is art. It's just laziness." Suddenly, I recognized how all of our discussions on the significance of rewritings and intertextuality might be boiled down to a simple and inaccurate explanation: lack of imagination. As a way of countering this charge, I broke the class up into small groups and asked them to rewrite their favorite song, poem, or story. By the end of the class, unsurprisingly, none of the groups was able to come up with a successful reworking. At this point, they were willing to concede that reinterpreting a familiar work—preserving its integrity while reshaping it in an unfamiliar way—was a difficult task. I was pleasantly relieved when the same student confessed, "this kind of laziness is too much work."

Initiating an intellectual discussion in the literature classroom about artistic inspiration and the process of creation might very well be the first step toward helping teachers and students genuinely engage with the question of plagiarism. Recent studies suggest that treating plagiarism as an unambiguous crime has not had successful results, but if literature professors can introduce plagiarism as an academic topic rather than a simple rule, then students can become part of the solution. Rather than imposing rules that may be difficult to grasp or care about, why not reflect together on our own creative processes and rethink the way we engage with other literary sources? This does not mean plagiarism cases should ever be treated nonchalantly; rather, it requires a shift in which plagiarism is integrated into the classroom: first by introducing plagiarism as something that is intellectually interesting, second by observing different forms of textual engagements and differentiating between borrowing and stealing, and finally, by creating opportunities to think about our own responsibilities as writers. In this way, we can appreciate creativity not necessarily as a manifestation of originality, but as a synthesis of ideas interpreted anew. As Malcolm Gladwell rightly points out, "Isn't that the way creativity is supposed to work? Old words in the service of a new idea aren't the problem. What inhibits creativity is new words in the service of an old idea" (13–14). By debating the distinction between different forms of engagement with earlier texts, we can create a learning environment that enhances the ability to analyze, synthesize, and recreate, while also maintaining personal responsibility. Such discussions can motivate us to reflect on the art of borrowing as an intellectual question, and allow us to recognize literary history as an interdependent process in which works stand in relation to one another rather than in isolation. This shift in perspective can undoubtedly benefit the development of each individual's own writing practices, and the appreciation of creativity and ownership.

WORKS CITED

Bakhtin, M.M. Glossary. *The Dialogic Imagination.* Ed. Michael Holquist. Austin: U of Texas P, 1981.423-434. Print.

Çetin, Mahmut. *Çalıntı Polemikleri.* Istanbul: Biyografi Net İletişim ve Yayın, 2005. Print.

Coetzee, J. M. *Foe.* New York: Penguin Books, 1988. Print.

Eira, Christina. "Obligatory Intertextuality and Proscribed Plagiarism: Intersections and Contradictions for Research Writing." *APEIC* December 2005. Web. 7 February 2008.

El Shabrawy, Charlotte. "Naguib Mahfouz." *The Paris Review* 1992. Web. 6 August 2008.

Erener, Sertab. "Music." *Crossing the Bridge: The Sound of Istanbul.* O.S.T., 2005. CD.

Gladwell, Malcolm. "Something Borrowed." *The New Yorker* 22 November 2004. Web. 4 August 2008.

Kolich, Augustus M. "Plagiarism: The Worm of Reason." *College English* 45.2 (1983): 141–48. Print.

Kristeva, Julia. "Word, Dialogue, and the Novel." *The Kristeva Reader.* Ed. T. Moi. New York: Columbia UP, 1986. 35–61. Print.

Mahfouz, Naguib. *Arabian Nights and Days.* Trans. Denys Johnson-Davies. New York: Anchor, 1995. Print.

Pamuk, Orhan. *My Name is Red.* Trans. Erdag Goknar. New York: Knopf, 2001. Print.

Rhys, Jean. *Wide Sargasso Sea.* 1982. New York: W.W. Norton & Company, 1998. Print.

Say, Fazil. *Gershwin.* Cond. Kurt Masur. Warner Music France, 2000. CD.

QUESTIONS FOR DISCUSSION

1. Esra Mirze Santesso writes: "Mahmut Çetin looks at the artistic process in literature, film, and criticism, arguing that the act of creation rests often on the ability to find inspiration in earlier works. He also notes that the line between inspiration and plagiarism often naturally blurs. This blurring raises questions about possible cases of plagiarism." Have you ever been so influenced by a writer's (or musician's) style or content that you tried to adopt that style, or were inspired by it

to create work of your own? How would you apply this artistic process Çetin describes to academic writing?

2. Though Santesso's chapter tackles the issue of plagiarism in the field of literature, many of its concepts can be applied across the disciplines, from the sciences to music, from engineering to architecture. How might you connect some of Santesso's points to one or more of these fields?

4 From Rules to Judgment: Exploring the Plagiarism Threshold in Academic Writing

Paul Parker

Before You Read: *Consider a page or two of something you've written that incorporates outside sources. Using different color highlighters or pens, identify those passages that are (a) your own ideas and own voice, (b) the ideas of someone else but expressed in your words (paraphrasing or summarizing), and (c) someone else's words (quotations). Do any patterns emerge? What do they suggest about your own writing?*

It is not uncommon to experience confusion and even fear when first attempting to incorporate the ideas or wordings of others in academic writing.[1] This is perhaps because many of us initially understand writing with academic integrity as simply a matter of demonstrating correct technical form, such as the accurate use of a specified citation system when quoting and paraphrasing from sources, or paraphrasing with words sufficiently different to those used in an original source. A preoccupation with technical form alone, however, can obscure the role of authorial judgment in producing academic writing that can withstand accusations of plagiarism. Writing with academic integrity involves more than just scrupulous management of information through strict adherence to rules and conventions. It also requires that authors operate as architects of analysis and argument who lead with independent critical judgment. This authorial judgment is particularly evident in the way academic writers construct a balance in their texts between an 'executive voice,' which presides over the flow of discussion throughout the whole text, and various 'expert voices' drawn from outside sources to lend support.

After establishing a basis in research for the confusion about plagiarism in academic writing, this article guides students and teachers through a series of citation examples that progressively build into a short passage of academic discussion. This progression not only allows us to interrogate the threshold separating plagiarism from legitimate borrowing but also reveals the important role of authorial judgment in managing the necessary uncertainty of original analysis in academic writing. A three-point criterion is subsequently proposed for producing academic text that can withstand accusations of plagiarism. The criteria prepares the way for an audit protocol we can use to investigate how this judgment has been applied in published academic texts from particular fields of study.

Mystery and Contradiction

Educational research has shown that academic writing, and plagiarism in particular, is often poorly understood by those entering higher education for the first time. Without explicit instruction in the scholarly values, assumptions, and practices of the Western academy, beginning students commonly experience academic writing as mysterious (Lillis 76). They can find themselves left alone to "invent the university" in their writing, slowly piecing together an understanding of scholarly expectations through a combination of osmosis, imitation, and guesswork (Bartholomae 134). Given the severe penalties associated with plagiarism, much of this effort may be spent puzzling over the boundary separating the legitimate use of borrowed ideas and wording from cheating. Empirical evidence has been available for at least a decade that suggests the majority of undergraduates are uncertain about this plagiarism threshold, especially with regard to adequate paraphrasing, and as a result, many plagiarize inadvertently (Roig, "Can" 113, 121). This problem is generally attributed to ignorance of convention or poor technical skills. Yet, the fact that even college and university professors can disagree about what constitutes plagiarism (see, for example, Roig, "Plagiarism" 313, 321) implies that the uncertainty is also conceptual in nature, which brings us back to the question of how academic writers first come to understand plagiarism.

The notion of plagiarism is likely to appear contradictory to those unfamiliar with the ways professional scholars use academic writing to analyze and test the propositions or "knowledge claims" made in published research (Penrose and Geisler 509–14). Academic writers perhaps experience this contradiction most acutely in relation to the Western academy's expectations of originality and corresponding disdain for imitation. Academic writing is expected to be "original" work, and yet a large part of its production ostensibly involves reproducing the views of established authors (Levin 4–7). Moreover, while it is recognized that imitation plays an important part in academic learning (Jensen and de Castell 325), particularly in a foreign language (Pennycook 225–26), the value of imitation for learning academic writing is undermined in an environment where copying from texts is strictly prohibited.

To move beyond these apparent contradictions and begin to demystify the plagiarism threshold it is useful to examine in turn the technical and conceptual considerations involved in writing with academic integrity. In so doing we will shift our understanding of plagiarism from questions of rigid compliance to those of delicate balance.

CITATION SYSTEMS AND TEXT MATCHING TOOLS

Since plagiarism places the reputation of an educational institution at great risk, the most common methods of informing students about how to use sources appropriately tend to be those that encourage the most visible compliance. Assessment by academic writing will almost certainly require that students demonstrate proficiency in one or more systems of referencing or citation. To this end, institutions will quickly direct beginning students to citation style manuals and perhaps also training sessions. With the growth of the Internet as a tool of plagiarism, many institutions have also begun to implement text matching software tools to scan student assignment submissions, sometimes on a mandatory basis, for text copied from electronic sources. We will now consider what these systems and tools tell us about what counts as plagiarism in academic writing.

Producing an Academic Audit Trail

The most apparent function of citation systems in academic writing is to provide readers with an audit trail of research sources. Credited sources need to be documented with consistency and precision so that an independent assessor (such as an essay examiner) can, potentially, locate and verify the information cited. While the preferred format for information varies with each system or "style," all provide conventions for three basic aspects of citation that scholars must observe to avoid plagiarism in their academic writing: citing ideas from outside sources by quoting select text from the original; citing ideas from outside sources by expressing those ideas in different words, that is by paraphrasing; and presenting the corresponding bibliographical details for each source in a list of works cited. These three aspects are modeled below in a manner similar to many style manuals. Such resources will often demonstrate each mode of in-text citation with isolated sentences, and also present samples of the bibliographical format to adopt for different types of publications. In this example, the bibliographical format of an academic journal article is presented in the Modern Languages Association (MLA) style used throughout this volume.

In-text citation for quotation:

Hendricks and Quinn conclude from previous studies of student academic literacy development that it is by "knowing when and how to reference that students demonstrate their ability to integrate, in their writing, knowledge they have gained from their reading with their own ideas" (448).

In-text citation for paraphrase:

As suggested by previous studies of academic literacy development, students' capacity to create in writing a synthesis of their own thinking and the evidence of published sources is apparent in the decisions they make about referencing (Hendricks and Quinn 448).

Bibliographical entry in list of Works Cited (Journal Article):

Hendricks, Monica, and Lyn Quinn. "Teaching
Referencing as an Introduction to Epistemological Empowerment." *Teaching in Higher Education* 5 (2000): 447–57.

Many academic libraries now provide citation management software that can automate these formatting operations while we write,
which highlights the essentially mechanical nature of citation systems.
Compared with the complexities of subject content and composition-
al subtleties of academic writing, the rigid and predictable nature of
these systems may be relatively comforting. Indeed, when combined
with the authoritative and procedural presentation of many style manuals, such qualities can create the impression that plagiarism is simply
the crime of failing to properly observe the formal "rules" of a citation
system. Yet, as will be shown in later examples, it is possible to properly
apply citation conventions to incorporate outside sources, but still produce academic writing that risks being accused of plagiarism.

Producing "Novel" Academic Text

While citation systems provide a means to expose the content of academic writing to external validation by manual means, text matching
software tools have been developed to automatically audit the technical novelty of the wordings used in paraphrases and in portions of text
presented as original writing. These tools measure novelty of linguistic form in purely differential terms, checking whether any portions
of text in electronically submitted work reproduce exactly (or, with
some tools, approximately) portions of text in existing electronic works
available to their search engine. To illustrate, if the journal article by
Monica Hendricks and Lyn Quinn quoted above was available to the
search engine of a text matching tool and Text 1 below was tested for
novelty of form, the tool would identify the text in italics as having
originated in that journal article.

Text 1:

By *knowing when and how to reference students* show
the capacity to combine in their essays *knowledge they
have gained from their* research *with their own ideas*
(Hendricks and Quinn 448).

Judgment must be applied to determine if such data provides evidence of plagiarism. While the source has been correctly cited, Text 1 would arguably constitute plagiarism on the grounds of insufficient paraphrasing. Portions of exact wording from the original source, the text in italics, have been seemingly "passed off" as paraphrased text. This is possibly because paraphrasing accrues greater academic merit yet is more difficult to produce than direct quotation. What this shows, in other words, is that the feedback provided by text matching software is only meaningful if we already have some understanding of what can count as plagiarism in academic writing. Moreover, these tools currently only highlight "verbatim copying" (Warn 201) of the kind illustrated on a small scale in Text 1. The following two examples serve to illustrate this limitation.

> Text 2:

> By understanding at what times and in what ways it is appropriate to cite, learners show they are able to combine in their essays information obtained from research sources with insights they develop themselves.

> Text 3:

> Students' capacity to create in writing a synthesis of their own thinking and evidence from published sources is apparent in the decisions they make about referencing.

In Text 2, the plagiarized text identified in Text 1 has been replaced with synonym words and phrases. The in-text citation has also been removed. An examiner would almost certainly regard this as a clear case of plagiarism due to the lack of citation and superficial paraphrasing. Although Text 3 offers a more substantial paraphrase that alters the structure of the original sentence (from active to passive voice), the lack of a citation means this unattributed paraphrase still constitutes plagiarism of ideas if not words. Yet, because the configuration of text used in both these examples of plagiarism is technically "novel," neither would be identified by text matching software. We can thus see that the feedback generated by text matching software needs to be approached with a critical appreciation of how the software functions.

While submitting assignment work for automated feedback can encourage authors to pay closer attention to their writing and academic skills (Green, et al.), this feedback does not in itself provide a complete picture of what can count as plagiarism in academic writing.

THE BALANCING ACT OF AUTHORIAL JUDGMENT

These standard methods of identifying what counts as plagiarism in academic writing have taught us two principles. Plagiarism is avoided if we (a) produce a reliable audit trail by correctly using a recognized citation system, and (b) ensure also that the text of our assignment work is novel in the sense that it does not reproduce any existing written text, except where properly identified as direct quotation. However, by applying these principles somewhat literally and in the extreme, as writers are sometimes prone to do, it is possible to see that a crucial element is still missing from the criteria. In Text 4 below, the by now familiar quotation from Hendricks and Quinn (448) has been supplemented with citations from two new sources[2] to form a paragraph of discussion. The paragraph reads coherently and complies with criteria (a) and (b), but does this place it safely outside the realm of plagiarism? The predominance of cited material over original wording from the writer may be cause for doubt, particularly if large sections of an assignment were composed in this way.

Text 4:

By "knowing when and how to reference [. . .] students demonstrate their ability to integrate, in their writing, knowledge they have gained from their reading with their own ideas" (Hendricks and Quinn 448). In so doing students approximate the judgment of professional academic researchers who cite previous work partly to acknowledge "a debt of precedent" but also "to display an allegiance to a particular community or orientation, create a rhetorical gap for [their] research, and establish a credible writer ethos" (Hyland 342). There is a preference for paraphrase over direct quotation in expressing this judgment. This is perhaps because we demonstrate a deep understanding of unfamiliar subject matter by writing about it rather than just copying verbatim. As Uemlianin argues:

> [P]araphrase is more than simply a test of or a result of understanding; paraphrase is part of what it is to understand. In practice attempts to understand often take the form of attempts to paraphrase: one attempts to understand something by trying to articulate it in different words, or to explain it to someone else. (347)

Text 5 is likely to raise similar concerns. While direct quotation has been replaced with paraphrase, arguably achieving greater coherence, this paragraph could still be accused of lacking a strong authorial "voice" that presides over the three cited sources.

Text 5:

> Students' capacity to create in writing a synthesis of their own thinking and evidence from published sources is apparent in the decisions they make about referencing (Hendricks and Quinn 448). In making these decisions students approximate the judgment of professional academic researchers who, as Hyland observes (342), cite previous work partly to give due credit but also to position themselves and their work to contribute to the ongoing discussion of knowledge in their academic community. There is a preference for paraphrase over direct quotation in expressing this judgment. This is perhaps because we demonstrate a deep understanding of unfamiliar subject matter by writing about it rather than just copying verbatim. As Uemlianin argues, it is not so much that the ability to paraphrase ideas follows from a prior understanding of those ideas but rather that ideas are fully understood or absorbed *through* the process of their paraphrasing (347).

These reservations about whether or not Text 4 and 5 cross the plagiarism threshold suggest that a third criterion is at play. The technical demands of compliance with criterion (a) and (b) can obscure an additional expectation to demonstrate 'authorial judgment' in academic writing. That is, effective academic texts communicate the author's control or authority over meaning in the text. This judgment, which we can label criterion (c), is strongly reflected in the way these texts are composed to achieve a balance of independent analysis and carefully staged citation of outside sources. By performing this balancing act in their writing, academic authors show they can confront and inhabit a space of uncertainty that requires intellectual work beyond the simple compliance with citation rules seen in Text 4 and 5. Academic research and learning are precisely about engaging with the boundary between what is known and what is unknown. The task of academic authors, both student and professional, is to manage this uncertain boundary by actively reviewing, positioning, and harnessing previous research in their writing to produce independent insight: an outcome that might otherwise be termed "originality" of meaning or interpretation.

To observe how this independent insight can be expressed in academic writing we will now examine a longer example of discussion. In Text 6, the sources cited in earlier examples have been supplemented with new material to build a more sustained discussion of the topic that extends across two paragraphs. While reading this example, consider the concerns about weak author voice raised above in relation to Texts 4 and 5. Does this new version seem more likely to resist the concerns about plagiarism raised by these previous examples?

Text 6:

The expectation that students reference appropriately in their academic writing needs to be understood as more than just a matter of acknowledging and authenticating outside sources. While it is necessary to give due credit when borrowing text in Western cultures that have evolved a "sense of the private ownership of words" (Ong, qtd. in Pennycook 205), referencing also plays an important role in the kind of learning students are expected to engage in by writing research papers. This is perhaps most apparent in higher education where students develop independent judgment by writing critically with and about the knowledge produced by their academic discipline. Hendricks and Quinn specifically highlight the place of referencing in this nexus of academic learning, knowledge, and writing. They draw on studies of university student writing to argue that in making decisions about "when and how to reference" in research papers, students develop their capacity to create a synthesis of their own thinking and evidence from published sources (448).

By applying referencing conventions in this way to integrate individual insight with established knowledge, writers approximate the authorial judgment of professional academic researchers. This learning has both social and cognitive dimensions. First, in social terms, writers gain the right to "legitimate peripheral participation" (Lave and Wenger 29) in the intellectual projects of academic "communities of practice" (Wenger 45). As Hyland observes in his study of referencing practices across different disciplines (342), academics cite previous work not only to give credit but also to position themselves and their work to contribute to the ongoing discussion of knowledge in their academic community. Second, the preference for incorporating the work of others through paraphrase rather than direct quotation is believed to enhance a writer's intellectual engagement with that material. It is assumed that a deep understanding of unfamiliar subject matter is better achieved by writing about this material than by just copying it verbatim. There is support for this view in Uemlianin's finding that the paraphrasing process engages students in basic analysis of source information. His results suggest the ability to paraphrase ideas in writing does not simply derive from a prior understanding of those ideas but rather that ideas are understood or absorbed *through* the process of their paraphrasing (347).

We can address this question through a more systematic analysis of the text's structure. Figure 4.1 presents the balance of author voice and supporting citations in Text 6 in the form of a diagram. Sentences and phrases containing citations have been separated into circles to reveal that the remaining sentences, shown as boxes, form a chain of controlling statements that spans the two paragraphs: the binding voice of

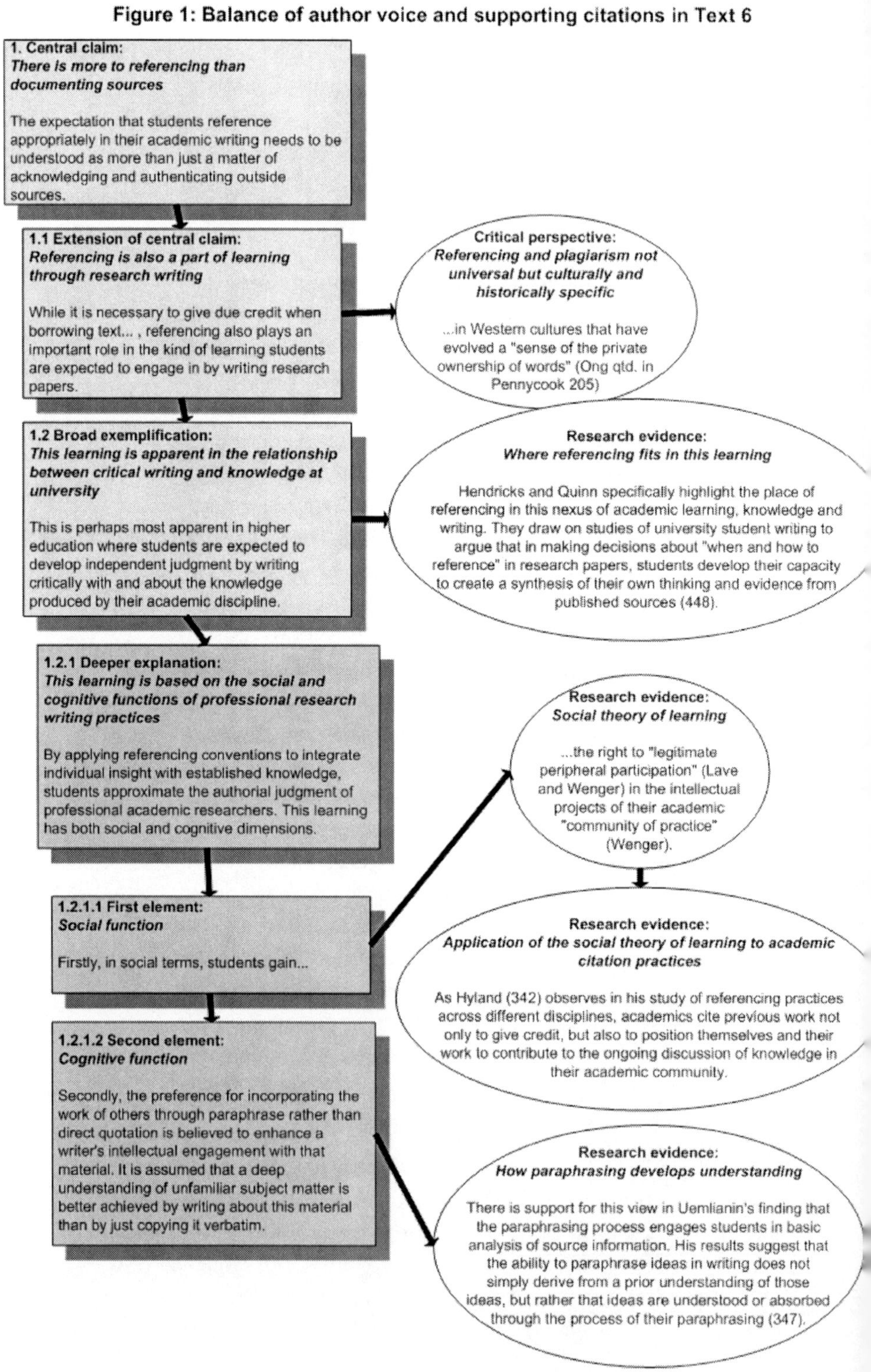

Figure 1: Balance of author voice and supporting citations in Text 6

1. Central claim:
There is more to referencing than documenting sources

The expectation that students reference appropriately in their academic writing needs to be understood as more than just a matter of acknowledging and authenticating outside sources.

1.1 Extension of central claim:
Referencing is also a part of learning through research writing

While it is necessary to give due credit when borrowing text... , referencing also plays an important role in the kind of learning students are expected to engage in by writing research papers.

Critical perspective:
Referencing and plagiarism not universal but culturally and historically specific

...in Western cultures that have evolved a "sense of the private ownership of words" (Ong qtd. in Pennycook 205)

1.2 Broad exemplification:
This learning is apparent in the relationship between critical writing and knowledge at university

This is perhaps most apparent in higher education where students are expected to develop independent judgment by writing critically with and about the knowledge produced by their academic discipline.

Research evidence:
Where referencing fits in this learning

Hendricks and Quinn specifically highlight the place of referencing in this nexus of academic learning, knowledge and writing. They draw on studies of university student writing to argue that in making decisions about "when and how to reference" in research papers, students develop their capacity to create a synthesis of their own thinking and evidence from published sources (448).

1.2.1 Deeper explanation:
This learning is based on the social and cognitive functions of professional research writing practices

By applying referencing conventions to integrate individual insight with established knowledge, students approximate the authorial judgment of professional academic researchers. This learning has both social and cognitive dimensions.

Research evidence:
Social theory of learning

...the right to "legitimate peripheral participation" (Lave and Wenger) in the intellectual projects of their academic "community of practice" (Wenger).

1.2.1.1 First element:
Social function

Firstly, in social terms, students gain...

Research evidence:
Application of the social theory of learning to academic citation practices

As Hyland (342) observes in his study of referencing practices across different disciplines, academics cite previous work not only to give credit, but also to position themselves and their work to contribute to the ongoing discussion of knowledge in their academic community.

1.2.1.2 Second element:
Cognitive function

Secondly, the preference for incorporating the work of others through paraphrase rather than direct quotation is believed to enhance a writer's intellectual engagement with that material. It is assumed that a deep understanding of unfamiliar subject matter is better achieved by writing about this material than by just copying it verbatim.

Research evidence:
How paraphrasing develops understanding

There is support for this view in Uemlianin's finding that the paraphrasing process engages students in basic analysis of source information. His results suggest that the ability to paraphrase ideas in writing does not simply derive from a prior understanding of those ideas, but rather that ideas are understood or absorbed through the process of their paraphrasing (347).

Figure 4.1: Balance of author voice and supporting citations in Text 6.

the author. In addition, each controlling and supporting element has been labeled with the function it performs in the text. From this view, it is possible to test the extent to which Text 6 meets the criterion of authorial judgment. If all of the citations were removed, the words that remain should still tell the basic "story" of the whole text. Ignoring the circles we can see that the linked sequence of controlling statements and functions shown by the boxes can indeed stand alone in this way. The chain begins with the topic sentence of the first paragraph, which also presents the central claim developed across both paragraphs (1: "There is more to referencing than documenting sources"); then proceeds to extend the central claim (1.1: "Referencing is also part of learning through research writing"); and finally closes the paragraph with a broad exemplification of where and how that extended claim occurs (1.1.1: "This learning is apparent in the relationship between critical writing and knowledge in university"). The topic sentence of the second paragraph continues to advance the central claim of the whole discussion by announcing two theoretical explanations for the extended claim (1.1.2: "This learning is based on the social and cognitive functions of professional research writing practices"). Finally, each of these perspectives (1.2.1: "Social function" and 1.2.2: "Cognitive function") is introduced and outlined in turn.

Returning now to the circles, Figure 4.1 also allows us to observe how, in stark contrast to Texts 4 and 5, these outside voices serve a secondary and supporting role in developing and substantiating the central chain of reasoning. At 1.1, the first expert voice is brought in to challenge the assumption that plagiarism is a universal concept. Next, the voice of Hendricks and Quinn is called upon to report research findings that elaborate on the meaning of 1.1.1 and also link to the new subtopic at 1.1.2. The controlling idea at 1.2.1 is first explained broadly with reference to concepts from Jean Lave and Etienne Wenger, before Ken Hyland is used to link these concepts to the academic context. Finally, the author summarizes the research findings of Ivan A. Uemlianin to provide some evidence for the assumption outlined in 1.2.2.

This simple analysis of structure in Text 6 has highlighted that the "multivoiced" nature of academic writing (Angelil-Carter, qtd. in Hendricks and Quinn 456) makes the balancing act of authorial judgment a necessary third component of maintaining a comfortable distance from the plagiarism threshold. If academic writing can be shown to have an "architecture" (Swales and Feak 122) of the kind illustrated by Figure 4.1, in which borrowed content is subordinate to the larger purpose of the argument, and this content has been cited accurately and with appropriate novelty of form, then this writing is very likely to withstand accusations of plagiarism.

FOLLOWING AN ACADEMIC AUDIT TRAIL
TO DEVELOP AUTHORIAL JUDGMENT

We can gather more specific data to inform our judgments about the plagiarism threshold in academic writing by actively researching and analyzing the citation and composition patterns favored in the work of published academic authors. This data will be more relevant if we choose examples of work published within our field of study. Hyland has shown (346–62), for example, that patterns of citation and attribution vary between academic disciplines in ways that reflect different approaches to knowledge.[3] In "hard" disciplines like the natural sciences and engineering, knowledge is acquired through the accumulation of unproblematic facts generated by research methodologies widely recognized by the discipline's community to remove human bias. As the following example illustrates, the dominant tendency therefore is to present citations in a form that is subordinate and structurally separate from the content of the statement. Moreover, it is very rare to see any use of direct quotation in these disciplines.

> The ability to paraphrase ideas in writing does not simply derive from a prior understanding of those ideas but rather ideas are understood or absorbed *through* the process of their paraphrasing (Uemlianin 347).

By contrast, so called "soft" disciplines like the humanities and certain branches of social science often treat knowledge as contingent upon particular theoretical perspectives and the application of these by individual scholars. To this end, there is a far greater tendency to cite in ways that acknowledge not only the source of the information reported but also the role of the originating author in producing this claim to knowledge. It is therefore common to find citations of the kind shown below in which the originating author is integral to the structure of the statement (in this case the grammatical subject of the sentence) and the controlling agent of a tentative reporting verb. Consider how the type of knowledge represented here would change if the tentative verb "argue" were replaced with a more definite verb like "find," "show" or "report." Finally, the greater value these "soft" disciplines place upon capturing knowledge in unique linguistic expressions means that we are more likely to see direct quotation of the author's original words, albeit very sparingly.

> *Hendricks and Quinn argue* that by "knowing when and how to reference [. . .] students demonstrate their ability to integrate, in their writing, knowledge they have gained from their reading with their own ideas" (448).

If set readings have been provided as part of a course of study, these texts should provide examples of citation and composition that are typical of that discipline. After locating suitable texts, we can select two or three and submit them to the following audit procedure:

> 1. Find a short passage in the text that contains several citations and make a photocopy. To ensure there is sufficient information to analyze, it is useful to examine a passage of discussion that spans at least two paragraphs, like Text 6 above. At this point, it is also useful to photocopy the list of works cited and attach this to the photocopied passage.

> 2. Identify all the sentences and phrases in the passage that cite outside sources and mark this text with a pencil or highlighter. Now answer the following questions about the passage:

> Does the unmarked text that remains function primarily to communicate the controlling voice of the passage? If so, in what ways is this achieved?

> What is the balance of controlling and subordinate voices in the passage? How does this balance relate to the author's purpose?

Are the cited sources linked to controlling statements, or to each other? What does this say about the function of each citation in the passage?

Do some citations seem to carry more weight or importance to the argument or flow of the passage than others do? How can we tell?

How has language been used to integrate each citation into the passage?

3. Select some of the citations from the passage. If the text includes both paraphrase and quotation, aim to select examples of both, including quotations of various sizes if these are available. Follow each citation to the bibliographical details of the source text presented in the list of works cited that was photocopied earlier.

4. With this information, visit an academic library to locate copies of the original source texts. Ask the librarians for assistance if these sources are difficult to locate.

5. Finally, compare the paraphrases and quotations that were selected from the passage with the corresponding content of the original source texts. Focus on the following in particular:

How much information from each original source has been cited in the passage?

Is there a relationship between the mode of citation in the passage, paraphrase, or quotation, and the amount of information cited from the original source? For example, do paraphrases in the passage correspond to specific sentences or phrases in the original source, or do they summarize larger sections or even main arguments that are developed throughout the whole source text?

A MATTER OF RESEARCH AND DISCUSSION

We have seen in this chapter that an important part of understanding what can count as plagiarism in academic writing is understanding when and how rules give way to judgment in the composition of academic texts. This authorial judgment is best learned by actively investigating and confronting the uncertainties of process in academic writing practice. By going beyond sentence-level examples to analyze progressively larger passages of academic text, it has been possible to observe how academic authors do more than comply with citation systems and produce technically novel text to keep their work clear of the plagiarism threshold. They also assert authority and control over the meaning in their texts by performing a careful balancing act of independent analysis and reference to outside sources. Moreover, by following the audit procedure outlined in the previous section, we can equip ourselves with data to better gauge where the plagiarism threshold manifests in particular fields of study. Textual research of this kind allows us to make more informed choices when incorporating outside sources in academic writing and to initiate a dialogue among students and teachers about the plagiarism threshold, and about where and how academic values and writing practices might be made more explicit. When student writers and their teachers approach the plagiarism threshold as a target of mutual inquiry (Haggis 530), that threshold is transformed from an arbitrary expectation or 'hidden curriculum' into a vehicle for critical engagement with academic learning.

NOTES

1. I would like to thank my colleagues Ros Martins and Maria Inglis for their valuable feedback during the drafting and revision of this article.
2. Bibliographical details for sources cited in the text examples appear in the list of Works Cited.
3. For detailed taxonomies of citation options and their rhetorical functions in academic discourse, see also Buckingham and Nevile, and Thompson and Tribble.

WORKS CITED

Bartholomae, David. "Inventing the University." *When A Writer Can't Write*. Ed. Mike Rose. New York: Guilford, 1985. 134–65. Print.

Buckingham, Joanna, and Maurice Nevile. "A Model of Citation Options." *Australian Review of Applied Linguistics* 20.2 (1997): 51–66. Print.

Green, David, Iris Lindeman, Kelly Marshall, and Grette Wilkinson. "Student Perceptions of a Trial of Electronic Text Matching Software: A Preliminary Investigation." *Journal of University Teaching and Learning Practices* 2.3a (2005). Web. April 2006.

Haggis, Tamsin. "Pedagogies for Diversity: Retaining Critical Challenge amidst Fears of 'Dumbing Down'." *Studies in Higher Education* 31.5 (2006): 521–35. Print.

Hendricks, Monica, and Lyn Quinn. "Teaching Referencing as an Introduction to Epistemological Empowerment." *Teaching in Higher Education* 5.4 (2000): 447–57. Print.

Hyland, Ken. "Academic Attribution: Citation and the Construction of Disciplinary Knowledge." *Applied Linguistics* 20.3 (1999): 341–67. Print.

Jensen, Jennifer, and Suzanne de Castell. "'Turn It In': Technological Challenges to Academic Ethics." *Education, Communication and Information* 4.2/3 (2004): 311–30. Print.

Lave, Jean, and Etienne Wenger. *Situated Learning: Legitimate Peripheral Participation*. New York: Cambridge UP, 1991. Print.

Levin, Peter. *Beat the Witch-Hunt! Peter Levin's Guide to Avoiding and Rebutting Accusations of Plagiarism, for Conscientious Students*. 2003. Web. May 2006.

Lillis, Theresa M. *Student Writing: Access, Regulation, Desire*. London: Routledge, 2001. Print.

Pennycook, Alastair. "Borrowing Others' Words: Text, Ownership, Memory and Plagiarism." *TESOL Quarterly* 30.2 (1996): 201–30. Print.

Penrose, Ann M., and Cheryl Geisler. "Reading and Writing Without Authority." *College Composition and Communication* 45.4 (1994): 505–20. Print.

Roig, Miguel. "Can Undergraduate Students Determine Whether Text has been Plagiarised?" *The Psychological Record* 47.1 (1997): 113–22. Print.

—. "Plagiarism and Paraphrasing Criteria of College and University Professors." *Ethics & Behavior: Special Issue* 11.3 (2001): 307–23. Print.

Swales, John M., and Christine B. Feak. *English in Today's Research World*. Ann Arbor: U of Michigan P, 2000. Print.

Thompson, Paul, and Chris Tribble. "Looking at Citations: Using Corpora in English for Academic Purposes." *Language Learning & Technology* 5.3 (2001): 91–105. Print.

Uemlianin, Ivan A. "Engaging Text: Assessing Paraphrase and Understanding." *Studies in Higher Education* 25.3 (2000): 347–58. Print.

Warn, James. "Plagiarism Software: No Magic Bullet." *Higher Education Research and Development* 25.2 (2006): 195–208. Print.

Wenger, Etienne. *Communities of Practice: Learning, Meaning and Identity.* Cambridge: Cambridge UP, 1998. Print.

QUESTIONS FOR DISCUSSION

1. Paul Parker discusses the difficulties students have with understanding academic writing, pointing out that "[a]cademic writing is expected to be 'original' work, and yet a large part of its production ostensibly involves reproducing the views of established authors (Levin 4–7)." Take another look at the highlighting activity you did before you read the chapter. How has your ownership over your own ideas (alongside, or compared to, those of the "authorities" you have cited in your work) factored into your perceptions of plagiarism? How do you perceive it playing out in your own work?

2. Locate a journal article within your discipline, and then identify a few passages that mix the writer's voice with other sources. Follow the same process with the different-colored pens that you did on your own writing in the "Before You Read" section. What patterns, if any, emerge? What insights did you learn about the way authorial voice and judgment are used in your discipline? How does this insight challenge your thinking about your own writing in the discipline?

Part I
Synthesizing What You've Read

1. In describing her process of explaining how creativity arises out of intertextuality, or borrowing from what has come before for the purpose of extending, reworking, or reinterpreting those ideas, Esra Mirze Santesso writes:

> I thought wrong. A student raised her hand and said: "I don't think this is art. It's just laziness." Suddenly, I recognized how all of our discussions on the significance of rewritings and intertextuality might be boiled down to a simple and inaccurate explanation: lack of imagination. As a way of countering this charge, I broke the class up into small groups and asked them to rewrite their favorite song, poem, or story. By the end of the class, unsurprisingly, none of the groups were able to come up with a successful reworking. At this point they were willing to concede that reinterpreting a familiar work—preserving its integrity while reshaping it in an unfamiliar way— was a difficult task. I was pleasantly relieved when the same student confessed that "this kind of laziness is too much work."

Test her argument here. Take a familiar song or poem and rework it by extending its meaning in an interesting and/or surprising way or providing new insight into its meaning. Did you find the process a creative one or a lazy one that should be punished as plagiarism? Explain.

2. Paul Parker writes:

> Academic research and learning are precisely about engaging with the boundary between what is known

and what is unknown. The task of academic authors, both student and professional, is to manage this uncertain boundary by actively reviewing, positioning, and harnessing previous research in their writing to produce independent insight: an outcome that might otherwise be termed "originality" of meaning or interpretation.

What similarities can you draw between the kind of originality of meaning or interpretation Parker is discussing here and the kind of reworking or reinterpreting that Santesso discusses?

IN PRACTICE

1. In groups, research and read several institutions' definitions of plagiarism and their policies on punishment for plagiarizing, really considering each word and the concepts presented (such as 'intention,' 'ownership,' and 'responsibility'). Write an academic integrity policy that you think effectively deals with these complexities.

2. Think about what motivates students to plagiarize or otherwise cheat. Write a statement, essay, or letter to the editor of the school paper, or create a presentation that will motivate students to *want* to work ethically and honestly.

Part II
Texts, Technologies, and Surveillance

As of this moment when we are writing this sentence, the fan fiction site, *CSI Forensics: From Out of the Lab* shows 12,233 reviews composed in response to 2,817 cases written by fans of the show. Elsewhere in cyberspace, the *Adbusters* homepage features "Blackspot Shoes: For Kicking Nike's Ass," a pro-grassroots campaign that aims to undermine the power of megacorporations. In the virtual neighborhood of film, producers, actors, and directors are gearing up to remake *Dirty Dancing*, *Carrie*, and *My Fair Lady*. What do all of these digital technologies have in common? They are all piggybacking on previous work in order to create new art, new ways of seeing the world and its characters.

Imitation has long been part of rhetorical practice and study. In fact, we often provide our students with writing exercises that ask them to model their writing on different samples we provide for them. As advancements in technology have occurred, opportunities for imitating or discovering inspiration are more prevalent. These innovative media have been integral in the production of novel and imaginative forms; however, technology is often the culprit that perpetuates both plagiarism and the culture of suspicion that surrounds it.

While some Web endeavors are helping to bring old narratives back to life in new ways, other websites—like *Turnitin.com*—are trying to catch students who are not doing original work in school. The result of this surveillance can be student and teacher paranoia: Students become concerned that they may be caught stealing, teachers become concerned that their students may be doing dishonest work, and both students and teachers may fear for how others will view their work and their character.

Part II introduces another complicated piece of this discussion about plagiarism: Academia and media technologies often send mixed messages to us about what constitutes new art and what constitutes plagiarism. It's confusing. We hear a rap remix that includes threads of an old 1980's tune, we don't take the time to read the fine print of the liner notes (where the artist has credited her influences), and we might think it's okay to weave someone else's work in and out of our own without documentation. Or, we may draw from the influences of academia and condemn that rap artist for "copying." We may feel encouraged to engage in creative borrowing in the classroom, but we may also become paranoid that we will borrow in illegal ways. The rhetoric of plagiarism in the academy can seem so harsh that students may be hesitant to build on the many pertinent aspects of pop culture that might help enhance their own arguments because they're afraid of citing them incorrectly; or because they don't want to have to engage the tedious work of documentation; or because they don't think they could do the kind of high-quality original work that teachers expect (so they may resort to less honorable means).

The technologically intricate and creative world we're living in now practically begs for us to analyze it, to construct new meaning out of old texts, to trace the merging of one idea into the next as we share in the evolution of intellectual and cultural change. Yet, as teachers and students who engage in the process of intellectual inquiry and composition, how do we negotiate the thicket of terminology and ethics while examining popular culture? How do we construct new meaning while paying homage to what has come before us? Perhaps most important of all—how do we begin to break down the culture of suspicion so that we can use new technologies to compose with integrity as we cultivate ingenuity?

5 Sampling Is Theft? Creativity and Citation after Hip Hop

Richard Schur

Before You Read*: Often musical artists include "thank yous" or "shout outs" in their liner notes; what function(s) do these serve?*

March 5, 2004 is known as "Grey Tuesday." On that day, over a million people downloaded copies of DJ Danger Mouse's *Grey Album*. The album was a mashup that blended The Beatles's *White Album* and Jay-Z's *Black Album* and transformed them into something completely fresh and new (Demers 139–42). Listeners loved hearing the eerie similarities between the two records and the fresh way DJ Danger Mouse arranged the two sets of music. It was funny, interesting, and different. Depending on the critic, *The Grey Album* initiated the mashup trend or rapidly accelerated its popularity.

Why did a million people decide to download those tracks on that particular day? Part of the answer involves how hip hop has transformed our notions about creativity. Hip hop, with its layered samples, has become so commonplace that it and its effect on MTV, commercials, and talk radio has changed how we understand creativity. In today's world, cutting and pasting sounds, images, and text is so commonplace that we do not think of such borrowings or sampling as theft. People just think of it as normal and feel free to add a sentence from one website, an image from another website, and a paragraph from a third website and call it his or her own. Contemporary hip hop artists, however, must pay a license fee to use samples in their work. When we use or borrow images, texts, and sounds, we may actually be engaging in copyright infringement, plagiarism, or both. The reason that all those people downloaded *The Grey Album* on March 5, 2004 is that DJ Danger Mouse had not paid for the right to copy either the Beatles's or Jay-Z's 121 albums. If he did not take his album off the Web by that midnight, he was going to be sued for copyright infringement. Because people wanted to protest copyright law and because they wanted copies of the album, word traveled around the Web that this would be the last chance to obtain *The Grey Album*—and people downloaded it in droves.

In this chapter, I clarify the distinctions between sampling and academic citation and between copyright infringement and plagiarism. First, I illustrate how hip hop sampling functions, using Kanye West's "Gold Digger" as my primary example. Second, I contrast West's use of sampling with academic citation. I argue that academic citation provides students and professors alike the opportunity to participate in academic or intellectual discussions, provided they recognize their sources and give "shout outs" or credit to the appropriate writers and thinkers.

In the 1970s, African Americans and Latinos created rap music and hip hop culture (George 1–21; Chang 103–07). Amid the decaying infrastructure of New York City, these youths searched used record stores for "phat" beats from whatever musical style they could find (Fricke and Ahearn 46). These early deejays took cliché sounds and transformed them into exciting dance mixes. Sampling, the art of locating the best sections of rhythms or melody from a recording, and layering, the practice of building a new song from sampled rhythms or melodies, became the heart of this new musical form and artistic style (Schloss 79–80).

The resulting creations overflowed with popular culture references and presented a thorough criticism of American society (Rose 100). Deejays, such as Kool Herc DJ, Afrika Bambaataa, and Grandmaster Flash, unleashed a barrage of sampled sounds, everything from *The Pink Panther* theme to James Brown songs, and helped audiences hear hidden similarities between songs, especially those from different styles, as they challenged one another to seek out new beats from old records (Fricke and Ahearn 49; Chang 97). Hip hop thus provided an aural retelling of American cultural history and offered a less violent venue for competition between rival crews.

Today, hip hop is one of the most popular forms of music, no longer confined to a particular racial or ethnic group or a specific city.

Hip hop-inspired sampling and layering now pervade all forms of American popular culture, even if only established hip hop artists, like P. Diddy and Kanye West, can afford to regularly use samples. Even people who claim to dislike hip hop music probably encounter its effect on television, radio, film, literature, and art on a regular basis. This hip hop-ification of American culture has fostered considerable confusion about intellectual property law and copying.

Kanye West's "Gold Digger" offers a nice illustration for how hip hop creativity interacts with copyright law and citation. It also can help us see the potential dangers of using hip hop music as a model for our own academic writing. For those who are not familiar with it, the song borrows Ray Charles's and Jamie Foxx's singing Charles's song "I Got a Woman." The song begins with Foxx mimicking Charles's voice, but with alternative lyrics. The new lyrics lament that his girlfriend is a "gold digga" rather than the supportive spouse or life partner who satisfies Charles. After the listener recognizes the fake sample as evoking the iconic sound of Ray Charles, West's voice cuts in and describes how women today only support men as long as their money or fame lasts. The song then alternates between the Charles version and Foxx's imitation of it, and West's updated take on gender relations. The song was released not long after Foxx's film *Ray* became wildly popular and has helped turn Kanye West into one of today's most popular music stars.

Most hip hop fans would probably identify West as the writer, producer, and performer. The savvy student who is familiar with copyright law and academic citation would know that the situation is probably more complicated. In fact, it is. When we look at the fine print in the liner notes of Kanye West's *Late Registration*, we find that West shares the copyright of "Gold Digger" with Ray Charles and Renald Richard. Charles and Richard wrote the original and own the copyright to it. As is customary in the recording industry, they receive ownership rights in any new song based on sampled material and a portion of the royalties. In addition, the compact disc states, "'Gold Digger' contains samples from the Ray Charles recording 'I Got a Woman,' produced under license from Atlantic Recording Corp."

By thinking about the fine print from Kanye West's compact disc, we can learn quite a bit about copyright infringement and how it is different from plagiarism. Copyright law regulates who can make copies of a song, book, poem, painting, etc., and under what conditions. According to copyright law, the person who composes an original work possesses a copyright in it. They are free to sell it, like they could sell a stick of gum or a car, and transfer their ownership rights in that work to another person or corporation. Frequently, music companies require musicians to transfer part or all of their copyrights as part of their recording contracts. Whoever owns the copyright can charge others for making a copy of, or performing their work. In the case of music, there is a statutory scheme where any time a song is played, whether on a radio station or in a dance club, both the performing artist, in this case Kanye West, and the copyright holders, West, Ray Charles, and Renald Richard here, each receive a predetermined royalty payment. In addition, any time a musician plays or records that song, the copyright holder receives a royalty payment. So, when people invoke copyright or intellectual property, they are referencing who owns a particular song, book, play, or artwork and possess the right to make money from the sale and distribution of that creative product.

Academic citation and plagiarism, by contrast, is concerned with recognizing the origin of ideas and offering documentation for one's arguments. In the case of quotations, it also acknowledges the source for a particular expression of an idea. Kanye West's "Gold Digger" uses the sample statement in the liner notes to inform listeners that Ray Charles constituted the source for some of the musical expression contained in his song. West, in effect, pays homage to the inspiration that Charles unknowingly provided for his song and acknowledges that his own creativity depended on that of Charles's. Although West's compact disc does not, it is commonplace that hip hop artists include a lengthy acknowledgements or thank you section, recognizing their families, their crews, other crews, and R&B and funk pioneers. Akin to the purpose of a Works Cited section, these "shout outs" help listeners locate the rapper's or deejay's music, including his or her primary influences and inspirations.

Although it may seem paradoxical, I am arguing that hip hop shares a concern with scholars and professors about recognizing the sources and individuals who shaped our thinking and creativity. In both hip hop and academics, "keepin' it real" is a primary concern. For hip hop, deejays and rappers attempt to depict their reality through their music. Hip hop frauds, such as Vanilla Ice and MC Hammer, who falsely invoke street credentials, quickly find themselves without an audience. Authenticity, the art of genuine and honest self-presentation, has become one of hip hop's most attractive features. Hip hop, unlike other musical forms, deflects attention from the individual and centers it upon the crew and others who have influenced the music. However, this emphasis on understanding the context of music's origin does not diminish the emphasis on creativity within hip hop. Todd Boyd notes, "The best producers [. . .] are those who though they may use samples and break beats, do so in a way as to disguise masterfully their origin and reinterpret their meaning in the process of the song" (82). In other words, one's reputation depends on how thoroughly the producer manipulates and reworks the appropriated samples. In fact, hip hop culture has developed its own ethical code for sampling. Through numerous interviews with hip hop producers, Joseph Schloss identified "biting" as "the appropriation of intellectual material from other hip hop artists" as a hip hop analog to plagiarism (106). Appropriating material without changing it or commenting upon it is viewed as dishonest and uncreative, and thus not considered worth listening or paying attention to. For example, Kanye West's use of "I Got a Woman" does not constitute "biting" Ray Charles's song and sound because he goes beyond the initial message and music by applying it to contemporary gender relations.

The academic world operates with a surprisingly similar set of assumptions about authenticity and creativity. First, participating in academic and intellectual life hinges upon trust. For education and research to succeed, professors and students must trust one another and have faith that a person's work is, in fact, his or her work and that he or she has honestly summarized the current state of the debate. "Biting" another's work undermines a person's credibility and is sufficient cause, at many universities, for dismissal. Second, creativity is best evidenced by first mastering existing arguments and then reshaping and applying them to a particular problem, issue, or text at hand. In other words, genius or academic excellence typically requires demonstrating complete mastery of the current literature. Citing sources allows writers to prove their understanding and apply that understanding to a new situation. Proper citation, thus, helps show the complexity of the writer's thought and the interesting way she or he arranged her or his sources to develop a novel argument. I would argue that the broad appeal of Kanye West's "Gold Digger" resulted not simply from its similarity to Ray Charles's song, but more from how he evoked the original even as he turned its meaning upside down.

One of the key distinctions in copyright law is the idea/expression dichotomy. Historically, copyright allows a person or corporation to own, not an idea, but a particular expression of that idea (Demers 32–37). This means, for instance, that Einstein could not own the idea that $E=mc^2$ or that there is a particular relationship between energy and matter. However, he could write a book elaborating on that idea through specific examples. That book could be copyrighted, even if the idea could not. This means that subsequent writers could discuss, analyze, or criticize his formula, provided they expressed their ideas in their own words.

Sampling, like composing a paper, clearly borrows or appropriates expressions, not just ideas, and therefore looks like it might violate copyright law. Within copyright however, there is a pretty well recognized exception for the Fair Use of copyrighted materials for critical or scholarly purposes. In other words, copyright law permits brief quotations, provided the writer then proceeds to analyze, criticize, or apply the ideas within the quotation. This exception was created, in part, because it enables the ongoing discussion of important ideas. As long as the writer is bringing his or her own creativity and thought to the topic, there would be no copyright infringement. This helps explain why legal decisions initially viewed sampling as theft: The courts did not understand hip hop as transforming the sampled music; they perceived it merely as copying. Consequently, copyright law has played an important role in changing the course of hip hop. Artists such as Public Enemy, De La Soul, and A Tribe Called Quest found that their method for creating music had been, in effect, prohibited because copyright owners began demanding outrageous fees for samples. Only the most successful hip hop producers, such as Kanye West and Sean "P. Diddy" Combs can afford to employ samples regularly.

The idea/expression dichotomy, although a legal concept, can help writers determine when and where they need to include citations. Whenever a writer copies words, images, or sounds, a license is needed because that writer is appropriating the expression of someone else's creativity. Thus, Kanye West had to indicate that he sampled Ray Charles in "Gold Digger," and a writer would be required to cite Charles as a source if she or he quoted his lyrics. Failure to do so—in West's case—would constitute copyright infringement because West would have copied the song without permission, even if he was attempting to transform its meaning. Because courts tend to view hip hop sampling as noncreative and because selling hip hop music can be quite lucrative, West is required to negotiate a license to produce copies of that sampled material, which obligates him to share the ownership rights with Ray Charles and Renald Richard. For most class-based writing assignments, the writer's primary concern is with citation or plagiarism, not copyright law, because few assignments will enrich their authors. Thus, copyright law should not, in itself, worry students in their writing for school. Once students enter the work force, however, appropriating another person's or corporation's work might have monetary implications. Borrowing a song, picture, or text without permission could result in a lawsuit, monetary damages, and even an employee losing his or her job. Plagiarism, however, is a much more important concern for writers, especially students in school and their professors. Scholars, like hip hop audiences, prize authenticity. Within both communities, artists and writers must be sure that their genuine voices shine through their work even if they are exploring existing ideas, songs, or books. While copyright permits the appropriation of ideas without citation, scholarly writing demands a higher level of conduct. In academic writing, even ideas must be cited because (1) writers must be absolutely clear about where tradition ends and their creative thought begins, and (2) readers want to be able to verify the accuracy of quotations and paraphrased material. This is where an important difference between hip hop and academic writing emerges. Again, take Kanye West's "Gold Digger" as an example. Despite his sampling and imitation of Ray Charles, West's voice shines through as he provides a new take on gender relations and translates the original into hip hop. As a result, most listeners could determine the boundary between Charles's and West's respective contributions to the song. Few listeners, however, probably concern themselves with whether West accurately quotes Charles because "Gold Digger" possesses Charles's musical sensibility, if not the actual words. While hip hop does not necessarily demand accuracy, a scholarly paper would. Thus, Jamie Foxx's revision of the lyrics would present a significant problem if he were claiming to provide an accurate summary of Charles's attitude toward women. In most academic papers, such attention to detail is crucial for persuading readers of an argument. False or imperfect evidence would taint the argument and the veracity of the paper and the speaker. From this perspective, academic honesty requires more than what copyright demands.

As technology improves, the market for sampled sounds, images, and texts has increased. Companies buy and sell sampled texts for advertisements, theme songs, and background imagery. It is not uncommon that the most recent episode of your favorite show might include all three: an advertisement for a soft drink, a verse from a popular song, and a poster of today's singer of the moment. Although viewers do not see the transactions, the television producers paid for the rights to use them in their show and create another hook to persuade us to watch. Precisely because the audience is likely to recognize them, producers want to appropriate their goodwill. Most importantly, the copyright owners were willing to sell their intellectual property for this use. Copyright law regulates the buying and selling of those intellectual properties.

Although students might be tempted to engage in similar practices when writing their papers, a different set of rules applies. Academic writing demands authenticity and creativity. Simply borrowing other's work does not allow the student's voice to come through, nor does it allow the student to demonstrate his or her ability to criticize, analyze, or apply the sampled material. Scholarly writing involves following a code of ethics, not simply the dictates of copyright law. Kanye West's "Gold Digger" ultimately complains about women who want him for his money, not his true self. In its own way, the song demands honesty and authenticity. That is exactly what academic writing demands, too.

Works Cited

Boyd, Todd. *The New H.N.I.C.: The Death of Civil Rights and the Reign of Hip Hop.* New York: New York UP, 2002. Print.

Chang, Jeff. *Can't Stop, Won't Stop: A History of the Hip-Hop Generation.* New York: St. Martin's Press, 2005. Print.

Demers, Joanne. *Steal This Music: How Intellectual Property Law Affects Musical Creativity.* Athens: U of Georgia P, 2006. Print.

DJ Danger Mouse. *The Grey Album.* Danger Mouse, 2004. Web. February 2004.

Fricke, Jim, and Charlie Ahearn. *Yes Yes Y'all: Oral History of Hip-Hop's First Decade.* Cambridge, MA: Da Capo, 2002. Print.

George, Nelson. *Hip Hop America.* New York: Penguin, 1998. Print.

Rose, Tricia. *Black Noise: Rap Music and Black Culture in Contemporary America.* Middletown, CT: Wesleyan UP, 1994. Print.

Schloss, Joseph. *Making Beats: The Art of Sample-Based Hip-Hop.* Middletown, CT: Wesleyan UP, 2004. Print.

West, Kanye. "Gold Digger." *Late Registration.* Island Def Jam, 2005. CD.

QUESTIONS FOR DISCUSSION

1. When an artist creates a song using the techniques of sampling, the song becomes part of a long musical tradition, or conversation. Explain why. Then think of academic writing in the same way. How might an academic text become part of a long tradition or conversation? What part does citation play in extending a tradition or a conversation?

2. Richard Schur writes: "[. . .] creativity is best evidenced by first mastering existing arguments and then reshaping and applying them to a particular problem, issue, or text at hand." How have your thoughts changed or not changed about *creativity*?

6 Teaching Plagiarism: Remix as Composing

Martine Courant Rife and Dànielle Nicole DeVoss

Before You Read: *Martine Courant Rife and Dànielle Nicole DeVoss ask the following questions: "How are writers developing skills and abilities when writing to fan fiction sites? When distributing their work across networks? When slickly merging textual and visual (and often motion and sound and more) elements—some of which they've created, some of which they've altered, and some of which they've downloaded—within their compositions?" Before reading the article, visit a fan fiction site to examine what goes on firsthand. Next, use Esra Mirze Santesso's discussion of intertextuality and reworking to consider Rife and DeVoss's questions.*

INTRODUCTION

We would argue that "writing"—especially writing planned, prepared, crafted, and/or delivered within digital realms and networked spaces—might more aptly be labeled *remixing* or *composing* (DeVoss and Porter, "Rethinking Plagiarism"; Heins and Beckles; Lessig; Manovich; McLeod).* A case in point: A student intern working at a local nonprofit is developing a press release for an upcoming event. He accesses the networked archives for the office and finds several older press releases and copies and pastes the general format and design from one older press release, along with the organization's contact information. He deletes the older contact information and replaces his own name as contact on the press release, then copies and pastes

---

* Note: This article draws from the research in a DigiRhet project.

a chunk of relevant text from another older press release and replaces some information with details for the upcoming event. His supervisor suggests some revisions, and eventually the press release is finalized and distributed. Another volunteer at the office, who does the organization's Web development work, accesses the networked archives for the press release and prepares it for Web publication, moving it from a word-processed document to a dynamic, Web-ready document. She again accesses the archives, this time looking for photographic content, and finds a photo from an earlier event. She adds this to the Web document, which is eventually reviewed by the office supervisor and published on the organization's website.

Our culture, especially our academic culture, clings to static and perhaps romantically unrealistic notions of the solitary author and his unique genius (Reyman; Robbins): The lone writer, alone in his or her study, a candle burning, a glass of brandy at the elbow, writing as the ideas flow through his or her mind. This focus on the single author and his or her solitary genius in academia is of the utmost importance in literary studies (think about the English classes you've taken, and the emphasis on the individual writer and their great works), for example, and is also evident in the teacherly focus on citation practices, which continually reconstitute the idea of original-author-as-most-important. The ways teachers draw on a field's canon, "great literature," or "key authors" also exemplifies the idea of author-as-solitary-genius. However, much of the writing we do beyond school is done in ways similar to how these writers prepared their press release—collaboratively, across time and space and documents, and with remix as a key practice for invention and composing—that is, writing by appropriation—taking bits, pieces, and ideas and compiling and remixing them in new and innovative ways. Sometimes these acts of appropriation, as the example above reveals, are in a spirit of sharing and within an environment where this use is expected (for another take on appropriation, that is, the appropriation of ideas, see Phillip Marzluf, this volume).

Sometimes, however, these acts of appropriation run counter to the initial intent of the original authors (or the companies representing them). Appropriation is a particularly prevalent act in terms of multimedia and multimodal composing, where writers can pull audio, video, images, sound, and more and choreograph them into rich compositions. A case in point: On websites like *SomethingAwful* (especially the "Photoshop Phriday" area of the site) and *Worth1000*, a variety of visual composers work with words and images to appropriate and remix existing cultural images. One author, for instance, has revised the iconic Dick and Jane texts, taking the original imagery and revising the images and text to question the white middle-class ethos of Dick and Jane, to revise the cultural script of the story, and more. In the richly intertextual example we've included here (see Figure 6.1), Dick and Jane play *The Lord of the Flies.*

Figure 6.1: "Misadventures of Dick and Jane." *SomethingAwful.*

The spaces in which this sort of composing is done are dramatically different from, for instance, older spaces of writing (think writing notes onto note cards to organize later while drafting, or composing on a typewriter with an inability to easily move words, sentences, and paragraphs, much less to include any graphical content without scissors and tape)—the copy-paste function, downloading, and peer-to-peer file sharing spaces change the context for, audiences of, and shape of writing. In these spaces, issues of copyright law, Fair Use, and plagiarism converge. If *plagiarism* is defined as the "unethical" taking of someone else's words, texts, or ideas without giving proper credit, in digital spaces, "plagiarism" is commonplace. If copyright infringement is defined as the "illegal" taking of someone else's copyrighted intellectual property through "substantial similarity," Fair Use is the main defense standing between acceptable writing-as-remix and writing that could be considered copyright infringement. That is, because United States law makes any use of another writer's or artist's copyrighted materials potentially an infringement of the law, specifically Title 17 U.S. Copyright Law, if a writer is not within the perimeters of Fair Use, that writer may have done something a court could deem illegal: infringed upon another's copyright. In terms of the examples above, who "owns" the press release that the student intern created? Who "owns" the photograph the Web developer selected to publish with the online version of the press release? Did either of these writers "plagiarize" when using existing press releases as templates, copying and pasting chunks of text from earlier press releases, or selecting a photo to reproduce from the organization's archives? Likewise, who "owns" the Dick and Jane revision? Did the author infringe upon copyright in his use of the Dick and Jane imagery?

As writers, students, teachers, researchers, and workers in a digital world, we need both theories and tools that are situated in today's complex networked writing environments that examine the blurred boundaries between plagiarism and Fair Use and that forge a new ethic of Fair Use that addresses writing-as-remix (see, for instance, Billings; Castner et al.; CCCC-IP; DeVoss and Porter, "Rethinking Plagiarism"; Logie, 2005 and 2006; NCTE; Rife; Stearns; Woodmansee and Jaszi). Theories help us understand and analyze practices and approaches; tools allow us to implement theory. So, for instance, we might theorize writing-as-remix. This means that we need to think differently about authorship and ownership of texts—to consider approaches that recognize and call attention to multiple-authored pieces, work that is written "collaboratively" with other artists and writers (living or dead, in physical proximity or across the globe), and work where ownership is shared across networks (of people and machines) and servers (Reyman). Thinking of writing in this way might help us choose a particular type of process and/or a specific digital tool for a particular writing situation. If we return for a moment to the press release example above, for instance, we might rethink it a bit and break down the writing activities into individual components where we can both add theory and see tools. In our initial example, a student intern working at a local nonprofit is developing a press release. The context here helps us abstract the student's writing process, and from that we might develop a theory. This student is working for a "nonprofit." This means the student is probably creating a document that will not be used for commercial gain. It would be different, of course, if the student was working for Microsoft or for Walmart—both clearly commercial, profit-oriented organizations. The second element relevant in the student's writing process is that the student is creating a "press release." Press releases have specific purposes that differ from, say, the academic essay, the research paper, the script to a play, a text message, and so on. Press releases are documents specifically meant to be widely disseminated to call attention to an event or issue. The important information in press releases is the event or issue rather than the author. We thus might theorize in a way that attends to the ethics and legality of a use, and both the purpose and the producer of a document might help us decide issues of ownership and authorship and how a document might be subsequently appropriated.

In this initial scenario, we can also examine the tools that facilitated the student's remix writing activity. The student accesses the networked archives for the office and finds several older press releases and copies and pastes the general format and design from one older press release along with the organization's contact information. To access the archive, the student had to use a number of technologically mediated tools such as the archive itself, the software permitting copying and pasting of the text, a computer, and so on. We can further develop our theory of remix writing by thinking about how the tools in this case have interacted with the purpose of the writing—this process might inform how we think about appropriation of others' materials and the act of writing itself in the digital age.

The processes this composer engaged during the preparation of a relatively typical workplace document, a press release, disrupt much of what we learn in school. For instance, there's no single author here coming up with an original idea all his own. There's no citing sources here; the resources used are part of the "commons" of the particular organization and don't necessarily require an explicit, MLA-formatted reference. In fact, most of our current teaching practices and institutional approaches would label these processes acts of plagiarism (see the introduction of this volume for a discussion about historical and contemporary notions of plagiarism). In addition, most of our current teaching practices and institutional approaches to plagiarism encourage a "detect and punish" approach, especially considering Internet sources, paper mills, and online services such as *Turnitin.com* (DeVoss and Porter, 2006a and 2006b; DeVoss and Rosati). Teachers are expected to identify instances of plagiarism and to appropriately punish the plagiarists. What we suggest, however, is that teachers and institutions adopt approaches that recognize how writing happens in the world, especially in our networked and digital world. Further, we suggest that teachers and institutions emphasize—and teach!—ethical sharing rather than the policies dictated within an antiquated "detect-and-punish" regime. Students, in turn, can help theorize what it might mean to engage in ethical sharing.

We thus situate our discussion of plagiarism in this chapter within recognizing larger intellectual property issues, guiding awareness of the issues surrounding digital composing choices, and framing writing-as-remix as part of larger digital literacy practices (DeVoss, Cushman, and Grabill; DeVoss and Porter, 2006a and 2006b; DigiRhet. org; Hawley; Martin; New London Group; Porter and Rife; Rife; Valentine; Whitaker). Specifically, we argue that remix is a critical, contemporary composing practice, and that remix is a skill teachers should *teach* and a skill that students, as writers and workers, should *learn*. We thus pull apart the blurred boundaries between plagiarism and copyright in order to reconverge these concepts and to suggest some practical ideas for ethically using others' work.

COMPOSING IN A REMIX CONTEXT

That's how creativity happens. Artists collaborate over space and time, even if they lived centuries and con-

> tinents apart. Profound creativity requires maximum
> exposure to others' works and liberal freedoms to reuse
> and reshape others' material. (Vaidhyanathan 186)

The workplace scenario we've included here is an illustration of remix—of an author taking bits and pieces, prompts and templates,
and creating a new piece of work. According to Lawrence Lessig,
the Director of the Edmond J. Safra Foundation Center for Ethics at
Harvard University and a Professor of Law at Harvard Law School,
remix culture is a culture of derivative works, a culture where everything and anything is up for grabs—to change, to integrate, to mix,
and to mash. Large-scale examples that have generated a good deal of
attention in the media include Danger Mouse's *The Grey Album* (see
Schur, this volume, for a discussion). However, the ability to remix has
been accelerated by the personal computer and by digital networks,
which allow many of us, not just media savvy professional musicians,
for instance, to more easily share, copy, download, and mix media.
Although many of today's teachers learned to write—and learned to
teach writing!—with paper, with typewriters, and with the specter of
the original, sole author looming over them, remix culture is the space
in which most of us compose today. Remix culture exists in tension
with what Lessig terms "permission culture," where copyright restric-
tions are everywhere and are rigorously policed. Permission culture
might be characterized by fee-per-use or cost-per-click approaches to
intellectual products, where each piece of intellectual property must be
licensed or purchased, and derivative works are virtually nonexistent
due to the costs of licensing. Mapped onto issues of plagiarism, permission culture is where citation and attribution practices are everywhere and often supersede an author's original work (think of writers
who perhaps spend more time MLA-checking and quote-evaluating
than attending to developing their own ideas).

Siva Vaidhyanathan, a media scholar and professor of law at the
University of Virginia, contextualizes remix culture within today's
"digital moment," a time during which information can, theoretically,
flow seamlessly, and also a time where the spread of information is
constantly policed and restricted. Thus, although this particular digital moment is characterized by the multiple ways people can "share
ideas, information, expressions, truths, and lies over vast distances in
virtually no time" (Vaidhyanathan 152), this moment is also characterized by a constantly increasing acceleration of the means to inhibit

such sharing. Copyright and intellectual property is rigorously policed by organizations like the Recording Industry Association of America (RIAA). The networks through which we research, remix, and write are spaces of surveillance, equipped with bandwidth detectors, for instance, that trigger if we're moving or sharing too many large files across the network. At Michigan State University, for instance, the network use of individuals who appear to be moving large files can be investigated by administrators. Users who are found to be sharing or moving copyright-protected files receive warning messages; unheeded warnings can lead to the suspension of the user's network account—which students need for everything from accessing class materials to paying tuition bills to checking their university email. Plagiarism is rigorously policed by sites like *Turnitin.com*, which schools pay a large fee to use (see Harris-Moore, this volume for an extended discussion of *Turnitin.com*; see also Lowe, Schendel, and White; Marsh; and the CCCC "IP Reports"). On these "plagiarism detection" sites, teachers upload student papers, and the site runs an "originality check" test to determine whether the paper—or portions of it—has been plagiarized.

Although these policies work against remix culture (at the same time that they supposedly work against plagiarism), at our schools and in our classrooms, remix culture often shapes perceptions of writing and notions of the products of writing. One example of a perception that sometimes emerges among students is the "you can, so you should" perception that arises from being able to easily, for instance, do a Web search for images and to either click-and-drag or download an image into another document, slideshow, or Web page. Another example of where this perception manifests is among the millions of remixers out there in cyberspace posting digital videos on *YouTube* and *Vimeo*—videos that might have a "soundtrack" of copyright-protected work or draw on culturally circulating images or sound clips. Other sites, like *LiveJournal, MySpace, Facebook*, and others facilitate the use of downloaded-and-edited visuals, movie clips, sound clips, and more. Remixing the words, images, and audio of others is, in fact, commonplace, expected, and *valued*—it is part of the heart and fabric of the Web.

Plagiarism(?): A Situating Example

> If a traditional twentieth century model of cultural communication described movement of information in one direction from a source to a receiver, now the reception point is just a temporary station on information's path. If we compare information or [a] media object with a train, then each receiver can be compared to a train station. Information arrives, gets remixed with other information, and then the new package travels to other destinations where the process is repeated. (Manovich)

On *FanFiction.net*, thousands of writers, designers, and composers borrow existing characters from anime/manga shows and comics, from books, from television cartoons, from video and console games, and from movies and television shows and extend the lives and activities of these characters. For instance, in the television category, in August 2011, there were sixty-seven submissions that extend the lives and times of the *Golden Girls*. There were more than 2,100 submissions that extend the plot of the television show *Highlander*, moving the characters and storylines out of television and into writing across the Internet. There were almost two thousand submissions rewriting and remixing *Prison Break* and more than nineteen thousand for *House, M.D.* In addition, in September 2008, there were four hundred submissions for *Prison Break*, and just under three thousand for *House, M.D.*, revealing the pace at which these fan fiction authors produce and contribute work. *Supernatural* is the most remixed and revised television show, with 51,254 submissions. *Buffy: The Vampire Slayer* is the second most remixed, with 42,387 submissions (particularly interesting given that the show was canceled in 2003). Not only does fan fiction revise and rewrite characters, plots, and other aspects of a variety of media in textual and narrative form but fan fiction—through the use of graphic-editing applications and savvy downloaders and users of images—also revises the visual storylines. For instance, there are revised screen stills from *Buffy* that feature a rapturous Buffy romantically embracing Giles (certainly a deviation from the original storyline on the show). In addition, these spaces are typically richly interactive. On *Fanfiction.net*, users are invited to respond to each other's stories, and discussion boards allow a space for authors and readers to assess the quality and reality of the stories posted to the site.

Personally, we are both writing teachers and composition scholars, and we're thrilled to see the level of engagement these writers have with different media, and their inspiration and abilities in taking, remixing, and re-presenting the storylines, character developments, and myriad aspects of the media they're working with. We also wonder, however, what it means in today's digital world that composers can easily find and download a television story script, for instance, and alter and edit it—remixing and revising, moving pieces around, adding some text, changing the plot, and more. Who is the author of such a product? Who "owns" this work? Is this practice what we might traditionally call *plagiarism*? Or is this, instead, a violation of copyright, as television scripts are copyright-protected intellectual property? Or are these activities *both*? What are the implications of these activities? How are writers developing skills and abilities when writing to fan fiction sites? When distributing their work across networks? When slickly merging textual and visual (and often motion and sound and more) elements—some of which they've created, some of which they've altered, and some of which they've downloaded—within their compositions? Perhaps most importantly, how will today's writers change tomorrow's ideas about plagiarism, copyright, and remix?

PLAGIARISM: IN OUR INSTITUTIONS

In his essay, "Visual Rhetoric in a Culture of Fear: Impediments to Multimedia Production," Steve Westbrook, an English professor and researcher who studies visual rhetoric and copyright, argues that writing teachers might differentiate between how notions of Fair Use apply to alphabetic texts (by this he means fairly typical, words-only essays) versus new media compositions—certainly an important question to ask as we transition from writing traditional essays with words only (and all the default formatting that goes along with them, such as one-inch margins, twelve-point Times New Roman type, etc.) to integrating multiple media into our work.

We mean "Fair Use" two ways here: First, the act of fairly or ethically using someone else's work; and second, following the provisions of the Fair Use clause in U.S. Copyright Law (sometimes a use fits both of these ways, but not always). In the piece, Westbrook reflects on the inability to publish his student's ("Sara's") work, a parody of a Maybelline advertisement. In her text, Sara challenges women's sexual objectification in visual culture. Sara's multimedia parody illustrates her ability to engage in the type of work that good writing does—that is, her composition engages a timely topic and draws upon her experiences, her knowledge, and existing cultural material to make a particular argument. By creating this text, Sara understood "composing as a cultural activity by which writers position and reposition themselves in relation to their own and others' subjectivities" (Trimbur 109). Yet Westbrook could not obtain permissions from the copyright holder in order to include Sara's parody in his text, and he felt that Fair Use was too uncertain to depend on in light of potential copyright liabilities (including the fact that the journal in which he published his piece and in which Sara's work would have appeared is read by thousands of readers). In other words, Westbrook was not willing to rely on the Fair Use doctrine to protect his right to publish Sara's parody without permission from Maybelline, Inc., the company that holds the copyright for the ads that Sara created a parody of. Therefore, Sara's work is not published in Westbrook's essay. Instead, Westbrook *describes* her visual parody with alphabetic text, positing that when using print, he can more easily incorporate other's print materials (e.g., a quote from someone's work) without fear of copyright infringement. It's interesting that if Sara had only quoted "copy" or text from the ads, Westbrook could have easily included her composition in his article, but because she used images from ads, her work caused a copyright concern. In his piece, Westbrook's concerns chilled his approaches and restricted him from including the media that would best support his claims and discussion. Yet, the Fair Use doctrine was created exactly for purposes such as Westbrook's—that is, showcasing a cultural critique created in a nonprofit, educational environment.

Similarly, the plagiarism policies of our institutions, as well as teachers' interpretations of those policies, chill the ways students approach the writing they are asked to do. A slippery vantage point that writing teachers and English departments typically cling to with respect to traditional alphabetic essays is that traditional notions of plagiarism still apply, seamlessly and unquestioned—regardless of how much the spaces in which students write, the media students select and include, and the writing tools students now use, have changed. It is important that we note that we are *not* arguing that plagiarism no longer exists.

Regardless of digital networks and multimedia affordances, regardless of the ways today's "digital generation"[1] comes to write, there are still clearly right and wrong approaches to textual composing. Purchasing and downloading a term paper on the Web, slightly altering it, and turning it in as one's own written product *is* wrong. We certainly wouldn't argue against that. Likewise, copying and pasting chunks of material from several different sources without attribution is also wrong, although typically less an issue of plagiarism and more an issue of students entering into the conventions and practices of academic writing (see Howard, 1993 and 1995; Minock; Pecorari; and Valentine, who provide ample evidence that students need to be taught and need to practice citation and paraphrasing, and often are "trying on" different voices and writing by taking snippets of others' work).

Identifying these practices as intellectual dishonesty is nothing new, and it is certainly reflected in the policies of our schools and colleges. For example, in the first-year writing course that Martine teaches at Lansing Community College, the official departmental language on plagiarism reads:

> You must avoid plagiarism on all papers. Plagiarism consists of taking words or ideas from an outside source without properly acknowledging the source, or submitting a paper written by someone else. Plagiarism will result in a 0.0 on the first graded activity on which it occurs, and a 0.0 in the course if it reoccurs. Plagiarism in the final portfolio will result in a 0.0 in the course. ("WRIT 121")

At Michigan State University, where Dànielle recently directed the undergraduate program in Professional Writing, the official university policy on academic honesty articulates the importance of integrity, truth, and honesty to the university and specifically identifies plagiarism as the act of claiming or submitting the academic work of another as one's own or allowing work to be completed for oneself by another person. Both of these policies assume that the concept of plagiarism applies in blanket form across *all* writing contexts and regardless of any given writing purpose or tool used.

As we know, however, plagiarism policies are easier written than followed and require a great deal of case-by-case assessment and in-classroom negotiation when applied. As teachers, we've found that our most appropriate methods are on a student-by-student, instance-by-instance basis that typically either complicates or transcends policies. Unfortunately, in terms of prevention, many instructors either adopt a detect-and-punish approach or fall back on a finger-wagging "just don't do it" approach to teaching and addressing plagiarism (see Zwagerman, this volume, for a discussion of the student-teacher relationship constructed in a detect-and-punish context; see Reyman, this volume, for an alternative and richer approach to the "don't steal" message). Teaching students to carefully and correctly summarize, paraphrase, and quote from sources is critical to academically sound approaches to plagiarism prevention. Likewise, helping students understand *why*, in American academic prose, we value citation principles and why we attribute ideas to others, is core to helping students understand and avoid plagiarism.

ATTRIBUTION, AUTHORSHIP, AND AFFORDANCES

Sarah Robbins, a feminist historian and American Studies professor at Kennesaw State University, extended the ways writing scholars are approaching plagiarism and asked why approaches value authorship and product, often at the exclusion of the teaching that can happen through writing itself. That is, some writing textbooks, as well as writing program courses and curricula, have more of an emphasis on teaching citation practices than on teaching invention. The focus is too often on producing a thesis-based, MLA-formatted finished product rather than on the writing strategies and tools that help writers produce the many kinds of texts situated to many purposes and audiences they will prepare in their lives as citizens and workers. In her essay, Robbins raises a critical issue pertaining to Fair Use of the work of others: she ponders whether it is paradoxical that while writing teachers value authorship, they tend to place themselves at odds "with publishers and some professional writers' interests in protecting textual ownership rights" (167). Robbins is concerned about the paradox that writing teachers often emphasize individual authors and their ownership of work when at the same time, teachers often distribute the work of others in their classrooms (e.g., a chapter or two photocopied from a book). In this example of sharing the work of others in the classroom, however, perhaps it is not so much a protectionist stance that writing teachers are taking toward authorship, but a desire to have students truly engage with and synthesize multiple sources of information. Teachers typically distribute copyright-protected material in the classroom with a desire to share resources and to facilitate student learning. If attention is paid to copyright issues—that is, to potential infringement of the original author's copyright by photocopying and sharing chunks of a text—most teachers assume this act falls under Fair Use protection. This same interest is really what is underneath the teacherly focus on plagiarism: protection of student learning. Teacher or institution focus on plagiarism may not be so much a protection of solitary genius as it is desire to see students critically engage with classroom discussions, activities, and texts.

With these definitions and complexities of plagiarism in mind, we want to return to the fan fiction examples from earlier in this chapter. Fan fiction challenges traditional definitions of plagiarism. Clearly, users of *Fanfiction.net*, for instance, can only obtain meaning and value from the site and from the fan fiction by entering with preexisting knowledge that the writings posted there extend *existing* stories. Typical MLA or APA citation would be somewhat redundant—because in order to understand a fan fiction story, a reader has to know the previous storyline and characters. In fact, quoting from earlier shows and including parenthetical citations would be disruptive to the composing practices related to fan fiction. Attribution, in this case, is therefore *implicit* via the affordances of digital technologies and interface design when connected to audience awareness and a shared community perspective (that is, we know these shows, and we know that this is fan fiction). The same is true with parodies, which have become easy to construct and share on spaces like *SomethingAwful* and *YouTube*. A reader's understanding of a parody is dependent upon knowledge of the underlying work. *The Shining Redux*—a parody movie trailer that remixes scenes from the original movie and adds upbeat music to indicate a storyline about family bonding—is meaningless unless the viewer is familiar with the original movie, *The Shining*, and recognizes how twisted the parody is. Traditional ways of citation in such cases seem inappropriate, even obsolete to the genre. Are these instances of plagiarism? Yes, maybe, perhaps; but regardless, they are certainly *something else*, too.

In the cases of fan fiction and of parody, copyright infringement is another issue to consider. Whether the kinds of work featured on *Fanfiction.net* and *YouTube* are copyright infringement is not a sim-

ple matter. Copyright protects derivations of an old work. Derivative
works such as those on *Fanfiction.net* may be infringing on the old
work's copyright, yet if the new work transforms the older work, the
new work could be within the Fair Use protections of Section 107
of U.S. Copyright Law. Recently, the U.S. Register of Copyrights,
Marybeth Peters, wrote a recommendation where she suggested that
noncommercial videos—cultural critique pieces like Luminosity's
Women's Work (where the composers merged scenes of women represented as victims in horror and supernatural movies to a soundtrack
of Hole's "Violet") and the 2007 anti-Clinton remix political video by
ParkRidge47, "Vote Different"—might be transformative enough to
be Fair Use, especially because only small, minutes-long portions were
used and because the remixed videos were "used for [. . .] new and
different purpose[s] from the original" (51). ParkRidge47's video is a
political parody of a 1984 Apple Macintosh commercial, and Peters
pointed out it might be a Fair Use, because Fair Use protects the right
to critique or comment on the work of another. Such critique may be
deemed not infringing based on the social good in preserving the ability to create new, transformative work (see, for instance, *Campbell*; Lessig; Vaidhyanathan). Peters also pointed out that some video remixes
might not be Fair Uses, especially when they use "multiple clips from
the same motion picture" and "larger percentages" of a single motion
picture (51). Luminosity's *Vogue/300* is one such remix, described by
Peters as "showing an extensive montage of scenes from the movie *300*
mixed with Madonna's sound recording, 'Vogue'" (51, footnote 187).

In recent years, with the explosion of digital media, file download
and file sharing spaces, and robust software applications that allow
writers to integrate not only the words of others, but also the sounds
of others and images created by others, and, because many writers live
and write within remix culture, defining plagiarism can be problematic. Attempting to convince today's digital writers that writing practices
that are seamless and may seem "natural" in and across digital spaces
are actually suspect and perhaps dishonest is difficult. It's important,
in light of changes in understanding authorship and ownership, that
we not assume that all writers, for instance students and teachers, have
the same notion of what "plagiarism" is. Perhaps teachers should not
define plagiarism *for* students, but instead enter into more appropriately complex discussions of how writing happens within digital spaces. Perhaps students should help teachers develop robust, appropriate

notions of authorship and ownership in consideration of large-scale, networked spaces in which copying-and-pasting and remix practices are prevalent—if not expected and valued.

REMIXING AS COMPOSING

We would argue that rather than "infringing," "stealing," or "plagiarizing" others' materials and ideas, remix can be the thoughtful, deliberate, ethical, and Fair Use of others' work. Such fair and ethical use must carefully consider the interplay of copyright and plagiarism. The comparison between copyright and plagiarism and how a writer might approach ethically and fairly using others' materials extends the work done on "patchwriting" (Howard, "Plagiarisms"; Klausman) and writing as imitation, and hopefully provides some starting points for teachers and students to recognize the complexity related to and issues involved with using the work of others—inside our classrooms, within our institutions, and in the professional world. As writing teachers, we have found some starting points to initiating fruitful and appropriately complicated discussions of the intersections of plagiarism and intellectual property. Some of the strategies we recommend to students also work well for teachers. They are as follows:

- Consider mapping your own writing processes, and identify and explain points where others' work intersects with your own. Perhaps start by digging deep and broad—for instance, do you listen to music while you write? How does that music influence your ideas or your writing processes? Continue by exploring when you seek sources and how you put those sources to work in your own writing.
- Define plagiarism, and provide example cases and repercussions; define copyright infringement and provide example cases.
- Review the academic honesty or plagiarism policies of your institution, and prepare a one-page overview to guide your work.
- Review copyright information on *Copyright.gov*, and prepare a one-page overview to guide your work. Review the copyright policies of your institution, and prepare a one-page overview to guide your work.

- Purposely plagiarize! For example, Martine asks students to read Jeffrey Klausman's article "Teaching about Plagiarism in the Age of the Internet." She then asks students to paraphrase their own definitions of direct and indirect plagiarism and patchwriting. Finally, using a select chunk of text, she asks students to purposely create their own examples of each type of plagiarism.
- Hold a debate where interested people present and deliberate upon the similarities and differences between plagiarism and copyright. Use of case examples are helpful here: Martine uses Tom Forsythe's "Food Chain Barbie" case to illustrate (visually and textually) the issues with copyright and Fair Use (Heins and Beckels; *Mattel*); she also uses Rasheed Wallace's tattoo to spur interest in the topic.[2]
- Read about and discuss the complexities of plagiarism in the digital age; then review and evaluate the usefulness, correctness, and/or adequacy of online tutorials such as Indiana University's "How to Recognize Plagiarism" and Butler University's "Understanding Plagiarism." As time permits, construct an online tutorial on plagiarism/copyright for your peers and colleagues.
- Interview working professionals in a field you're interested in as to how the professionals write on the job and where issues of plagiarism and copyright might intersect with your work.
- Select a piece of digital media (e.g., the *YouTube* phenom "Internet People" or Weezer's video for "Pork and Beans," also available on *YouTube*), and trace the sources drawn upon and/or remixed—including recognizable influences, sampled work, quoted text, others' photographs or artwork, etc.
- Explore sites like *Turnitin.com* and *Plagiarism.org*, coupled with brief readings on plagiarism; once you're situated in the larger, national, and corporate landscape of plagiarism approaches, work in small groups and develop an "ideal" plagiarism policy to guide your work as a writer.
- Create an online or other glossary of intellectual property terms. Consider publishing this online and adding to it regularly.

CONCLUSION

We began this chapter by claiming that writing in digital environments may more aptly be labeled as remixing. Although today's academic culture tends to cling to stale notions of the solitary author, and continues to oversimplify definitions of plagiarism in academic policies and standards, writing in digital environments causes a convergence of plagiarism and issues of copyright. Because of the fundamental ways writing has changed over the last decade or so (particularly due to the Web coming into common use around 1995), the way we perceive, teach, describe, and understand plagiarism must reflect the remix culture that is inherent in writers' life experiences—experiences both inside and beyond school.

We argue for an ethic of Fair Use that takes into account the complexities of how students and teachers exercise agency, dialogue, and engage in critical awareness of composing processes via acts of appropriation. This is complementary to the "acceptable" or "allowable" copying approach that Jessica Reyman describes in this book. Although downloading a paper and turning it in as one's own is obviously unethical, other acts of appropriation—as some of our examples illustrate—are done in a spirit of sharing and expected use, and simply raise our awareness and affirmation of "a belief in the social aspects of all writing" (Robbins 168–69). By acknowledging the changed nature of writing along with the "complexity inherent in all collaborations" (Robbins 169), we can use this moment as one for launching dialogue with other writers about the ethical use of others' materials.

Acknowledging our own attitudes and assumptions—and where they originate and how they might be made more complex within digital spaces—provides a space from which we can explore issues of plagiarism and copyright. We want to make sure that all writers, students, and teachers are critically engaging with others' materials and discoveries and with each other. Students and teachers together work toward this shared goal of accomplishing learning and the acquisition of new skills. Complicating traditional understandings of plagiarism and layering in discussions of copyright and Fair Use will help writers understand and negotiate authorship decisions in our digital, networked world.

How we understand what constitutes the ethical use of others' materials in school and in our classrooms has effects that travel beyond

our schools and classrooms as writers continue their educations, develop professional personas, and apply what they have learned in school
(Ahrenhoerster). We have found that plagiarism, copyright, and Fair
Use instruction is rare in schools and in colleges. The kind of approach
we have offered in this chapter, one that relies on a conversation that
will continually develop an ethic of Fair Use that meets the needs of
today's writers, may be a move in the right direction to protect writers' learning, understanding of processes, uses of tools, and abilities
to participate in the kind of writerly exchanges taking place in digital
environments.

NOTES

1. We use this term with some trepidation and skepticism. Although
myriad popular press articles and reports are quick to associate today's college students as digital elites and savvy users of computers and multimedia
technologies, this is certainly not the case for all students, especially those
returning to college, and particularly those who have not had regular access
to computers and to the resources to learn to use computers and digital tools.
See Oblinger and Hawkins; Morgan; Owen; Prensky, 2001a and 2001b; and
Windham for an extended discussion of the promises and perils of typifying
today's students as "digitally literate."

2. In the "Food Chain Barbie" case, Tom Forsythe was sued by Mattel
for copyright infringement because of his Barbie parodies, through which
he challenges the objectification of women's bodies and sexuality. After a
long battle, the court ordered Mattel to pay Forsythe for bringing a frivolous
lawsuit. In the Rasheed Wallace scenario, the Pistons' star paid a tattoo artist to create an original design that was then inscribed on Wallace's upper
arm. Subsequently, Wallace signed a multimillion-dollar contract with Nike.
Nike then took photographs of Wallace in its apparel, prominently featuring
the tattoo. The tattoo artist alleged copyright infringement. Both of these
cases provide robust, engaging visuals for classroom use and come out of the
visual/remix culture that students are already familiar with before they reach
our classroom doors.

WORKS CITED

Ahrenhoerster, Greg. "Will They Still Respect Us in the Morning? A Study
    of How Students Write after They Leave the Composition Classroom."
    Teaching English in the Two-Year College 34.1 (2006): 20–31. Print.

Billings, Roger. "Plagiarism in Academia and Beyond: What is the Role of the Courts?" *University of San Francisco Law Review* 38 (2003): 391–430. Print.

Campbell v. Acuff-Rose Music, Inc. 510 U.S. 569. Supreme Court of the United States. 1994. Print.

Castner, Joanna, Michael Donnelly, Rebecca Ingalls, Tracy Ann Morse, and Anne Stockdell-Giesler. "(Mis)Trusting Technology That Polices Integrity: A Critical Assessment of *Turnitin.com*." *inventio* 1.8 (Fall 2006). Web. 12 March 2007.

CCCC. "IP Reports." n.d. Web. 9 June 2012.

CCCC-IP. "Plagiarism Detection Services Bibliography." n.d. Web. 21 September 2006.

DeVoss, Dànielle Nicole, Ellen Cushman, and Jeffrey T. Grabill. "Infrastructure and Composing: The *When* of New-Media Writing." *College Composition and Communication* 57.1 (2005): 14–44. Print.

DeVoss, Dànielle Nicole, and James E. Porter. "Rethinking Plagiarism in the Digital Age: Remixing as a Means for Economic Development?" *WIDE Research Center 2006 Conference.* Web. 24 June 2006.

DeVoss, Dànielle Nicole, and James E. Porter. "Why Napster Matters to Writing: Filesharing as a New Ethic of Digital Delivery." *Computers and Composition* 23 (2006): 178–210. Print.

DeVoss, Dànielle, and Annette C. Rosati. "It Wasn't Me Was It? Plagiarism and the Web." *Computers and Composition* 19 (2002): 191–203. Print.

DigiRhet.org. "Teaching Digital Rhetoric: Community, Critical Engagement, and Application." *Pedagogy: Critical Approaches to Teaching Literature, Language, Composition, and Culture* 2.1 (2006): 231–59. Print.

Fanfiction.net. 2012. Web. 12 March 2007.

Hawley, Christopher S. "The Thieves of Academe: Plagiarism in the University System." *Improving College and University Teaching* 32 (1984): 35–9. Print.

Heins, Marjorie, and Tricia Beckles. "Will Fair Use Survive? Free Expression in the Age of Copyright Control, A Public Policy Report." Brennan Center for Justice. December 2005. Web. 27 February 2006.

Howard, Rebecca Moore. "A Plagiarism Pentimento." *Journal of Teaching Writing* 11.3 (Summer 1993): 233–46. Print.

— "Plagiarisms, Authorships, and the Academic Death Penalty." *College English* 57 (1995): 788–806. Print.

—. "Sexuality, Textuality: The Cultural Work of Plagiarism." *College English* 62 (2000): 473–91. Print.

Klausman, Jeffrey. "Teaching about Plagiarism in the Age of the Internet." *Teaching English in the Two-Year College* 27.2 (1999): 209–12. Print.

Lessig, Lawrence. *Free Culture: How Big Media Uses Technology and the Law to Lock Down Culture and Control Creativity.* New York: Penguin Press, 2004. Print.

Logie, John. "Copyright in Increasingly Digital Academic Contexts: What it Takes." WIDE Research Center, Paper #7. Web. 24 June 2006. 12 March 2007.

—. "Plagiarism and Copyright—What Are the Differences?" *The Council Chronicle* (5 November 2005). Web. 12 March 2007.

Lowe, Charles, Ellen Schendel, and Julie White. "Issues Raised by Use of *Turnitin* Plagiarism Detection Software." *cyberdash.com.* 7 September 2006. Web. 24 June 2012.

Manovich, Lev. "Remix and Remixability." *Rhizome.* 2005. Web. 5 September 2006.

Marsh, Bill. "*Turnitin.com* and the Scriptural Enterprise of Plagiarism Detection." *Computers and Composition* 21 (2004): 427–38. Print.

Martin, Brian. "Plagiarism: A Misplaced Emphasis." *Journal of Information Ethics* 3.2 (1994): 36–47. Print.

Mattel v. Walking Mountain Productions. 353 F.3d 792. United States Court of Appeals, Ninth Circuit. 2003. Web. 3 August 2006.

McLeod, Kembrew. *Freedom of Expression: Overzealous Copyright Bozos and Other Enemies of Creativity.* New York: Doubleday, 2005. Print.

Minock, Mary. "Toward a Postmodern Pedagogy of Imitation." *JAC: A Journal of Composition Theory* 15.3 (Fall 1995): 489–510. Print.

Morgan, Glenda. "The Myth of the Net-Generation." *Accidental Pedagogy.* 16 August 2006. Web. 8 October 2006.

NCTE. "Plagiarism and Copyright—What Are the Differences?" *NCTE.* Web. 21 September 2006.

New London Group. "A Pedagogy of Multiliteracies." *Harvard Educational Review* 66 (1996): 60–92. Print.

Oblinger, Diana G., and Brian L. Hawkins. "The Myth about Students." *Educause Review* 40.5 (2005). Web. 8 October 2006.

Owen, Martin. "The Myth of the Digital Native." *Futurelab.* 2004. Web. 8 October 2006.

Pecorari, Diane. "Good and Original: Plagiarism and Patchwriting in Academic Second-Language Writing." *Journal of Second Language Writing* 12 (2003): 317–45. Print.

Peters, Marybeth. Recommendation of the Register of Copyrights in RM 2008–8; Rulemaking on Exemptions from Prohibition on Circumvention of Copyright Protection Systems for Access Control Technologies. Web. 2 September 2010.

Porter, Jim, and Martine Rife. "*MGM v. Grokster*: Implications for Educators and Writing Teachers." WIDE Research Center, Paper #1. Web. 28 June 2005.

Prensky, Marc. "Digital Natives, Digital Immigrants." *On the Horizon* 9.5 (2001): 1–6. Print.

—. "Digital Natives, Digital Immigrants Part 2: Do They Really Think Differently?" *On the Horizon* 9.6 (2001): 1–6. Print.

Reyman, Jessica. "Copyright, Distance Education, and the TEACH Act: Implications for Teaching Writing." *College Composition and Communication* 58.1(2006): 30–45. Print.

Rife, Martine Courant. "The Fair Use Doctrine: History, Application, and Implications for (New Media) Writing Teachers." *Computers and Composition* 24.2 (June 2007): 154–78. Print.

Robbins, Sarah. "Distributed Authorship: A Feminist Case-study Framework for Studying Intellectual Property." *College English 66.2* (2003): 155–71. Print.

Something Awful Forum Goons. "Misadventures of Dick and Jane." Work of Art. *Something Awful*, 2012. Web 12 March 2007.

Tearns, Laurie. "Copy Wrong: Plagiarism, Process, Property and the Law. *California Law Review* 80 (1992): 513–53. Print.

Student Academic Integrity FAQ. Michigan State University. n.d. Web. 12 March 2007.

U.S. Copyright Law. Title 17, Chapter 1, Section 101. U.S. Copyright Office. <http://www.copyright.gov/title17/>. 2 September 2010. Web. 12 March 2007.

Trimbur, John. "Taking the Social Turn: Teaching Writing Post-Process." *College Composition and Communication* 45 (1994): 108–18. Print.

Vaidhyanathan, Siva. *Copyrights and Copywrongs: The Rise of Intellectual Property and How it Threatens Creativity.* New York: New York UP, 2001. Print.

Valentine, Kathryn. "Plagiarism as Literacy Practice: Recognizing and Rethinking Ethical Binaries." *College Composition and Communication* 58.1 (2006): 89–109. Print.

Westbrook, Steve. "Visual Rhetoric in a Culture of Fear: Impediments to Multimedia Production." *College English* 68.5 (2006): 457–80. Print.

Whitaker, Elaine E. "A Pedagogy to Address Plagiarism." *College Composition and Communication* 44 (1993): 509–14. Print.

Windham, Carie. "Getting Past Google: Perspectives on Information Literacy from the Millennial Mind." EDUCAUSE Paper 3. 2006. Web. 8 October 2006.

Woodmansee, Martha, and Peter Jaszi, eds. *The Construction of Authorship: Textual Appropriation in Law and Literature.* Durham, NC: Duke UP, 1994. Print.

"WRIT 121 Official Course Syllabus." Composition I (WRIT 121) Official Course Syllabus. Communication Department. Lansing Community College. 2005. Print.

Questions for Discussion

1. Before reading this chapter, would you have described the work of writing as solitary? How would you describe it now? List all the *voices* involved in the act of writing.

2. If writing is not a solitary act, what does that mean for a definition of *original work*? What does it mean to have *original work*?

7 Instructors as Surveyors, Students as Criminals: *Turnitin* and the Culture of Suspicion

Deborah Harris-Moore

Before You Read*: What does the existence of programs like Turnitin suggest about how plagiarism is taught? If you haven't explored Turnitin.com, visit it now.*

Most of us have seen signs outside and in retail spaces that present warnings like "Surveillance Cameras in Use," "Stealing will be Prosecuted," and the more ironic "Smile, you're on camera!" Many of us have glanced up at the cameras perching above doors or ATMs, aware that we are being recorded. If you are like me, you worry that by naturally glancing at the displayed cameras or peering about to find an obscured camera, you look somehow suspicious no matter how ethical you are. For a moment, even if you have never committed a crime, you might feel like you have done something wrong.

Even though many of us have had similar experiences in public spaces, you may have never imagined that plagiarism detection in educational institutions can operate in the same way as surveillance systems and subsequently can have the same effects. Plagiarism detection software has been developed in response to an increase in recorded plagiarism cases. That is, with the rise of available information on the Internet and the development of online paper mills through which students can purchase full papers online, many schools are noting an increase in the number of plagiarism cases and are developing preventative and punitive measures. As a result of increased access to the Web and the purported rise in plagiarism rates, educational institutions have tried several approaches to deterring plagiarism: emphasizing their academic codes; increasing the punishment for academic dishonesty; establishing departments or student clubs devoted to educational integrity; and purchasing or developing plagiarism detection software that allows instructors to enter student papers into the Web to find matching text. While most institutions approach the rise in plagiarism cases with a variety of preventative and punitive techniques, more and more institutions are utilizing plagiarism detection software as a practical tool to discourage and detect plagiarism. The implementation of the software in educational settings has prompted discussions regarding the assessment of plagiarism, representations of student identities, and invasion of student privacy. Detection software, some argue, serves as a surveillance mechanism that can create and maintain detrimental power structures between administrators, instructors, and students.

For the purposes of this discussion, I frame current debates regarding plagiarism detection software, specifically *Turnitin*, within recent conversations about its implications for power and privacy. I explore French philosopher Michel Foucault's concepts in *Discipline and Punish: The Birth of the Prison* such as observation, judgment, and examination in order to examine the culture of surveillance that detection software creates and maintains. I define and use these terms to analyze the format and implementation of *Turnitin* software, the language in the company's training materials and on its website as it was presented in 2006 (which marked the ten year anniversary of the software creation in 1996), and the resulting power structures that have continued to develop between administrators, instructors, and students as a result of its integration in educational settings. I have chosen to address all of the individuals involved in this structure in the third person; the reason for this choice is that Foucault offers us a theory of systems where *each individual*—in this case, students, teachers, and administrators—takes on a fundamental role in the functioning of the institution and its power hierarchy. As a reaction to the potentially detrimental institutional framework that plagiarism detection software creates and maintains, I argue that a more preventative and educational approach to avoiding plagiarism, which I will describe, can help make detection software more productive than punitive. In other words, I take the student's role very seriously in this discussion. In order for students to understand their crucial role in this debate, I have constructed an argument that allows them to see the system from the outside in.

Foucault has written about many different social systems, namely those that regulate medicine, psychiatry, sexuality, education, and deviance. In his book *Discipline and Punish*, Foucault informs the reader about the history of torture, discipline, prisons, and surveillance systems starting in eighteenth century France. In this historical overview, he includes the contributions of Jonathan Bentham, an English jurist and philosopher, who planned for a prison called the Panopticon, which never came to fruition. In the original design, the prison was to be shaped like a circle with an open space in the middle for prisoners to engage in physical activity. The structure would be several stories high, with cells making up the walls of the structure and the bars facing in toward the center. The prisoners would not be able to see each other from their cells, however, because a central tower—a small nucleus in the central space—would block their view to the other side of the prison. The tower would be as high as the prison, and a balcony for armed guards would crown the top. The purpose of this design, Bentham argued, was to give the prisoners the illusion that guards were always watching and to isolate the prisoners from each other. The prisoners would think that surveillance existed everywhere, all the time, and subsequently they would behave according to the rules (200). Foucault uses this plan for a prison as an analogy for the way all surveillance systems work; that is, the power of surveillance is that the average person does not know where the surveillance technology exists, has no access to the technology, and is forced to believe the threats of punitive action in the case that the surveillance catches them in a deviant act. In *Discipline and Punish*, Foucault attempts to trace the relationships between power, knowledge, and punishment in the institutional context using a history of the modern penal system.

The power of plagiarism technology can often be similar to the surveillance system described by Foucault. Many instructors do not challenge the use of the technology and allow it to become an apparatus of power in that "it assures its efficacy by its preventative character, its continuous functioning and automatic mechanisms" (206). In other words, if students know that the technology exists and that instructors are free to use it at any time, they may constantly fear the prospect of writing. They may be concerned that some of their language may sound similar to other sources or that they failed to cite their work properly. This is the "preventative character" Foucault describes in his work. The existence of the technology alone is advertised to prevent any temptations, any mistakes in citation, or any attempts to plagiarize. I must qualify my argument before I continue: By considering plagiarism software in educational contexts according to Foucault's theories of punishment, I do not mean to suggest that academic institutions are the same as prisons. Rather, Foucault's theories regarding power and surveillance speak to the channels of power in other institutions, and one can see that observation, judgment, and examination are simultaneously enforced by and on individuals within many different institutions. That is, prisons and schools are institutions with very different social and cultural functions, yet both are discrete, organized spaces that operate according to their own constraints and regulations. Think about all the layers of power in various schools: In high school, there is the local school board, the superintendent of schools, the principal, the vice principal, the teachers, the counselors, the students, and others. College hierarchies can be even more complicated because these layers of power exist in larger institutions generally.

Foucault's historical study of the development of prisons is a useful lens for reading the media surrounding plagiarism and the resulting criminalization of those involved in plagiarism cases. Foucault famously illuminates how during the eighteenth century, before the traditional prison space was conceived, reformers sought their own media—a theater of punishment—where the public could witness the treatment of criminals in the hopes that those in power could maintain control over and through representation. In these "theaters," disciplinarians marched accused criminals to public spaces, displaying them in front of crowds in order to punish them through physical and verbal abuse. The audience members would internalize the punishment of others and maintain discipline in their daily lives in order to avoid the same punishment they witnessed. The recent media attention devoted to plagiarism cases and punishment, especially because the media is so public and pervasive, similarly provokes fear and maintains behavior in the viewers; in fact, students and instructors who see and hear about these cases in the media can adopt similar language and perspectives as the media on plagiarism. This is how those in power—administrators and creators of the technologies adopted by the school—maintain control over and through representation. The misidentification of students as criminals results, in part, from the kind of value-laden language used to describe cheating and plagiarism on the *Turnitin* website and in related media. The *Turnitin* homepage clearly engages mass media perspectives on plagiarism by presenting incendiary news headlines including "High Tech War Against Plagiarism" and "Fighting Plagiarism One Professor at a Time." The presence of these headlines on the *Turnitin* homepage directly implicates the technology itself and its use in a greater "values war." The technology, as an instrument in the larger battle against plagiarism, becomes the powerful weapon with which the war is fought and won.

The use of war imagery on the homepage clearly separates two opposed sides: The educators are construed as pitted against the students who plagiarize. Based on these terms, the technology assists the "good guys" and is the all-powerful weapon in the larger battle, as demonstrated in the "Media: News and Press" link, where the first two of four headlines (listed vertically) use the word "fight" in the title and mention it at least once in the news flash. Yet, the good/evil distinction is often formulated as administrators against the instructors who resist the technology, or instructors who use the technology and the students who resist it. These complex relationships remind us that other institutional factors and demands are at work; manufacturers are appealing to institutions; institutions are sometimes putting pressure on instructors, and instructors have complex relationships with students. Because the pressures are often not communicated among these levels, the technology and its use remain largely unexamined. Surveillance is reduced to technologies that are in place, but human factors often become secondary to the principle of efficiency.

Systemization and Teaching

To begin, let us compare plagiarism detection technology and Foucault's theories of discipline and punish in order to investigate how plagiarism detection software mirrors the practices described by Foucault in eighteenth century prisons. The development of norms and rules and their ability to function independently from human interference promotes the systemization of discipline, where people create and maintain a system because it is ordered, efficient, and gives the appearance of productivity. Specifically, the use of established techniques and technologies that help maintain discipline, like the techniques used in Foucault's theaters of punishment, ensure the success of any disciplinary system or institution. Though the traditional prison did not yet exist in the late eighteenth century, according to Foucault's research the notion of discipline was developing as a system of techniques that could control a person's body and behavior. The prosecutors of crimes maintained discipline by forcing systematic regulations of time (like timetables), physical action (exercise and military drills), group procedures, and final assessments (148–64). Throughout these procedures, those in power observed the prisoners and monitored their actions. Over time, norms developed based on the repeated behavior of prisoners and the expectations of prisoners and administrators. This form of discipline was maintained without traditional cells or prison bars; the surveillance created a prison existing outside physical domains. The fear itself became a crime deterrent because those who witness disciplinary practices internalize the notions embedded in those practices; stated simply, they begin to regulate their own behavior. Some scholars concerned with plagiarism have similarly critiqued recent assessment and disciplinary techniques regarding plagiarism cases because they are often abstracted from authentic cases and are arbitrarily created, but serve as a deterrent that promotes fear in students.

Teaching based on the punitive model could be interpreted as a technology of surveillance. Rebecca Moore Howard, a leading critical scholar on the topic of plagiarism, argues that plagiarism and students who plagiarize can only be defined and categorized in relation to larger institutional signifiers for copyrighting, ownership, and authenticity ("Plagiarisms, Authorships, and the Academic Death Penalty"). Copyright laws determine how much teachers, for example, can copy from an original text for distribution to their classes when they depend on a company to make the copies. Usually the amount is limited to approximately one chapter or a limited number of pages. In "Could There be a Right to Own Intellectual Property?" James Wilson argues that public work is especially difficult to own given its exposure and availability; the very fact that the text is public implies public *use* of the text. He says that objects of intellectual property are "abstract and socially mediated" and "[t]his makes it even more difficult to think of ownership of intellectual property in terms fundamentally of a relationship between the owner and a thing, rather than as fundamentally a set of rights against others with regard to a specific type" (398–99). Given the widespread publication of text on the Web, ranging from information on college and university websites to personal blogs, students may find it hard to figure out what is bound by copyright law and what is free to cite and distribute. Moreover, the difference between scholarly sources that are credible in academic papers and popular sources (which are not credible sources) becomes blurry.

The software is also difficult for administrators and teachers to use at times, forcing them to evaluate the results carefully, because the detection software often uses one limited method for a variety of different cases. In "Sexuality, Textuality: The Cultural Work of Plagiarism," Howard argues that teachers judge texts for plagiarism based solely on the sources included in the texts. Based on these factors, plagiarism could be defined only by textual comparison, and one could apply a quantitative formula to count the number of plagiarized words. In other words, what if a student only used a single source for all of his or her research when the teacher did not assign a specific number of sources? It would appear that the student plagiarized from that source solely based on the quantity of information he or she cited directly or indirectly from a single source. These sorts of categories have not been clearly defined by administrators or teachers, so the use of plagiarism software can unfairly present cases of plagiarism. Still, many teachers will continue using the software because many are compelled to decrease their overwhelming workload by using pedagogical technologies that cut their work time considerably.

Academic codes of conduct are often a means to advise students not to plagiarize and outline institution-wide consequences, but generally do not outline the process or standards of *assessing* individual plagiarism cases for individual departments. Instructors, therefore, often have no method to compare the software-specific reported rates of copied material against larger institutional standards unless their respective departments train them. Bill Marsh argues that plagiarism detection software like *Turnitin* fails to educate instructors and students on definitions of plagiarism, so instructors often take a role in maintaining surveillance without understanding what they are actually seeking. Marsh describes the software's process of plagiarism detection, explaining that it scans students' papers by changing text into hypertext to detect similarity (137). What Marsh is describing is how the software changes the student's text into code and seeks the Internet for matching code. The problem is that the software searches only for surface similarity, not analyzing how the copied material is used or situated within the work. For example, a student may have supplied information about the source earlier in the text or paragraph but forgot to include the page numbers. The software will not note the earlier introduction of the material, and an instructor may not check the paper closely for earlier references once the software has matched the text with its original source. The instructor is limited to the software's line of sight, which is not situated in the classroom. The technology cannot adapt itself to a particular context or account for culture. While many people use technology because it limits the possibility for error and the time it takes to complete a task, they often fail to see how the technology limits them.

The software scanner, moreover, does not include particularized personal or educational context in its search: neither the class from which the paper was created nor the student's individual situation. As a result, the software can find a student guilty without assessing all the factors of individual cases. For example, imagine that a student may have been confused about a particular citation practice and emailed an instructor or teaching assistant prior to the paper due date, but never received a response. If that were the case, the instructor might be more forgiving of the student's failure to cite correctly. The program, however, does not take specific cases into account, and an overworked professor may enter a few papers into the database and simply trust the results without recalling these details. Many instructors and students therefore resent the use of technologies and feel that it eliminates interpersonal relationships with students and promotes a business model of education. The technology helps process plagiarism cases using a systematic method and potentially weeds out the students who plagiarize, but it does not teach students individually or motivate students to complete their own work. This processing of potential plagiarism cases can create an environment where efficiency is valued over human intervention, thereby echoing a business model. Because the program cannot account for these individual cases, Marsh is also concerned with the way the program's website constructs plagiarizing as an unethical and criminal activity (11). Students are often misidentified as criminals when the terms of plagiarism are ill-defined or not defined at all and when the individual cases are ignored.

One can think of the *Turnitin* detection software website and the publicity surrounding its use in universities as creating a similar space as the Foucaultian theater of punishment, where the presence of the technology alludes to the constant possibility of criminal behavior and potential punishments. The descriptions used to characterize plagiarism and those students who plagiarize serve as not only social commentary, but as a warning to others. According to Foucault, behavior is maintained through the techniques of observation, judgment, and examination. We will investigate these terms and how Foucault defines them in *Discipline and Punish* in order to further read plagiarism cases and *Turnitin* technology in the terms of these definitions.

HIERARCHICAL OBSERVATION AND PLAGIARISM DETECTION

Observation serves to maintain discipline because those who are observed often cannot see the viewers or the surveillance technologies, so the observed individuals maintain acceptable behavior in order to avoid potential punishment. Foucault discusses how observatories developed during the classical age, and the access to new lines of sight translated into new knowledge for the viewers. He argues that those in power observed subordinates in order to enforce and maintain certain behaviors in the individual or group. These observatories were situated in a similar fashion to military camps; other institutions (schools, hospitals, and prisons) developed similar observational modes following this model (171). Foucault claims the most powerful surveillance would be achieved by the least-fragmented lines of sight, where the viewing mechanism could see everything at once as an omniscient eye (173). Imagine, as I described earlier, a guard on that watchtower in the Panopticon, observing prisoners without being seen. The prisoners are vaguely aware that the guard is there, but they control their behavior based on the fear of being watched. This concept serves as an interesting theoretical framework to read current practices in plagiarism detection, where the technology is owned and accessed solely by the instructors and administrators. One can see how plagiarism detection software operates with similar surveillance methods.

The *Turnitin* software provides a single site used to detect plagiarized material, but it does so by observing great tracts of cyberspace. The user uploads papers written by students, and the software "crawls" through the Web, looking for similar text. It may be true that the instructor can enter a section of a student's essay on any search engine and essentially scan the Web, but the software serves as a more piercing gaze because it actually highlights all copied sections of the piece when it reports "hits" upon completing the search. The instructor who searches using a regular search engine may not be able to easily "see" all parts that are plagiarized at once, as the various plagiarized sections may come from different sources. The detection software seems to have a more accurate and efficient eye and a wider range of sight.

The software is available on the Web from any personal or public computer (when one has an account with the company), which actually unifies the space rather than fragments it. Fragmentation would indicate barriers and walls, and the space of the Web presents only a few walls (such as password-protected sites, copyright-regulated sites, and private databases). Users of this software do not have to travel to specific locations on campus in order to use it. Therefore, the software does create an omniscient line of sight and is not limited by physical space. According to Foucault, discipline is achieved through a calculated gaze, where surveyors carefully watch all the actions of the surveyed. Discipline is not achieved through force, as Foucault argues that disciplinary power "was also organized as a multiple, automatic and anonymous power; for although surveillance rests on individuals, its functioning is that of a network of relations" (176). The students do not know when their work is being observed and processed through this surveillance system, nor do they always know when or how it is being used. Thus, as Foucault explains, the surveillance apparatus as a whole produces power and enables the disciplinary power to be absolutely indiscreet, since it is everywhere and always alert (by its very principle, it leaves no zone of shade and constantly supervises the very individuals who are entrusted with the task of supervising) and at the same time absolutely 'discreet,' for it functions permanently and largely in silence (177). Those in educational settings who do not have access to plagiarism detection technology, but know it exists, can be left feeling powerless against it. The power of the technology lies in the simultaneous knowledge that it exists and that it cannot be seen.

Students could then, based on their generally limited access as students, develop a fear of the software, where this technology becomes an immanent *thing*—an elusive, unseen, and lurking watcher. Often, that is part of the software's power to deter plagiarism rather than just detect it. A student's fear of the technology itself becomes a powerful preventative force in plagiarism deterrence, but when institutions use methods that promote fear, they do not reflect or advocate their greater, supposedly proactive educational goals. Using fear as a deterrent does not reach the potential roots of the issue: a student's lack of education regarding research methods and knowledge concerning correct citation practices and his or her overload of work. One might argue that this use of fear is unethical because it forces students into behaviors based on their perceived powerlessness. While many instructors may view the software as a neutral instrument, students may see it as an all-seeing, determining, and surveying mechanism.

EXAMINATION OF THE PLAGIARIZED MATERIAL, EXAMINATION OF THE INDIVIDUAL

Often the assessment standards for discipline are based on completely subjective categories, since the issue is concerning socially acceptable behavior and social constructions of normalcy. Based on Foucault's argument, in the examination, the person or mechanism that gazes upon its object is able to classify what is deemed deviant behavior and punish according to those standards (181–84). Examination procedures emerged in hospitals and schools officially in the eighteenth century and further solidified the positions of those in power and also those who were treated as objects for viewing and judging (189–92). The power of the examination is that it allows judgment against the individual based on a set of standards (norms) that are created, shaped, and owned solely by the examiners. The examinees are tested against these sets of norms and objectified in the process (187). Often the judging criteria are rigid and determined not by individual differences in the examinees, but by categories and general scientific description (191). These categories are generally unknown to the examinees and protected by the examiners because hiding the examination criteria offers a source of power and control over the tested subjects.

The examination becomes another form of power, knowledge ownership, and control, serving as a crucial part of surveillance. Instructors, then, can potentially use examination to modify and enforce behavior rather than test for comprehension of educational material. The examination procedures used to determine deviance and misbehavior are often hidden as well. Foucault argues,

> [t]he entire criminal procedure, right up to the sentence, remained secret: that is to say, opaque, not only to the public but also to the accused himself. It took place without him, or at least without his having any

knowledge of the charges or of the evidence. In the
order of criminal justice, knowledge was the absolute
privilege of the prosecution. (35)

The power of the examination lies in the hidden standards of judgment. Howard poses similar concerns regarding the process of defining, detecting, and punishing plagiarism, arguing throughout her
article "Plagiarisms, Authorships, and the Academic Death Penalty"
that plagiarism has not been clearly defined, and its boundaries are
still contested. If this is the case, how are instructors and administrators defining and assessing real cases of plagiarism? Do they have a
standard approach to identifying and assessing plagiarism?

One weakness of detection software is that it identifies matching
text but does not define the boundaries of plagiarized versus non-pla-
giarized papers for the user. This is similar to the concept of examination outlined by Foucault because instructors are forced to create
standards and become instruments of disciplinary codes based on the
very terms they cannot define. The software does not define these
terms either but presents broad categories in its results. In the final report, *Turnitin* displays a split screen, where the student's work is posted
on the left, and the original text is on the right. Areas where students
have copied text are highlighted in both screens. In order to rate the
occurrence of plagiarism, *Turnitin* supplies a feature that places the results (the amount of highlighted plagiarized text) on a colorized scale
represented by the following categories: red, no plagiarism; green,
some plagiarism; and yellow, entire paper copied. These categories
leave much room for individual interpretation. The scale of *some* plagiarism could vary from two paragraphs to seven in a six-page paper.
What is the difference between these cases? Is one plagiarized, and one
not? Is a paper only plagiarized when the entire paper is copied?

While an instructor is not often formally trained to judge individual plagiarism cases in terms of a scale—rather, they judge based on
the often vague provisions of academic codes—they are trained how to
use the software. The instructor is limited to the categories established
by the software itself. He or she is trained to identify the categories
but not how to decipher what the categories mean. The instructor's
lack of guidance for assessing individual cases further mystifies the
detection and punishment process for the students. In his discussion
of litigious procedures in the eighteenth century and their theoretical
considerations, Foucault argues, "[T]he secret and written form of the

procedure reflects the principle that in criminal matters the establish-
ment of truth was the absolute right and the exclusive power of the
sovereign and his judges" (35). Strangely, the situation is the same for
many twenty-first century students who have no clue, often, of the
criteria used to judge them. Furthermore, if instructors cannot define
plagiarism, they will surely struggle to teach students the methods of
avoiding it. They haven't been trained to be critical of these weaknesses in the program but only trained to follow the results.

Foucault outlines the significance of training in creating and maintaining discipline and power. Often in institutions, the surveyors can
become the surveyed (the instructors, who survey the students, are
also monitored by the administrators); all of those involved are servic-
ing the larger power structures. Foucault argues that this phenomenon
is made possible by two elements: "First, the definition of behavior
and performance on the basis of the two opposed values of good and
evil." Second, as a result, "the disciplinary apparatuses hierarchized
the 'good' and the 'bad' subjects in relation to one another" (180–81).
These categories are evident on the *Turnitin* homepage, most apparently in the separate links to training materials for students, instructors, and administrators. Each group serves a different function in
maintaining this apparatus and therefore must be trained differently.

This training is based on gratification and punishment. The instructors receive the gratification of knowing they are enforcing the
code of academic integrity, saving time (and money), and successfully
identifying "criminals." The scenario is not without irony, however,
for though instructors may feel the power of police-force mentality,
they are also indoctrinated into a system not unlike the students. They
are often overworked when grading papers and find the software an
easy replacement for arduous Web searches. They are under similar
pressures from administration to uphold academic honesty in their
classrooms and enforce codes of conduct. Though instructors may feel
they have a choice in the use of the software, they are often inevitably
bound by disciplinary rules, procedures, and codes. If they choose to
reinterpret the code or make exceptions, they have the potential to feel
subversive rather than liberated.

Of course, Foucault might argue that any image of liberation and
empowerment is an illusion. The illusion of individuality in fact often
maintains hierarchies and gives the impression of power to the "individual" only to perpetuate his or her position. He would not pose

any seemingly productive alternatives that would appear to empower students because he would see power as constructed as well. However, this does not have to be the inevitable conclusion. Like media, technologies can be used in ways that consider ethical implications on users and their contexts. As Andrew Feenberg argues in *Critical Theory of Technology*, users should perceive technologies as situated in certain cultures, places, and times, and never as isolated. He argues, "[P]erhaps the computer is neither good nor evil, but both. By this I mean not merely that computers can be used for good or evil purposes, but that they can evolve into very different technologies in the framework of strategies of domination or democratization" (7). Feenberg argues that new, major technological inventions offer the opportunity to transform the power structures in and of which they operate (*Critical Theories of Technology*). A more proactive, rather than reactive, approach to plagiarism is accordingly needed, where detection software can be included as part of a more comprehensive educational curriculum.

AN EDUCATIONAL APPROACH TO PLAGIARISM PREVENTION

The first step toward promoting an educational approach to plagiarism prevention would perhaps be to define plagiarism and offer models and clear categories for assessment. Most importantly, students must have an active role in creating these definitions and establishing agreed-upon procedures. To cite one promising example, the University of Arizona's Eller College of Management created the Ethics Program in 2003 as a way to combat the problem of unethical business practices, and to help instill strong ethical behaviors in K–12 and college students. As part of the Ethics Program, a student committee has been formed to deal specifically with plagiarism policies, procedures, and education. The committee and administration are part of the Eller integrity (E-tegrity) program, which hosts an E-tegrity week and related website, and offers a plagiarism deterrence toolkit ("E-tegrity"). During the E-tegrity week, college students are challenged with ethical dilemmas, and their responses to those dilemmas are judged. The winning team is often awarded with supporting funds. Plagiarism is one of the major issues highlighted in the comprehensive E-tegrity program each year. The E-tegrity program also includes the use of *Turnitin* at the Eller College of Management, but it is framed as only one component of a multifaceted approach to plagiarism.

The emphasis on academic integrity in business education is extremely important for establishing general business ethics and sound business practices. In the *Journal of Business Ethics*, Rafik Elias cites studies proving that business students are more likely to cheat and those who do are at risk for unethical business practices later in life:

> The overall conclusion is that business students cheated more often than other students and were less likely to disapprove of it (McCabe 1997) and that they had more lax attitudes on what constituted cheating (Klein, et. al. 2007). Lawson (2004) also showed that business students who admitted to cheating were more likely to accept unethical workplace behavior. (200)

With cases like the Enron scandal, academic integrity can serve as an ethical foundation for students going into the business world. Further, the E-tegrity program sets a standard for students in other disciplines and even in public schools. The High School Ethics Forum was developed by Eller College to reach out to high schools in Arizona and offer a context for discussing business dilemmas and conducting ethical debates. At the college level, Eller College holds an annual Ethics Case Competition in which students debate an ethics case and try to come up with the most effective solution. In order to maintain ethical standards year-round, Eller College has developed a hotline for students to report any suspicious activity on campus or within their classes. Student reports are completely anonymous, and students can also use the hotline to discuss any concerns or ask questions about plagiarism ("Demonstrating").

At the very least, universities and high schools might pose critical questions when implementing plagiarism detection software and assessing its efficacy, so that they critically consider its implementation and use. Rosalind Tedford's article, "Plagiarism Detection Programs: A Comparative Evaluation" offers several exemplary questions to consider for further research on the development, use, and assessment of plagiarism software: Does the faculty, for instance, tell their students that their papers may be submitted to the program? Does the faculty require their students to submit their papers themselves—and if so, does this practice promote a culture of suspicion or a leveling of the playing field for all students? (118). In order to address these questions and suggestions, students and instructors should take an active role in the process of integrating and using technology like *Turnitin* within the educational context. One simple approach would be for schools to offer a link to the software's homepage on a library website, spatially situated near plagiarism prevention resources. Instructors could also offer that link on their syllabi and walk students through the software if they have access to technology, or they can create print documents with screen shots.

Since 2006 when I first analyzed the *Turnitin* website, the company has changed its image and the rhetoric displayed on the site. The look in 2010 became far more market-oriented and student-centered. The homepage boasts in large letters: "Prevent Plagiarism. Engage Students." Links to purchase the software and to see pricing plans are readily available on the homepage. The new software is also more comprehensive, offering peer review capabilities and feedback functions for teachers. The news headlines that were once so boldly posted are no longer found on the site and are replaced with news of which schools, states, regions, and countries have now adopted the software. The more recent rhetoric is focused on the program's popularity and usability rather than the criminality of plagiarism. There may be several reasons for these changes. Perhaps the company was made aware of critiques of the program, especially in academic circles. The company became more popular and may have assumed that the popularity alone would sell the product. Perhaps current subscribers asked for more functions as part of their package, and the company responded by developing the functions and advertising the changes on the site. While the emphasis on collaboration and student involvement is a generally positive step, the popularity of the product serves to mask many of the ideological assumptions behind the program and its uses. In other words, popularity alone does not mean that the program is ideologically neutral or that the basic functions of the program are different. More importantly, what gives a for-profit company the right to impose definitions of plagiarism within educational institutions? Should academic institutions be responsible for making and enforcing those definitions instead?

These questions and suggestions take into consideration the larger institutional context and the effect of the software on faculty and students, but they do not eliminate considerations of power; even if we define plagiarism, we are still (perhaps even more so) bound by that definition and its established categories for examination. Still, I favor Feenberg's view that change is possible and that people have opportunity for resistance. By discussing technology—especially its implications and the way that power is maintained through fear of punishment or technologies themselves—we can begin to discuss methods for more responsible technology use in the schools. Given that the future promises more advancements in pedagogical technologies and greater access to them, we should start to consider the ethical implications of their use and effects.

WORKS CITED

"Demonstrating College Social Responsibility." Ethics Program, Eller College of Management. Web. 8 November 2010.

Elias, Rafik. "The Impact of Anti-Intellectualism Attitudes and Academic Self-Efficacy on Business Students' Perceptions of Cheating." *Journal of Business Ethics* 86.2 (2009): 199–209. Print.

"E-tegrity." Eller College of Management. Web. 4 October 2006.

Feenberg, Andrew. *Critical Theory of Technology*. New York: Oxford UP, 1991. Print.

—. *Transforming Technology: A Critical Theory Revisited*. New York: Oxford UP, 2002. Print.

Foucault, Michel. *Discipline and Punish: The Birth of the Prison*. New York: Vintage, Random House, Inc., 1995. Print.

Howard, Rebecca Moore. "Plagiarisms, Authorships, and the Academic Death Penalty." *College English* 57 (1995): 788–805. Print.

—. "Sexuality, Textuality: The Cultural Work of Plagiarism." *College English* 62.4 (2000): 473–91. Print.

Marsh, Bill. *Plagiarism: Alchemy and Remedy in Higher Education*. Albany, NY: SUNY P, 2007. Print.

Tedford, Rosalind. "Plagiarism Detection Programs: A Comparative Evaluation." *College and University Media Review* 9.2 (2002): 111–18. Print.

Turnitin.com. Web. 2010.

Wilson, James. "Could there be a Right to Own Intellectual Property?" *Law and Philosophy* 28.4 (2009): 393–427. Print.

QUESTIONS FOR DISCUSSION

1. Deborah Harris-Moore writes: "Many instructors and students therefore resent the use of technologies and feel that it eliminates in-

terpersonal relationships with students and promotes a business model of education." What does Harris-Moore mean here? Brainstorm all the ways that the business of plagiarism detection software may influence the relationships students have with their teachers to get at an answer.

2. Harris-Moore writes: "The development of norms and rules and their ability to function independently from human interference promotes the systemization of discipline, where people create and maintain a system because it is ordered, efficient, and gives the appearance of productivity." Why might it be important to professors and/or administrators to give the impression that plagiarists are being caught and punished in an orderly, efficient, productive manner?

8 A Marked Resemblance: Students, Teachers, and the Dynamics of Plagiarism

Sean Zwagerman

Before You Read: *As a student or a teacher, when you learn that a student has plagiarized and gotten away with it, how do you feel? What do you wish would happen?*

Though it is not clear if academic plagiarism is becoming more common, it is certainly receiving widespread attention.[1] High profile cases, like that of student novelist Kaavya Viswanathan, make the national news (Smith and Motoko). Many schools require new students to sign honesty pledges. Teachers routinely cite their school's plagiarism policy on course syllabi and warn students of the punishments. Though we should be concerned about willful acts of plagiarism, the following excerpt from an academic integrity website at Rutgers University suggests that our concern may itself be cause for concern:

> Plagiarism is the basest form of parasitism. A leech may make a living from other organisms, but even a leech doesn't take credit where credit is not due. Thievery of words, scourge of the intellectual arena, plagiarism festers most prominently on college campuses worldwide. The Internet has ensured the profusion and accessibility of this germ, this disease that debilitates creativity and scholastic equality. (*Plagiarism and Honor Module*)

We might expect a tone like this if the topic was terrorists or kidnap-
pers, but it seems rather extreme as a reaction to plagiarism. When we
see otherwise reasonable people speaking this way, it's worth asking:
What's at stake here? If I copy an essay from the Internet and submit it
as my own, who and what am I threatening? Plagiarism is not a brute
fact like carbon or gravity, but a social fact, like traffic laws, good
manners, and college degrees—humans have, so to speak, invented
it. We can thus ask of plagiarism, as we can of other inventions like
diplomas and good manners, what does it do for us, and why do we
need it? Conversely, what does plagiarism—or more specifically, our
obsession with, and policing of, plagiarism—do *to* us? How might it
be working against us? My goal is to address some of these questions
and perhaps challenge a discourse of academic integrity that actually
threatens integrity by fostering divisiveness. Setting teachers against
"plagiarists" and "good" students against "bad" creates subgroups that
are not just antagonistic (and largely fictional) but symbiotic, turning
the student-teacher relationship into "a repeated game between plagiarizers and faculty" (Weinstein and Dobkin 1).[2] These opposing roles
function within a context of shared assumptions about the nature and
the consequences of academic dishonesty—assumptions understood
and acted upon by teachers, "good students," and "plagiarists" alike.

It is often noted that "plagiary" comes from the Greek word for
kidnapping. More precisely, it means the kidnapping of someone else's
children or slaves. Given the relationship we as students and teachers
have to language, this etymology is wonderfully appropriate; for although plagiarism is imagined as stealing words from their true and
original author, plagiarism is in fact taking words that were working
for a different master in their previous assignment. As for words and
children (and words as children), if we consider the tension between
the offspring and the parent, the derived and the authentic—with
attention to the etymological relationship of "authentic" to "authorship" and "authority"—we may appreciate how our enactment of the
vocabulary of academic integrity as policy and pedagogy resembles
the dynamics of a dysfunctional family. Students are divided amongst
themselves, suspicious that their classmate-siblings will sneak into
their room and take their words: The block quotation in the first paragraph was not written by a Rutgers professor but by a *student*. Meanwhile, the teacher-student relationship devolves into a spy-versus-spy
game in which the authorities of authenticity try to catch plagiarists,

and plagiarists—that small percentage of students who are willfully dishonest—become craftier.

The parent/child analogy, by which plagiarism is something students do against, or in spite of, teachers, obscures the experiences students and teachers share, experiences of competition, comparison, and evaluation. Like students, teachers have an anxious relationship with words and marks: marks in the form of grades and evaluations, and the marks which together form those words we wish to call our own, the writings upon which we are evaluated, ranked, and graded—in a word, marked. Though teachers are not given letter grades, they are constantly evaluated, in part by their students, and given—or not given—performance-based promotions, raises, and tenure. Our commonality is, at its root, a shared relationship to language. We are all the masters and the servants of language, the scribes and the inscribed, right down to the level of individual letters: those A's we hoard and desire, and those F's that scare us into compliance. It seems we would do well to reconsider the consequences of continuing to perform our roles in the drama of academic integrity as currently scripted, in order to imagine some alternatives.

Thinking of plagiarism as a clearly defined behavior allows us to see the student body as neatly divided between those who cheat and those who don't.[3] A fascinating study conducted at the Rochester Institute of Technology found that 27.6% of students surveyed admitted to plagiarizing "often," "very frequently," or "sometimes." But 90% believed that other students were doing so "often," "very frequently," or "sometimes" (Kellogg). Now if 27.6% of students are plagiarizing, that is indeed troubling behavior; but if 90% of students *think* everyone else is plagiarizing, that is a troubling misperception—and beliefs, as often as facts, lead to policy. The following excerpt from a report by Simon Fraser University's Task Force on Academic Honesty and Integrity shows how the rhetoric of academic integrity can disunite the student body by constructing two distinct groups of students, the honest, and the dishonest:

> Those [students] who follow the rules [. . .] want the discipline students receive for confirmed cases of academic dishonesty to [. . .] send a clear message that cheating is a risky business and those who engage in academic dishonesty should expect to be caught and punished. (Task Force 2)

Against these black and white perceptions, James R. Kincaid suggests, "We might try to entertain the idea that plagiarism, and even original- ity, are relative concepts" (97); Rebecca Moore Howard recommends abandoning the term "plagiarism" altogether because it lumps together such disparate acts as "fraud, insufficient citation, and excessive rep- etition" ("Sexuality, Textuality" 475). The "plagiarist," however, is a useful character in academic integrity discourse, one who embodies an array of written acts—some unethical, some not—in a clear, simple, disreputable identity.[4] Once we accept this splitting of the student body into "plagiarizers and non-plagiarizers" (Wilgoren A1), we can more easily justify an authoritarian countermeasure like plagiarism detection software by saying "it prevents good kids from taking the easy route" (iParadigms, *Turnitin*). The plagiarist is useful too in that he allows the rest of us—"those who follow the rules"—to imagine ourselves as the embodiment of honesty and integrity. However, the absolute goodness of the good student is as dubious as the badness of the plagiarist. The University of California at Davis promotes academ- ic integrity in a number of ways, including publishing in the school newspaper "all the embarrassing details—except for names" of crimes against integrity (Weiss A17). The university feels its actions are work- ing: One Davis student says, "'I would never want to cheat here—it's just too scary'" (A17). If this student is typical, then the honesty being fostered does not seem very honorable: The student behaves because she fears being caught misbehaving.

In addition to dividing the student body, simplistic perceptions of and responses to plagiarism harm the teacher-student relationship, as manifested in teachers' use of unethical means to police unethical behavior. The banner of academic integrity is sullied by the glaring, ironic contrast between the rhetoric of ethical values and some of the actions taken in the name of those values. As worries about plagia- rism—if not actual incidents of plagiarism—increase, "many profes- sors are putting less faith in honor and more in fear" (Gilgoff 51), in particular the fear inspired by plagiarism-detection products such as WordCheck and *Turnitin*. *Turnitin*'s website features letters such as these praising the product:

> Now I simply threaten them with (like—"You just
> wait till your father gets home"), "I'm going to submit
> this to *Turnitin.com*!" [. . .]

> I think the product is great. Just the threat of a pla-
> giarism system has forced a change in my students'
> behavior. It has forced my students to create their
> own work and forced them to learn the real way. (iP-
> aradigms, *Turnitin Testimonials*)

No doubt threats and force can bring about change, but as in the
UC Davis example, this changed behavior may not deserve to be
called integrity, nor do the means qualify as education; rather, what
we have is invigilated obedience, the unfortunate but unsurprising
result of "replacing the student-teacher relationship with the crimi-
nal-police relationship" (Howard, "Plagiarism, Policing" 1). A recent
Primetime television report on cheating and plagiarism provides the
following case. Complaining that students "think they can outsmart
the teacher," a high school history teacher submits her students' essays
to *Turnitin*. Determined to "get a more honest result," she does not
tell the students beforehand ("A Cheating Crisis"). The irony of using
the word "honest" in connection with her action went unremarked by
both the teacher and *Primetime* host, Charles Gibson. Neither recognized the ideology common to both a suspicious teacher and a student
who cheats to get a higher mark: the ends justify the means. Louis
Bloomfield of the University of Virginia believes plagiarism detection
programs "make dishonest students realize that it doesn't pay to use
any means necessary to get ahead" (Foster A38). As above, the irony
of making such a claim while endorsing surveillance would be comi-
cal if the consequences were not so detrimental to the teacher-student
relationship.

Donald McCabe, founder of The Center for Academic Integrity
and an oft-cited authority on these issues, would be the last person
to be lenient toward plagiarism; however, McCabe warns that an atmosphere of mistrust undermines learning: "[McCabe] expressed his
concern that requiring students to use plagiarism-detecting software
promotes a lack of trust, and resentment on the part of students toward their instructors. McCabe points out that feeling respected and
trusted is a major deterrent to academic dishonesty" (Task Force 23).
In addition to being vulnerable to ethical objections, arguments for invigilated obedience are weakened by the unequal distribution of punishment. Like McCabe, Gregory J. Cizek, author of *Cheating on Tests:
How to Do It, Detect It, and Prevent It,* wants to help teachers catch
cheaters, but Cizek concedes, "I suspect that only those who choose

the rather simplistic methods [of cheating] are likely to get caught. [. . .] This is not particularly a good thing, but it is the reality of the situation" (38). In other words, it is not bad students who are caught but bad cheaters. The truly brilliant cheaters will avoid detection, graduate with honors, and be elected to high office. The situation is the same for plagiarism: "The ethical paradox that we must acknowledge is that the more serious forms of plagiary are those that are most difficult to detect and for which the intent to plagiarize would be hardest to prove" (*Plagiary*). The loss of trust and the unequal distribution of punishment undermine the calls for increased surveillance and punishment and the praise bestowed on panoptic technologies of plagiarism detection.

I was long puzzled by the fact that calls for harsher punishment for plagiarism and support for invasive technologies are often voiced by people I know are opposed to abuses of authority such as warrantless searches, and manifestations of mistrust such as the proliferation of security cameras in public spaces. What makes plagiarism seem so important that it must be controlled at all costs, and what else might we be trying to control at the same time? A couple of years ago, a professor caught a student plagiarizing early in the semester. The professor asked the dean for authority to drop the student from her course rather than assign an F on the assignment and allow the student to stay. This professor feared that if the student stayed in the course, he would get his revenge by writing a negative course evaluation. This anecdote points to an important connection between the pressure of evaluation and faculty outrage against plagiarism. Not only are students and teachers constantly evaluated but we are also in large part evaluated on our writing and evaluated through the writing of others, in the form of grades, reports, reviews, etc. Students know all too well the anxiety of being "marked." Once a student's writing is reduced to a graded product, it serves "the calculation of the gaps between individuals, their distribution in a given 'population'" (Foucault 190). The course evaluation does the same to teachers, becoming part of "the mass of documents that capture and fix them" (189). The course evaluation is the one instance in which the pyramid of evaluation is inverted: It is the one opportunity for the pupils to administer the exam, to write an evaluation rather than write to be evaluated. The consequences of the "regulatory fiction of the autonomous author" (Howard, "Plagiarisms, Authorships" 791) find teachers once again in the same position as students, even while plagiarism policies keep teachers and students at odds, for the valorization of original *authority* within a context of evaluation creates anxiety for both students and teachers. Plagiarism threatens both our acts of writing and our acts of evaluation, acts vital to the integrity of the academy: The specter of plagiarism makes us doubt both the imagined authenticity of writing, and the imagined objective validity of grades. Suddenly every essay, every word—and thus every letter from A to F written upon that writing—is suspect.

Maybe that's a good thing. The identities of the good student and the plagiarist are further discredited by the fact that the behaviors they embody are themselves a dubious binary: "doing your own work" versus plagiarizing. Though a more thorough discussion is beyond the scope of this essay, it is important to note that contemporary—and indeed much historical—work in philosophy, psychology, rhetoric, composition, and education renders suspect any simple definition of "authorship," "authenticity," "originality," "meaning," and, consequently, "plagiarism." The field of writing and rhetoric so long ago dismissed as myth the Romantic notion of the poetic genius that it is astonishing to find the myth still going strong in discussions of plagiarism, as in the belief that there are two kinds of writing: one's own and plagiarized, the owned and the stolen. In reality (given the scarcity of poetic geniuses), most of us learn to write—and continue to write—by working with preexisting phrases, genres, and conventions. Linda Shamoon and Deborah H. Burns write, "When a student authors a 'good' paper [. . .] she may feel she is, indeed, being original. Rhetorically, however, her text probably imitates, elaborates, and applies ideas and forms from the various sources that are hers to use legitimately" (191). Howard reminds us that "patchwriting" is often the norm in the lower grades, and students new to higher education are sometimes surprised to learn that lashing together a paper by combining chunks from various sources is not only bad writing, but punishable conduct.[5] The issue of patchwriting demonstrates the ambiguity of plagiarism not only at the fuzzy margin between acceptable and unacceptable amounts of borrowing, but in the extent to which the rules about writing, and writing itself, are always conventional and contextual. Within this "social-rhetorical perspective" on writing, the evaluation of a student's writing is really the evaluation of that individual's performance in the role of student, in response to "the values and expectations of a specific reader or audience" (Shamoon and Burns 191). Since most instructors and students do not think of writing and evaluation in this way, however, the evaluation of student writing ranks and fixes that individual herself: We tend to believe that the letter grade says something about the person's innate abilities. Therefore the fear of plagiarism is the fear that a student will leap ahead through the ranks by mimicking authenticity in the stolen voice of authority and authorship, subverting the student-teacher power relation and stealing its currency, the grade.

Plagiarism may be feared even more as a threat to the imagined legitimacy of evaluation than it is to the authenticity of writing. Here again though, as it does in subverting Romantic ideas of authorship, plagiarism renders suspect that which to some extent deserves to be rendered suspect: the significance of the mark as a measure of a student's "aptitudes or abilities, under the gaze of a permanent corpus of knowledge" (Foucault 190). Even in the complete absence of cheating and plagiarism, the validity and integrity of the mark, the imaginary gold standard of rigor and excellence the A is supposed to signify, would be suspect. Nevertheless, the Official Transcript continues to invest grades with a near-scriptural authority and permanence, supposedly quantifying such qualities as "capacity"—a Romantic conception of how much the student has "in him"—and "promise," a word that takes intellectual potential and wraps it in a moral covenant, a commitment to produce. "Higher education," Robert Briggs writes, "has been increasingly reconceived over the last few decades as involving the cultivation of professional skills rather than the provision of knowledge" (20). As higher education becomes increasingly focused on preparing students for the work world, grades become less significant as indicators of academic performance than as coupons redeemable for graduate school and high-paying jobs (or so students hope). As Candace Spigelman writes, "Because student work is academic 'capital' traded for grades (which are themselves academic capital), ideas, words, and texts are forms of intellectual property with associated property rights for owners and elaborated punishments for 'trespassers' and 'thieves'" (30). Now that grades have become so valuable, plagiarism prevention seems even more urgent. In turn, monitoring students so vigilantly that students and teachers are always conscious of dishonesty's actual or potential presence endorses the supremacy of grades, intensifies the obsession, and furthers the disintegration of the student-teacher relationship. Teachers might pause to consider the ethics of encouraging students to be grade junkies and then punishing them for trying, if at times by unethical means, to get their fix.

If students and teachers alike are burdening marks with such grand and unpredictable ends as future social and economic success, we are right to ask just how valid these marks of evaluation really are. While we try to tell ourselves that they're fair and meritocratic, based upon clear grading rubrics for students and promotion criteria for teachers, we all fear that our grades may be more arbitrary than that, a fear expressed in the oral culture of both students and teachers. Students tell of getting poor grades because a teacher didn't like them, and teachers tell of colleagues denied tenure for personal or political reasons. These stories reflect our fear that success on exams and evaluations—and, more importantly, the currency of that success in the form of grades, diplomas, and promotion—is not in our control. Though some instructors find distasteful the obsession with grades and the commodification of knowledge, they still perform alongside students in an evaluative context, and thus, as Janice R. Walker points out, "[Teachers'] own attitudes and ideologies may be adding to the concept of knowledge as commodity, as students trade finished products for grades in the classroom, and we barter intellectual property for academic rewards in the tenure-and-promotion review process" (249). All university teachers know that publications, more than teaching, are the measure of professional success; writing is the tangible, gradeable product upon which faculty are evaluated, and it is on the basis of that evaluation that professors are or are not allowed to "graduate" to the next level. The slogan "publish or perish" is the teacher's equivalent of "do your own work" and "grades can determine your future." These expressions show the extent to which we still reduce "the power of writing" to its use in "the 'formalization' of the individual within power relations" (Foucault 189–190), still succumb to the Romantic idea of authorship, and still shortchange the opportunities to learn during the writing process in the interest of generating markable and marketable product.

At the beginning of this essay, I suggested some significance in the etymology of plagiary. I turn now to the definition of that which plagiarism threatens: integrity. It turns out that integrity is not synonymous with obedience or individual virtue but is rather the quality of soundness and unity within a body. While integrity should be a value that unites the students and teachers, the moral/punitive response to

plagiarism actually inhibits integrity by sowing its opposites: divisiveness and an isolating individualism. Unity implies collaboration and
trust, and an atmosphere of trust encourages us to take risks, to try on
new roles in the form of courses, majors, and—most importantly—
ideas and opinions: How does it feel to think like this, or to write
like that? What new possibilities emerge? Inflammatory rhetoric and
panoptic policies cannot but diminish intellectual play, creativity, and
risk-taking, activities that continually reinvigorate the roles—and the
writing—of student and teacher. Margaret Price writes, "[O]nce we
have acknowledged to students and ourselves that plagiarism is part
of an ongoing, evolving academic conversation, we can invite students
to add their own voices to that conversation" (90). An article in *U.S.
News and World Report* states, "85% of college students say cheating
is necessary to get ahead" (iParadigms, *Research*). We might be so
alarmed by this statistic that we start using plagiarism detection software. Instead, let's use the statistic as an opportunity for conversation:
What exactly does it mean to "get ahead?" Who is left behind? What
alternative futures—places to get to—can we imagine, and how do
they allow us to reimagine education?

The benefits of assuming most students are honest far out-
weigh the costs, while the opposite is true for assuming all are
suspect. Kincaid writes, "The plagiarism proctor, after all, doesn't
have it so good. He lives in a nightmare world filled with thieves
or, worse, abductors. All his neighbors lie in wait to snatch and
misuse, pollute and defile his words" (97). Who wants to learn
or teach in a place like that? Teachers too benefit from an atmosphere of trust. Teaching is a vulnerable act, especially in a
critical curriculum that exposes and questions the identity of
those things closest to hand: the classroom, the essay, the student—and the teacher! Within such a pedagogy, writes Ira Shor,
"The teacher surrenders the mystique of power and expertise,
while using his or her critical understanding of reality to provoke
critical consciousness in the students" (84). Surrender may be
humbling for a teacher, but the alternative (and probably more
familiar) role, that of the invulnerable expert, has its problems
too, such as "alienation from students, a need to appear formi-
dable, a fear of failing to meet the expectations of colleagues and
students, the constant pressure to put on a good show, [and] the

defensiveness that accompanies the exercise of power over others" (84). Finally, Briggs makes the crucial observation that "the ethical competencies that apparently animate the desire to produce 'one's own' work may actually arise as an effect of the process of mastering relevant research and writing techniques" (21). In other words, if teachers put less energy into catching cheaters and more into teaching writing and critical thinking, we should achieve the very objective of academic integrity: students more invested in their learning *and therefore* less inclined to cheat or plagiarize. The reduction of plagiarism surrenders its leading role in the teacher's engagement with students and their writing, and instead takes its proper place as the desirable byproduct of a collaborative, trusting relationship. Understanding plagiarism as a contextual phenomenon and a pedagogical opportunity encourages us all to respond in the roles we are best equipped to play: not as moral enforcers, but as thinkers and writers, students and teachers.

Notes

1. Compare, for example, the findings (or even the titles) of the television program, "A Cheating Crisis in America's Schools," and Alex P. Kellogg's essay, "Students Plagiarize Less Than Many Think, a New Study Finds" (see Works Cited).

2. I am not attempting herein to "deconstruct" plagiarism in order to conclude that it doesn't exist or doesn't matter, for although plagiarism is far from being a black-and-white issue, the vast grey area does not invalidate the distinction between, say, writing an essay and buying one. Honesty may be "only" a social construct, but then so are we; and here in the social world, we take honesty seriously. However, I find the vast grey area far more interesting.

3. Cheating and plagiarism are often mentioned in the same breath. I recognize that they are not synonymous, that cheating need not involve plagiarism and that many—in my experience, most—acts of plagiarism are not acts of cheating. I mention them together here not to condemn both equally but rather to try to avoid the urge toward condemnation long enough to consider the extent to which we all at times transgress the expectations and conventions of the academic community. Such transgression is often fruitful: We can appreciate "academic freedom" as a built-in protection and recogni-

tion of the extent to which certain acts of transgression are necessary for the continued vitality and relevance of the academy.

4. See references to "plagiarists" in Bugeja; Kolich; Lang; and throughout iParadigms's plagiarism.org website.

5. See Howard, "Plagiarisms, Authorships, and the Academic Death Penalty." *College English* 57 (1995): 788–806.

WORKS CITED

Briggs, Robert. "Shameless! Reconceiving the Problem of Plagiarism." *Australian Universities Review* 46 (2003): 19–23. Print.

Bugeja, Michael. "Thwarting Plagiarism." *Character Clearinghouse*. 2001. Web. 6 July 2004.

"A Cheating Crisis in America's Schools." Narr. Charles Gibson. *Primetime Thursday*. ABC. KOMO, Seattle. 29 April 2004. Video.

Cizek, Gregory J. *Cheating on Tests: How to Do It, Detect It, and Prevent It.* Mahwah, NJ: Lawrence Erlbaum Associates, 1999. Print.

Foster, Andrea. "Plagiarism-Detection Tool Creates Legal Quandary." *Chronicle of Higher Education* 48 (2002): A37–38. Print.

Foucault, Michel. *Discipline and Punish.* New York: Vintage, 1995. Print.

Gilgoff, Dan. "Click on Honorable College Student: Will Computers Make Honor Codes Obsolete?" *U.S. News and World Report* 21 May 2001: 51. Print.

Howard, Rebecca Moore. "Plagiarism, Policing, Pedagogy." (or "Forget About Policing Plagiarism. Just Teach.") *Chronicle of Higher Education* 16 November 2001. Web. 4 January 2006.

—. "Plagiarisms, Authorships, and the Academic Death Penalty." *College English* 57 (1995): 788–806. Print.

—. "Sexuality, Textuality: The Cultural Work of Plagiarism." *College English* 62 (2000): 473–91. Print.

iParadigms, LLC. *Research Resources.* 2003. Web. 16 June 2004.

—. *Turnitin Testimonials.* 2004. Web. 16 June 2004.

Kellogg, Alex P. "Students Plagiarize Less Than Many Think, a New Study Finds." *Chronicle of Higher Education* 1 February 2002. Web. 20 June 2004.

Kincaid, James R. "Purloined Letters." *New Yorker* 20 January 1997: 93–97. Print.

Kolich, Augustus M. "Plagiarism: The Worm of Reason." *College English* 45 (1983): 141–48. Print.

Lang, James M. "Dealing with Plagiarists." *Chronicle of Higher Education* 14 May 2002. Web. 6 July 2004.

Price, Margaret. "Beyond 'Gotcha!': Situating Plagiarism in Policy and Pedagogy." *College Composition and Communication* 54 (2002): 88–115. Print.

Plagiarism and Honor Module. The IDLE Project, Virginia Tech. Web. 8 August 2004.

Plagiary and the Art of Skillful Citation. Baylor College of Medicine. 31 July 1996. Web. 9 August 2004.

Shamoon, Linda, and Deborah H. Burns. "Plagiarism, Rhetorical Theory and the Writing Centre: New Approaches, New Locations." *Perspectives on Plagiarism and Intellectual Property in a Postmodern World.* Ed. Buranen, Lise, and Alice M. Roy. Albany, NY: SUNY P, 1999. 183–92. Print.

Shor, Ira. *Critical Teaching and Everyday Life.* Chicago, IL: U of Chicago P, 1980. Print.

Smith, Dinitia, and Motoko Rich. "A Second Ripple in Plagiarism Scandal." *New York Times* 2 May 2006. Web. 10 September 2006.

Spigelman, Candace. "Lessons from Forrester: Nurturing Student Writing in a Climate of Suspicion." *Issues in Writing* 13 (2002): 27–57. Web. 3 August 2005.

Task Force on Academic Honesty and Integrity. *Final Report.* Simon Fraser University. 15 February 2004. Web. 9 April 2004.

Walker, Janice R. "Copyrights and Conversations: Intellectual Property in the Classroom." *Computers and Composition* 15.2 (1998): 243–51. Print.

Weinstein, Jeffrey W., and Carlos E. Dobkin. *Plagiarism in U.S. Higher Education: Estimating Internet Plagiarism Rates and Testing a Means of Deterrence.* 2002. Web. 7 August 2004.

Weiss, Kenneth R. "Focus on Ethics Can Curb Cheating, Colleges Find. *Los Angeles Times* 15 February 2000: A1+. Print.

Wilgoren, Jody. "School Cheating Scandal Tests a Town's Values." *New York Times* 14 February 2002: A1+. Print.

QUESTIONS FOR DISCUSSION

1. Both Deborah Harris-Moore and Sean Zwagerman argue that there is something wrong with attempting to create academic integrity in students by surveillance and the fear of being found out. Zwagerman writes: "The University of California at Davis promotes academic integrity in a number of ways, including publishing in the school newspaper 'all the embarrassing details—except for names' of crimes against integrity (Weiss A17). The university feels its actions are working." Do you agree with Harris-Moore and Zwagerman or universities like the University of California at Davis? Explain.

2. Zwagerman writes: "Unity implies collaboration and trust, and an atmosphere of trust encourages us to take risks, to try on new roles in

the form of courses, majors, and—most importantly—ideas and opinions: How does it feel to think like this, or to write like that? What new possibilities emerge? Inflammatory rhetoric and panoptic policies cannot but diminish intellectual play, creativity, and risk-taking, activities that continually reinvigorate the roles—and the writing—of student and teacher." In your coursework, do you feel free to try new things? Or do you feel fettered by the possibility of a bad grade? What would your education look like if you felt free to experiment? If you do feel free to experiment, provide some examples of your most productive experiments.

Part II
Synthesizing What You've Read

1. While Richard Schur contrasts *sampling* and *layering* in song development with the practices that make up source incorporation in academic writing, Martine Courant Rife and Dànielle Nicole DeVoss draw connections between what they call *remixing* (which would include *sampling* and *layering*) and writing that is composed for and with digital environments (which would include academic writing). How many contrasts and parallels can you list between remixing and academic writing? You might begin by brainstorming lists of examples that would represent a remixing and then academic writing.

2. Rife and DeVoss ask the following questions: "How are writers developing skills and abilities when writing to fan fiction sites? When distributing their work across networks? When slickly merging textual and visual (and often motion and sound and more) elements—some of which they've created, some of which they've altered, and some of which they've downloaded—within their compositions?" Visit one of the fan fiction sites mentioned in their chapter, or another fan fiction site, to examine what goes on firsthand. Next, use Esra Mirze Santesso's discussion of intertextuality and reworking to answer Rife and DeVoss's questions.

IN PRACTICE

1. Deborah Harris-Moore suggests that technology can allow us to employ plagiarism detection software in educational ways. Explore this possibility by creating a writing assignment that includes plagiarism detection in a way that will help the writer.

2. Sean Zwagerman quotes this passage:

> Plagiarism is the basest form of parasitism. A leech
> may make a living from other organisms, but even
> a leech doesn't take credit where credit is not due.
> Thievery of words, scourge of the intellectual arena,
> plagiarism festers most prominently on college cam-
> puses worldwide. The Internet has ensured the pro-
> fusion and accessibility of this germ, this disease that
> debilitates creativity and scholastic equality. (*Plagia-
> rism and Honor Module*)

This quote is just one good illustration that plagiarism has become
a hot button issue. Plagiarism has become a focus not just in schools
but also in larger society. Why do you think that is? In groups of 2–4,
create a map of the societal factors you believe have converged to put a
spotlight on plagiarism. The map can be constructed in whatever way
makes visual sense to your group.

Part III
Authorship and Ownership: Cultural and Cross-Cultural Perspectives

Definitions of plagiarism are useful to help us categorize information; definitions help us create initial frameworks for understanding terms. While a definition can help enforce the rules, it can also make understanding plagiarism seem pretty simple: Just document the sources you use, and everything will be fine. What else does a student need to know?

Who are the students we're talking about? Where are they from? What perspectives on texts do they bring with them to the classroom? This section complicates simple definitions of plagiarism such as the one above, illuminating the reality that definitions don't necessarily help us understand how human beings comprehend, inhabit, and even resist them.

People inhabit definitions through cultural beliefs, material realities, and resulting practices. In the United States, for example, we have transferred beliefs and practices surrounding private property to intellectual property. Plagiarism, as a result, is considered a serious offense here, a violation of the rights afforded property owners. However, even in the U.S., as myriad artifacts from popular culture would suggest, we send messages about copying and cheating that are inconsistent with the rules of the academy. Now let's add another layer of complexity to this discussion: Doesn't the United States include people from around the world, people who value intellectual and physical property in very different ways, perhaps in ways that focus on the collective good rather than on the individual, for example? Wouldn't the dynamic cultural interchange among people from around the world change ideas about plagiarism? What about a group's material realities? How might writing through poverty and political turmoil change documentation practices and ideas about plagiarism?

As you read the chapters in Part III, consider how language and the many cultural influences shaping students' lives and histories necessarily impact their differing views of and attitudes toward using sources in texts. What is the role of the student who is a non-native speaker, or whose native culture is not American, in learning the standards of academic integrity that his or her American teachers maintain? Consider, too, how writing pedagogy can embrace the challenge of making space for multiple textual cultures *and* the teaching of academic discourse. What should be expected of teachers? Of programs?

More broadly, how do such questions challenge the responsibilities of the field of composition and rhetoric as one of the leaders on this issue? In the field, the national standards for writing and rhetorical awareness are articulated by the Council of Writing Program Administrators. The first sentence of the introduction to the "WPA Outcomes Statement for First-Year Composition" reads, "This statement describes the common knowledge, skills, and attitudes sought by first-year composition programs in American postsecondary education." As the chapters in this section demonstrate, however, American postsecondary education is heavily populated by students who are from cultures outside of America. How, then, should scholars in the field make recommendations to teachers and administrators about how research and documentation should be taught to address the many cultural layers of plagiarism?

Works Cited

Council of Writing Program Administrators. "WPA Outcomes Statement for First-Year Composition." *Council of Writing Program Administrators.* 2000. Web. 3 February 2010.

9 Who Cares about Plagiarism? Cheating and Consequences in the Pop Culture Classroom

Bridget M. Marshall

Before You Read*: How influential do you think popular culture is on our perceptions of cheating and plagiarism? What responsibilities do films, books, and television shows have to create consistent messages about these issues?*

In the classrooms we see portrayed in popular culture—whether on television, in movies, or in book series—students regularly plagiarize or cheat on their assignments. Such portrayals sometimes have an "after school special" tone to them, scolding students not to do such things, but they just as frequently treat plagiarism as an acceptable way to get through school; sometimes the cheating student is even portrayed as admirable—someone who has defied authority and triumphed over foolish teachers and administrators. Popular culture provides numerous examples of academic dishonesty, but little in the way of a consistent message about the consequences of cheating and plagiarism; this only further complicates the misunderstandings about plagiarism, copyright, and the "allowable copying" Jessica Reyman explains in an earlier chapter. Television and film storylines about cheating and plagiarism are not hard to find. In a 1998 episode of *Felicity*, Felicity rewrites a paper for her friend (and object of her crush) Ben ("Cheating"). In a 1999 episode of *Dawson's Creek* a group of students consider using crib sheets for the PSAT ("None"). A 2006 episode of *House* reveals that Dr. House attempted to cheat on an exam in medical school ("Distractions"). A 2006 episode of *Studio 60 on the Sunset*

Strip portrayed a professional television writer caught stealing jokes written by another comedian ("West"). The films *Ferris Bueller's Day Off* and *Cheats* both portray students cheating their way through high school. Many of these plotlines involve humorous capers and a triumphant end; sometimes viewers even identify with the "cheaters," who are frequently likable heroes. This essay explores three contemporary popular culture portrayals of student plagiarism: the movie *The Squid and the Whale*, the "Weight Gain 4000" episode of *South Park*, and the *Harry Potter* book series. Each of these fictional examples of plagiarism is loaded with a variety of responses—from students, teachers, and the plagiarists themselves; they reveal our culture's frequently conflicting messages about what plagiarism is and the appropriate consequences for it.

PLAGIARISM AND PERFORMANCE:
THE SQUID AND THE WHALE

In the 2005 movie *The Squid and the Whale*, the main character, Walt, plagiarizes a song and reacts with defiance and disdain when confronted by his teacher and parents. Early in the movie, Walt is shown wearing headphones and listening to the song "Hey You" by Pink Floyd, and practicing the song on his guitar using printed music that clearly displays the title and author. When he later performs the song, Walt's mother asks "Did you write that?" and he responds "Yes." Prior to performing the song at his school talent show, he announces to the audience that he wrote the song; the judges are impressed with his performance of what they believe to be his original song and award him the prize. Only later do school authorities realize the deception, contact Walt's parents, demand the return of the prize money, and place Walt in sessions with the school counselor. When the counselor asks why Walt claimed the song as his own, he replies, "I felt I could have written it so the fact that it was already written was kind of a technicality." Walt's response is a laughable moment in the movie; his excuse is ridiculous. His claim that he "could have written it" is rather beside the point, since he didn't write it. Saying he "could have written it" might mean he identified so deeply with the lyrics that he felt they could have come out of his own head. It might also mean Walt thinks that writing the lyrics couldn't have been so difficult—he could have written them himself. Notably, he says that the song was "already written," a turn of phrase that conveniently ignores the fact that someone else did the work of writing it. In effect, Walt disrespects the work of the original writer, dismissing it as something already completed that he could have completed. Walt's belief that it was just a "technicality" further shows his disregard for the hard work of the real writer.

Although Walt fooled his parents, the judges, and some members of the audience, the camera also shows several students in the audience who recognize "Hey You" and know Walt did not write it. Like these uncomfortable and disbelieving students, the viewer of the film does not see Walt as a hero; instead, we see him for the fake he is. Walt's "technicality" excuse just doesn't ring true: He knowingly chose to deceive his audience. He didn't just "forget" to say that someone else wrote the song; in fact, he chose at least twice to mislead his audience (first his parents, then the talent show viewers). Nonetheless, it's important to note that Walt's performance required a good deal of work: He studied the song, learned the chords and the words, and perfected his performance. One might even say that he performed his own interpretation of the song, as many artists do when they perform (or "cover") the work of another artist, but Walt claimed he wrote the song, making his performance an act of plagiarism. Walt was being evaluated by the judges for not just his performance but also for his (presumed) songwriting. Walt could have introduced his song by giving credit to Pink Floyd, and his performance would have been legitimate; in fact, he still might have won the talent show for his performance. In the setting of a school talent show, by properly acknowledging the original writer of the song, he could provide his viewers (both the audience of his peers and the judges of the talent show) with the information necessary to judge his own rendition fairly against the other performers in the show. Although Walt has misrepresented himself, he hasn't done the author of the song any direct harm; it's not as if Pink Floyd could or should have won the talent show. Still, his misrepresentation has certainly harmed his own reputation (with his parents, teachers, and peers) and may have harmed other performers in the show who were honest about their performances. Walt's deception also betrays a certain disdain for his audience; it's rather ludicrous for him to think no one else in the school has heard the song, which is from Pink Floyd's 1979 album, *The Wall*, one of the best-selling albums of all time.[1]

If Walt had been assigned to write a poem, and turned in the lyrics to "Hey You," it would obviously be a case of plagiarism, for which he would face the school's punishment. Although Walt's plagiarism involves a musical performance (rather than a written assignment), his case is much more typical of the kind of plagiarism that happens in schools than the kind that happens in the music industry. Musicians are sometimes accused of plagiarism, but more frequently, the problem—legally at least—is that their plagiarism is deemed to be copyright infringement. As Reyman's essay in this volume helpfully explains, "plagiarism is an academic offense," while "copyright infringement is a legal offense." This distinction between plagiarism and copyright infringement is complicated, but can be illustrated by one of the most well-known cases of plagiarism in the music industry, in which the musical tune to George Harrison's 1970 song "My Sweet Lord" was found by his audience and the courts to be identical to the song "He's So Fine," performed by the Chiffons in 1962. The judge described what Harrison had done as "unconscious" or "unintended" plagiarism, but it was not the plagiarism itself that was the legal issue; rather, Harrison's plagiarism violated the copyright of the original song. Harrison lost all royalties for his song and even a portion of the royalties for the entire the album on which it appeared ("Bright"). Harrison was required to pay $587,000 in damages, although an earlier ruling set the bill at $1.6 million (Krebs and Thomas). Harrison, unlike Walt, explained that he had not intentionally stolen the other artists' work, but copyright laws protected the creators of the earlier song from what was—musically at least—a copying of their idea. Professional musicians use other artists' songs all the time, but they must properly license their use of copyrighted material, or face legal action. While there are certainly large financial interests at stake for the music industry, musicians also show respect to each other's work and to their audiences when they appropriately acknowledge (and oftentimes pay) the creators of the songs they borrow. While Walt's plagiarism at the talent show isn't worthy of a lawsuit, he has nonetheless deceived his audience by taking credit for work he did not do; this is the problem at the heart of plagiarism.

PLAGIARISM IN THE CLASSROOM: CARTMAN VERSUS WENDY ON *SOUTH PARK*

Walt's case is like most cases of plagiarism involving young people in school: Such cases don't end up in court or involve copyright suits;

rather, they are matters dealt with within the community of students, teachers, and administrators. In an episode from *South Park*'s first season called "Weight Gain 4000," the character Eric Cartman wins the national "Save Our Fragile Planet" essay contest for his essay on environmentalism. His classmate, the conscientious student Wendy, believes he has plagiarized it, and searches the school's files to discover that Cartman simply took a copy of Henry David Thoreau's *Walden*, crossed out Thoreau's name, and put his own over it. In this case, unlike Walt's situation in *The Squid and the Whale*, there is no question of "interpretation" because there is no level of performance. Walt did put some serious work into perfecting his version of "Hey You"; Cartman, however, did nothing in his plagiarizing of *Walden*: He didn't even rewrite it! Obviously, simply recopying *Walden* wouldn't be acceptable, even if it did take a long time. The point is that Cartman did none of the thinking or writing required to complete the essay. Even if Cartman had put quotes around the entirety of *Walden* and properly cited Thoreau as the author, he still hasn't done the assignment. Turning in an essay written by someone else provides no level of interpretation (as Walt's performance of the song did); indeed, it's doubtful that Cartman even read Thoreau's essay. Cartman's case is similar to Walt's in that there is no question that Cartman and Walt intentionally and knowingly claimed credit for someone else's work. They intend their deception all along, and when they are discovered, they seem unconcerned that they did something wrong. Indeed, they blame their accusers or punishers. Like many *South Park* scenarios, Cartman's behavior is a bit ridiculous, and it's hard to imagine this happening in the real world.

Cases of cheating in television and movies tend to be portrayed in a simplistic manner, with characters who have very clearly done something wrong, and who are (in most cases) punished for that behavior. This simplification shows a general consensus that taking credit for someone else's creative work is unacceptable. These fictional plagiarists are not sympathetic characters; when they are punished for their plagiarism, the audience believes they deserve it. In real world incidents of plagiarism, which typically involve small passages rather than wholesale works, it's not always clear that the plagiarist is a villain, or even that he or she has done anything wrong. In a widely reported case of literary plagiarism, Kaavya Viswanathan's 2006 novel, *How Opal Mehta Got Kissed, Got Wild, and Got a Life*, included many passages identical to those found in novels by Megan McCafferty, Meg Cabot, and Sophie Kinsella (Mehegan A1). After the revelation of the similarities, Viswanathan's publisher recalled all unsold copies of the book and canceled her two-book contract, worth $500,000 (A1). At only nineteen years old, Viswanathan was the subject of numerous unflattering articles and editorials in newspapers across the nation and around the world. Her notoriety started after Viswanathan's readers contacted the publisher and her own college's newspaper, the *Harvard Crimson*, about the plagiarized passages they found. Viswanathan's story went on to be featured prominently in multiple articles in the *New York Times*, New Delhi's *Hindustan Times*, Canada's *Globe and Mail*, and London's *Independent*, to name only a few.

Unlike Cartman, Viswanathan did not take an entire book and claim credit for it; instead, she used passages from several different books, and included them within her own creative work. The majority of the book was in fact her own original writing, but as readers pointed out, she failed to give credit to the original writers, and misrepresented the book as being entirely her own creation. Notably, Viswanathan probably won't be the subject of a copyright suit, as the passages she borrowed are probably short enough to constitute Fair Use (see Reyman's essay for further discussion of the four principles used to determine Fair Use). However, by claiming these phrases and sentences by other writers as her own, she committed plagiarism; she could be sued by her own publisher for breach of contract since she misrepresented the writing as her own (Bhayani and Zhou). The legal ramifications of the plagiarism are certainly a serious issue, but what is notable about the case is the degree of public outcry, which spread first through academic newspapers and then through national and international news. The public discussion about this case was not about damage done to the other writers, since sales of the other novels were not affected by Viswanathan's plagiarism; rather, readers were upset that Viswanathan misrepresented herself by claiming to have written passages that she actually copied. Viswanathan has repeatedly explained that she did not intend the plagiarism, but even in cases of unconscious or unintended plagiarism, such as George Harrison's case, where the judge's ruling included the opinion that his borrowing was unconscious, plagiarists pay a price. Some fans—whether readers or listeners—support artists who have been accused of plagiarism, citing the fact that all writing borrows its ideas from other sources. Often, cases of plagiarism lead writers into murky territory. Many writers are inspired by a previous author's work, and in many cases, borrowing, revising, and expanding on a previous work is considered Fair Use, both artistically and legally. Most cases of plagiarism in the real world are less clear-cut than Cartman's stealing of Thoreau's *Walden* or Walt's performance of "Hey You."

High profile cases like Viswanathan's show the strong reactions authors and readers have to plagiarism not just on campuses but also in the larger world. One of the notable things about the *South Park* plagiarism case is that no one except the students seems to care about the plagiarism. Mr. Garrison pays no attention to the students who expose Cartman's cheating. When Stan tells Chef, "Cartman cheated and won the environmental essay contest," Chef says, "Yeah, yeah, whatever." Wendy tells the mayor, "You might want to review the essays. We think Cartman might have cheated," but the mayor's response is, "Who cares?" When Wendy announces from the stage that Cartman turned in Thoreau's *Walden* as his own essay, several adults in the audience also ask, "Who cares?" All of the adults are focused on the impending arrival of Kathie Lee Gifford, who will give the essay prize to Cartman at a televised ceremony. In their excitement about a celebrity and eagerness for publicity, they completely ignore the concerns of the students, who are increasingly dismayed to realize that Cartman will receive a prize for an essay he did not write. Of course, in the world of *South Park*, the adult characters are always portrayed as idiotic, incompetent, or worse; it is the children of *South Park* (excepting Cartman) who have a real sense of right and wrong. Still, it is notable that it is the students who feel the most anger about Cartman's plagiarism, since they are the ones who have been treated unfairly by being cheated out of a chance to win the essay prize (and the fame that goes with it). Although Cartman gets his comeuppance, it is for reasons having nothing to do with his cheating, and in fact, Wendy's concerns about the plagiarism are never addressed.

While in *South Park*, the students faced apathy when they raised their concerns about a fellow student's plagiarism, in the real world, authorities take action based on student concerns. Several recent news stories about student plagiarism show that students and those in authority both care quite a lot about plagiarism. In 2006, a graduate student at Ohio University, Thomas A. Matrka, discovered that almost thirty theses turned in for degrees were actually plagiarized; this led to the dismissal of faculty members and the revoking of several students' degrees (Wasley). In 2002, at the University of Virginia, physics professor Lou Bloomfield was alerted by a student that other students in his course were copying papers written for previous semesters (Argetsinger A01). In response, Bloomfield developed a computer program to scan papers for plagiarism, which led to a total of forty-five students being dismissed from the school and three students having their degrees revoked (Kahn). Both students and schools have a stake in making sure plagiarism is caught and punished, since reputations and academic integrity are on the line. Students want to know that they are being evaluated fairly by their teachers; this sense of fairness is violated by acts of plagiarism that go unnoticed, unreported, or unpunished.

Plagiarist Heroes and Villains: Harry Potter and Plagiarism

Both Cartman and Walt are fictional characters that aren't particularly likable; we might laugh at them, or find them a bit sad, but we aren't meant to see them as role models for how to be a good student (or a good person for that matter). When Cartman and Walt commit plagiarism, it is in keeping with their roles as young men of questionable ethics. In the fictional worlds where Cartman and Walt live, there are at least some characters who seriously object to their plagiarism, and there are consequences to their acts; in a very different fictional world, however, plagiarism seems to be just as common, but causes much less consternation. Throughout the fantastically popular *Harry Potter* series, Harry and Ron repeatedly copy Hermione's homework assignments with her permission. Unlike Cartman, Harry and his friends aren't repulsive people; unlike Walt, they are in fact likeable heroes of their stories. Harry, Ron, and Hermione are smart, kind, and loyal; they are the admirable characters of the books. Their friends don't make accusations regarding their copying to the school administration the way Wendy does; indeed, they let each other copy work freely. Since they are never caught or punished for their plagiarism, it might seem that the message of the books is that plagiarism is acceptable, or at least, that it's not a serious concern. However, a close reading of the books shows that there are consequences for cheating aside from being caught or punished by school authorities, even if the motive for cheating seems reasonable and the characters are otherwise "good."

Typically, Ron and Harry find themselves very busy with homework, social lives, and fighting the Dark Lord. Although Harry obviously has quite a lot on his mind other than schoolwork, it is also clear that he doesn't always make the best use of his time and doesn't practice very good study skills. In *Harry Potter and the Order of the Phoenix*, the boys come to rely upon Hermione to get through their classes: "Harry and Ron had so far managed to scrape passes in [History of Magic] only by copying Hermione's notes before exams" (229). All the students find History of Magic, taught by Professor Binns, especially boring. During one of Binns's lectures, Harry spends an "hour and twenty minutes playing hangman on a corner of his parchment with Ron" instead of paying attention to the teacher (229). The boys don't do a good job of focusing on their work, and then they try to avoid the consequences by using Hermione's work to get by. The boys know that they need to work harder, and that their huge piles of weekend homework are the result of their own poor time management. Harry says to Ron, "You know, we probably should try and get more homework done during the week" (295). Harry and Ron know they could be better students, but they prioritize their time in other ways. Poor time management or lax study skills aren't good things, but they're not plagiarism, either. However, they are practices that lead Harry and Ron to plagiarize their work instead of doing it themselves.

In *Harry Potter and the Sorcerer's Stone*, Harry's busy schedule with Quidditch practice takes precedence over his schoolwork, and Harry realizes, "It was really lucky that [he] now had Hermione as a friend. He didn't know how he'd have gotten through all his homework without her" (181). Harry and Ron both come to rely upon Hermione for her help, which at times goes beyond helping as she begins to actually do their work for them. In *Harry Potter and the Order of the Phoenix*, when their assignments include an essay on "the Inanimatus Conjurus spell" assigned by Professor McGonagall and "Professor Sinistra's equally long and difficult essay about Jupiter's moons," Ron and Harry immediately want to ask Hermione for help: "Listen [. . .] shall we just ask Hermione if we can have a look at what she's done?" (295). At this point, Ron doesn't even want to begin writing on his own; he has come to rely so much on Hermione that before he even considers the assignment, he wants to copy hers. Ron finds that he can get Hermione to help him, even when she doesn't want to do so. Exasperated with the boys a short while later, Hermione says, "Give them to me,

I'll look through them and correct them" (299), an offer that comes as a huge relief to Ron and Harry. Hermione then proceeds to "scratch out sentences here and there on their essays" and "check various facts in the reference books" (299). She then instructs Ron, "Okay, write that down [. . .] and then copy out this conclusion that I've written for you" (300). These scenes seem to show that plagiarism isn't something that's wrong; rather, it's helping a friend in need. Harry, Ron, and Hermione aren't villains, and readers may even sympathize with their plight, since the teachers' assignments seem unreasonable and excessive. Indeed, Harry and Ron are doing *some* work; their plagiarism isn't as egregious as that of Cartman or Walt, and yet, they are still earning grades and passing courses without actually doing the work their teachers believe they have done. Unlike Cartman and Walt, Harry, Ron, and Hermione are never caught, and it seems unlikely that they have any regrets about how they got through their Hogwarts classes.

In *Order of the Phoenix*, the workload gets harder; Professor Snape assigns "twelve inches of parchment on the properties of moonstone and its uses in potion-making" (234). The fact that Snape's assignments are dictated in inches is also a clue that these assignments are long and tedious with little real educational value. Notably, they don't have to write twelve points or arguments, but twelve *inches*—it is simply length of writing, not content that seems to matter to the much-reviled Professor Snape. The pointlessness of the exercise (at least from the perspective of the students) seems to be a prime motivation for the cheating; this, too, differs from both Cartman and Walt, who plagiarized in order to win a public prize rather than simply to pass a course. Exhausted from his other homework, Ron says, "There's no point in trying to finish this now, I can't do it without Hermione, I haven't got a clue what you're supposed to do with moonstones" (255). Ron's plagiarism has a snowball effect: Because he has skipped writing his own smaller assignments, he is completely incapable of completing the larger ones, and so he repeatedly turns to plagiarism to deal with his problem. Ron and Harry eventually become quite casual about copying work. In *Harry Potter and the Prisoner of Azkaban*, when an exhausted Harry realizes late one evening that he still has to complete his star chart for Astronomy homework, Ron offers, "You can copy mine, if you like" (146). Ron and Harry start plagiarizing not only longer essays but also short homework assignments. When Hermione won't provide help, they copy off each other. Copying homework becomes the way to get by in their classes, and both Harry and Ron's grades suffer for it when they are unable to perform in their exams.

It is understandable that Harry and Ron have difficulty completing their assignments; when they have spent half the night fighting the Dark Lord, it's hard to expect them to have their homework ready. Rather than accept the consequences of an incomplete, late, or missing assignment, Harry and Ron turn in work that is not their own and get credit for work they didn't do. Since their frequent and repeated copying is never caught, it seems plagiarizing is no big deal—but in their cavalier attitude toward their own plagiarism, Ron and Harry are being hypocritical. At the climax of *Chamber of Secrets*, Harry and Ron discover that Professor Lockhart, a teacher who has written several books about defeating various dangerous creatures, didn't do any of the things he described himself doing in his books. Instead, he stole the stories of other witches and wizards, erased their memories, and took their stories as his own to publish in several best-selling books. Like Walt and Cartman, he has brazenly taken credit for work other people did, and reaped rewards he would not have otherwise received. Harry demands of Professor Lockhart, "So you've just been taking credit for what a load of other people have done?" (297). Harry is furious, and rightly so: Lockhart's deception has serious consequences for the children and Lockhart himself, since he is not capable of taking on the monstrous creatures he claims he can. Lockhart has misrepresented himself in his writing; he has garnered fame and financial gain by stealing other people's stories. Lockhart's plagiarism has been a lifelong project, and it all comes crashing down on him the moment he actually has to do something for himself. Harry and Ron are right to be angry with him; however, they too are guilty of taking credit for work that others did. While the stakes might be smaller, they are still misrepresenting themselves to their teachers and classmates.

While Lockhart's plagiarism is in the form of published books, and Harry and Ron's plagiarism is only on school assignments, real world examples show that plagiarism in the less public academic setting is still cause for concern and punishment. For instance, Elizabeth Paige Laurie, a student at the University of California, voluntarily returned her diploma ten months after her former college roommate, Elena Martinez, revealed in an interview on the television show *20/20* that Laurie had paid her almost $20,000 to write her papers for her (Miller). Laurie has never spoken publicly about what happened, but she was savaged in newspapers and on the Internet. Her parents even chose to remove her name from a stadium at the University of Missouri at Columbia in response to that school's concern about the scandal (Carlson and Suggs 16). While not every plagiarism case is as high profile as this, plagiarism in the academic world damages reputations and careers. In 2006, a sophomore at Duke University, Zack Asack, was suspended from the school for a year for plagiarism and lost his position as starting quarterback on the football team (Vega E15). When such cases are discovered, they garner national media attention, often followed by a slew of letters to the editors and commentaries about plagiarism. When caught, plagiarists inevitably end up in serious trouble and cause serious angst in popular culture about originality and academic integrity.

Both inside and outside of academia, people have strong reactions to cases of plagiarism, but these responses to plagiarism—whether in the real world or in the fictional worlds of movies, television, and books—are complicated and often contradictory. Some plagiarists are painted as cheats and villains, while others are simply students trying to fight back against what they see as an overbearing educational system. While Walt, Cartman, and Professor Lockhart are portrayed as unrepentant and unsympathetic plagiarists, Harry, Ron, and Hermione are portrayed as students trying to get by in their classes. What all of these cases have in common is that the characters deceive their audience with a claim that they have done work that they haven't. As in many of the real world cases of musicians, writers, and students who used others' work, the issue isn't entirely about what they stole but rather that they misrepresented themselves. The *Harry Potter* case seems to show that some plagiarism (for instance, on a homework assignment) isn't a big deal, while other plagiarism (for instance, in a published book) is a serious breach. This too supports the idea that it is the audience that ultimately matters in cases of plagiarism. Harry and Ron don't care about their school assignments, and they don't think their teachers do either, since it's not clear that their papers are ever actually read. Thus, the message seems to be that turning in a plagiarized homework assignment that won't be read and that doesn't really matter to either the writer or the reader isn't a big deal. Where plagiarism really seems to matter, in pop culture and in the real world, is when writers plagiarize for an audience that is actually paying attention to the writing or performance. The message that the culture sends, through news stories and fictional examples, is that audiences who notice plagiarism care very much about the deception and will seek the punishment of plagiarists.

NOTES

1. *The Wall*, with twenty-three million copies sold, is currently ranked third among the top selling albums of all time by the RIAA.

WORKS CITED

Argetsinger, Amy. "Technology Snares Cheaters at U-Va.; Physics Professor's Computer Search Triggers Investigation of 122 Students." *Washington Post* 9 May 2001: A01. Web. 23 June 2012.

Bhayani, Paras D., and David Zhou. "Sophomore Novelist Admits to Borrowing Language from Earlier Books." *The Harvard Crimson* 24 April 2006. Web. 23 June 2012.

"Bright Tunes Music v. Harrisongs Music." *Columbia Law School Arthur W. Diamond Law Library Music Plagiarism Project.* 2002. Web. 10 December 2002.

Carlson, Scott, and Welch Suggs. "U. of Missouri Rechristens Sports Arena in Wake of Cheating Accusations Against Walton Heir." *The Chronicle of Higher Education* 51.16 (10 December 2004). *Thomson Gale Academic OneFile.* Web. 23 June 2012.

"Cheating." *Felicity.* WB Network. WLVI, Cambridge, MA. 3 November 1998. Television.

Cheats. Dir. Andrew Gurland. New Line Cinema, 2002. Film.

"Distractions." *House.* Fox. WNACDT. Lowell, MA. 14 January 2006. Television.

Ferris Bueller's Day Off. Dir. John Hughes. Paramount Pictures, 1986. Film.

Kahn, Chris. "UVA Plagiarism Scandal Ends with 48 Students Dismissed." AP State and Local Wire. 25 November 2002. *LexisNexis.* Web. 23 June 2012.

Krebs, Albin, and Robert McG. Thomas Jr. "Notes on People: Less Damage." *The New York Times* 27 February 1981: 7. *LexisNexis.* Web. 23 June 2012.

Mehegan, David. "Harvard Novelist's Book Deal Cancelled; More Signs Emerge of Duplications." *The Boston Globe* 3 May 2006: A1. *LexisNexis.* Web. 23 June 2012.

Miller, Greg. "Laurie Gives Up Diploma." *Columbia Daily Tribune* (Missouri) 19 October 2005. *LexisNexis.* Web. 23 June 2012.

"None of the Above." *Dawson's Creek*. WB Network. WLVI, Cambridge, MA. 13 October 1999. Television.

Rowling, J. K. *Harry Potter and the Chamber of Secrets*. New York: Scholastic, 1999. Print.

—. *Harry Potter and the Order of the Phoenix*. New York: Scholastic, 2003. Print.

—. *Harry Potter and the Prisoner of Azkaban*. New York: Scholastic, 1999. Print.

—. *Harry Potter and the Sorcerer's Stone*. New York: Scholastic, 1997. Print.

The Squid and the Whale. Dir. Noah Baumbauch. Samuel Goldwyn Films, 2005. Film.

Vega, Michael. "Asack is paying for costly mistake." *The Boston Globe* 12 November 2006: E15. *LexisNexis*. Web. 23 June 2012.

Wasley, Paula. "The Plagiarism Hunter." *The Chronicle of Higher Education* 52.49 (11 August 2006). *Academic OneFile*. Thomson Gale. Web. 23 June 2012.

"Weight Gain 4000." *South Park*. Comedy Central. 27 August 1997. Television.

"The West Coast Delay." *Studio 60 on the Sunset Strip*. NBC. WHDHDT, Lowell, MA. 8 October 2006. Television.

Questions for Discussion

1. Now that you have read the chapter, go back to the responses you had to the prereading question. Do you think the popular culture examples Bridget M. Marshall uses in this chapter actually reflect reality? Has this chapter changed the way you think about the responsibility of popular culture?

2. Talking together in small groups, discuss some other examples of films, television shows, or literature that depict cheating or plagiarism. How do these examples impact your relationship to your academic work?

10 Finding the Source: The Roots and Problems of Plagiarism

Rachel Knaizer

Before You Read*: Knaizer writes, "both a second language and plagiarism are more likely to be learned and not acquired." As you read, consider the unique perspectives of those who are learning about composition and plagiarism in a language—and culture—to which they are not native.*

Imagine this: Your best friend calls to tell you that his/her brother's girlfriend heard a damaging rumor about you. Your best friend doesn't quite believe the rumor and so calls to verify the information with you. The rumor is completely unfounded and false. You decide to confront the source of the vicious rumormongering. Whom do you confront? Your best friend? Your friend's brother? The girlfriend? Another source beyond your immediate social circle?

While this scenario may sound like a fantastic soap opera storyline, it is also analogous to the complexity of plagiarism. Just as finding the source of the rumormongering is difficult, authentic composition is more complicated than most people think. It's as if the long history of composition and publication is the long trail of a rumor, and citation is the individual in search of the rumor's source. Consequently, plagiarism is like accusing the wrong person as the rumor's source or not accusing anyone at all. Most studies of plagiarism focus on how to avoid it or why it occurs (Pincus and Schmelkin); these studies suggest a range of inappropriate composition behaviors—from wandering eyes during an exam to submitting another's project as your own, from copying a published text unknowingly to purchasing a paper sold on the Internet—that are generally referred to as plagiarism. However, plagiarism studies should seek to rethink and redefine the term and its application because writing itself is quite layered and complicated. While you may never figure out who exactly initiated the rumor, there is a way to confront the difficult process of composition: Ask those who actually write.

To examine just how complicated the process of composition and plagiarism is, I went directly to a struggling source: middle school students who were just being introduced to the complexities of writing and plagiarism. My intention was to replicate Faun Bernbach Evans's and Madeline Youmans's ethnographic study of college-level English as Second Language (ESL) students. Evans and Youmans organized discussion groups of college-level English Language Learners (ELLs) to determine what problems existed surrounding plagiarism and how students may be able to learn from one another.

In replicating their project, the volunteers who participated in my project were those with whom I worked closely and am particularly concerned—ELLs. As a secondary education teacher and researcher, I primarily encounter students whose first language is Spanish, but who may have also been designated as proficient English speakers, readers, and writers as demonstrated on standardized tests. Even though the students may have demonstrated proficiency on a state test, they often identify themselves by their native language and culture. Since these participants constantly negotiate their learning in two languages, they may be the most helpful in identifying ways all writers understand composition and plagiarism; these students offer both an insider and an outsider perspective on writing and plagiarism. Two discussion groups comprised of five volunteers each—eighth graders—were convened from a large, urban middle school at which I taught. In 2005, 72% of the 1,420 students were Latino, and 92% were eligible for a free lunch program (*NYCENET*). Almost 20% of the student body is ESL (*NYCENET*). All of the study's participants, who ranged in age from twelve to fourteen, speak a language other than English at home and were enrolled in an academically advanced program designed to ensure ELLs improved their scholastic achievement. Of the seven girls and three boys who participated in this study, four of these students were not born in the United States and three moved to the U.S. during their elementary or middle school years.

Originally, I presupposed plagiarism happened when students were not exposed to citation rules. However, through the participants' comments and reflections coupled with theoretical underpinnings, my own limited and simplistic views of plagiarism were changed. First, I came to realize that plagiarism is not explicitly an act of defiance. Students do not always plagiarize because they are lazy or unwilling to do the work. Secondly, my preconceived definition of plagiarism was challenged when I came to realize that how we all write, the rules we invoke when we write, and how we evaluate writing can be different in different cultures. If this study is but one example, plagiarized work is not mutually exclusive to authentic writing and composition, nor does it show an unwillingness to work and understand a subject. Ultimately, it becomes necessary for both educators and students to (re)examine and (re)define plagiarism because it clarifies the writing process and may help educators better teach writing, which, in turn, may produce better writers.

Common understandings of plagiarism approach it like a malignant growth reflective of the disease of poor scholarship; plagiarism is also treated like a negative correlative associated with composition and language studies. Generally, plagiarism is understood as a misuse of communication by not crediting a source or author; however, the theories and terms that underlie plagiarism studies are far more complicated and nuanced than are easily reduced to an issue of right and wrong. The foundation of language and communication is referred to as discourse. Discourse is a far-reaching term that includes all the different ways humans communicate, including the spoken word, the written word, and even gestures. According to the preeminent theorist Mikhail Bakhtin, discourse, our means of communication, is a highly charged term: "Language is not a neutral medium that passes freely and easily into the private property of the speaker's intentions; it is populated—overpopulated—with the intentions of others. Expropriating it, forcing it to submit to one's own intentions and accents, is a difficult and complicated process" (294). Wanting to make words our own and use them in a way that suits our needs and purposes is critical. We want our language to say what we mean, mean what we say, and represent who we are as people. In essence, what Bakhtin highlights is that discourse reflects both the author and the author's desire. Think of how celebrities trademark phrases they use. Rosie O'Donnell trademarked "cutie patootie" so that the phrase would be continuously associated with her and her unique mode of communication. In this case, her invention of the phrase, and its consequential trademarking, isn't about protecting her phrase from misuse by the general public, but permanently connecting her to the phrase. What is being said is almost as important as who is saying it and from where she comes. According to George L. Dillon in his article, "My Words of an Other," the speaker or author, through personal experiences, gives additional meaning to the pure black and white letter of the word (61). It is not what is written or what is said that simply communicates ideas and meaning, but what the speaker brings to it; "cutie patootie" wouldn't mean the same thing had O'Donnell not broadcasted it repeatedly on her television talk show.

Generally, the subtle implications of letters and words on a page are the difference between denotations, dictionary definitions, and connotations, the socially accepted definitions and uses of a word. Speakers and writers are more likely to rely on inexact connotations than the literal denotations because they are communicating based on their experiences. Another celebrity's phrase can be used as an example to emphasize the difference between intents, general understandings, and literal meanings. Paris Hilton's phrase, "That's hot," is just as (in)famous as the heiress herself. Literal meanings may prescribe that the phrase refers to the temperature or spice, but the connotation invokes a popular meaning particularly associated with the heiress. The phrase does not refer to spicy food or the temperature in a given room but rather the ineffable cool factor in a situation. Like Rosie O'Donnell's phrase, Paris Hilton's suggests the nuances of denotation, connotation, identity, and the use of language to make us unique. If the general understanding of a short phrase warrants this much discussion and illuminates Bakhtin's discussion of discourse, imagine how difficult it is to unravel the rest of the writing process and plagiarism.

Bakhtin also suggests that the difficulty with discourse is not just that an author or speaker is trying to create something different and unique, but that language and communication are filled with others' uniqueness, desires, and intents. Add to the speaker's or writer's intent the "overpopulated" terrain of discourse, and, suddenly, not only is the writer or speaker manipulating language for herself, but she is also trying to negotiate all that was said previously. Even in an everyday example, there is difficulty in extracting one speaker's or writer's intent from another: During a shopping excursion with a friend, he or she tries on a shirt that is quite flattering. When your friend calls you to the dressing room to ask for your opinion, you reply, "That's hot."

You may literally be telling your friend that the shirt looks good on her/him, but you are also alluding to Paris Hilton's use of the phrase. Her use of the phrase may be different from exactly how it's being used in this instance, but your statement can no longer be extracted from her usage. In this example, one previous and very famous user can be a source; however, discourse is much broader than one example with one particular source.

Language, and all forms of communication, is charged with others' meaning and is not filled with empty symbols or letters and words meant to describe a distant, objective reality. When inspiration strikes an author or anyone who is wishing to communicate, they take, reuse, and revise language to fit their needs. Even the study's participants recognized that writing is about being unique and authentic, but is based on information acquired previously. Student Four, for instance, began to question herself on how copying could be useful in helping a writer create their own new meanings:

> Student Four: When you're inspired, you learn part of something, use part of something, from what you copied.

While each person makes of language what they will, changing it to suit individual needs and experiences, they are also engaging with others' intentions and communication, even through possible misuse. The question about plagiarism becomes whether or not it is really misuse if you are now charging the language with your personal intent.

Suddenly, we understand writing and communicating to be a highly intricate process. Think about this chapter, for instance: As a writer, I am trying to uniquely define plagiarism and the results of my research while I am referring to theorists, writers, and researchers who have come before me and created a foundation for my research. Then, hopefully, I am writing so that someone following me may use my writing to help him in his own writing. That's a lot of writers and communication embedded in one paper. Startlingly, producing and using language becomes a complex process that is more than just recording words on a page. Writers, because they are engaging in discourse, do not simply record their thoughts but also try to place their ideas in relation to other ideas that have been spoken or published before.

What is more, when trying to produce unique, innovative writing and research, citing sources becomes increasingly questionable. How much of what I've written in this chapter is entirely my own? How much is influenced by all that I've read or what the students said in our discussion groups or what professors and other researchers have taught me? This text, in and of itself, is "overpopulated" by others' words and phrases. To whom do I attribute all of this information? Traditional citation, consequently, becomes almost too programmatic, too rigid for the free exchange of ideas in discourse. Yet, traditional citation is a method to which writers and speakers are bound. If the two previous sentences seem contradictory, they are; it is this contradiction that produces the gray terrain of plagiarism studies.

The thorny landscape of discourse and plagiarism studies is especially difficult to relatively inexperienced writers, like middle and high school students, and doubly difficult for students who are attempting to communicate in a new language with unfamiliar words and expectations. Inexperienced writers must establish their own voices, learn new information and vocabulary, and compose writing that communicates their intent. Student Three in my study discussed his difficulty in negotiating learning, authentic writing, and using information from reliable, authoritative sources:

> Student Three: [. . .] Let's say I need to write an essay or something, and I need to research on it, if the research is just fine and it has words that I would use, then I say it's okay. You could probably word it differently, but the words you can use them too, if you know, like what to use them correctly or know their meaning. But, let's say, there's these whole bunch of words that you don't know [. . .] If I came through a word like that, I would first go to the dictionary or something, then write it down. But I wouldn't write it down without knowing. I did that a few days ago. I was writing something, and then I noticed that the word I didn't even know, I didn't even know what I was writing, so I went to the dictionary and found out what the word was. Then, I said, 'Oh, now I know.' Now I get the sentence, and I worded it a bit differently.

Generally, Student Three discusses paraphrasing—how to select a passage and reword it to fit into his own writing, but Student Three is also articulating how difficult it is just to use language. The student explains that a writer must "know [words'] meaning[s]," as well as how "to use them correctly" in order to use language that "I would use." In essence, the student defines the very basis of discourse: knowing what you want to say, knowing how to say it, and knowing the various meanings, especially of other authors. These three elements exist every time a writer or speaker begins, whether he or she realizes it or not.

Mastering these parts of discourse becomes exponentially more difficult for a student who is trying to express herself in a language that is not her first language or mother tongue. An English Language Learner's difficulty in negotiating discourse exists because her second language—English—is learned and not acquired. How people demonstrate mastery over a particular language by using it is theoretically referred to as discourse and occurs through two complementary processes. The first method is "acquisition" (Gee 5), and mastery is gained through interacting with our immediate surroundings and the people who are present in those surroundings. Gaining language from those around us does not require much study or effort and is what James Paul Gee calls "primary discourse" (7). Think of how we learn our first words. We do not really work at it; we can barely recall how it happened. All we know now is that we used those first words to get what we needed or wanted from our environment. For instance, one's first words may be "No" or "Daddy" or "Mommy," which all acknowledge either those around us with whom we may need to communicate in order to meet our needs or a situation's circumstances that will get us what we want. Communication, at this state of language acquisition, is so easy we do not even realize we are doing it. Communication that uses primary discourse through acquisition is out of necessity, simply to get along in our surroundings.

By contrast, "learning," or the gaining of language through "secondary discourse" (Gee 8), involves significant practice and work. Secondary discourse is the information and language that exists outside of our immediate surroundings, often in a place of learning like school. Primary or secondary discourse can be contrasted, for example, by thinking of how a child might explain the shortest route between their house and their grandmother's house versus a geometric proof of the Pythagorean Theorem. A child may know that the shortest route to grandma's house is a shortcut through the woods. The child would have acquired this information after several trips to grandma's house, most likely with an adult modeling the route. However, a child would not learn a proof of the Pythagorean Theorem until they were enrolled in school because learning requires explicit instruction that breaks down the information into analytic parts. In this example, discussing the Pythagorean Theorem requires an additional set of terms and phrases that an individual would not need to use to survive and communicate in their immediate surroundings. The topics and language found in secondary discourse are not necessary to communicate with those closest to us but rather to communicate with a larger audience with whom we may not see or directly interact. Both the need and the audience are less immediate, so communication within secondary discourse is often the less authentic of the two methods (Gee 5). The child from the previous example would not give the directions to grandma's house using the terms found in the geometric proof. The proof's language would seem stilted and, probably, pretentious. Although both the child's route and the theorem's proof describe knowledge of the same topic, the proof and its language would seem disingenuous if not presented to the appropriate audience.

The previous example sets acquisition and learning, as well as primary and secondary discourse, in contrast with one another. However, acquisition and learning, as well as primary and secondary discourse, often work in accord with one another. Acquisition may produce ease, comfort, and familiarity, while learning may produce a deep understanding of a subject:

> [. . .] [W]e are better at what we acquire, but we consciously know more about what we have learned. For most of us, playing a musical instrument, or dancing, or using a second language are skills we attained by some mixture of acquisition and learning. But it is a safe bet that, over the same amount of time, people are better at these activities if acquisition predominated during that time [. . .] Acquisition and learning are differential sources of power: acquirers usually beat learners at performance, while learners usually beat acquirers at talking about it, that is, at explication, explanation, analysis, and criticism. (Gee 6)

Essentially, people who excel in a given area, such as music, have both acquired and learned about the subject. They possess a talent for the subject, as well as analytic skills that deepen their understanding and ability to communicate that understanding. A composer, for instance, must have the acquired talent to hear the subtleties of tone and melody, and also must have learned to replicate those tones and sounds on the musical staff by studying time signatures, keys, fingering, and so on. A combination of acquisition and learning are required for a person to become an authority.

For an English Language Learner to excel in English, according to Gee, an individual must have spent more time acquiring the language. That is, a person must use English to communicate in his immediate surroundings without formal instruction. Often, however, ELLs do not acquire English, but learn English in formal settings. As a result, they may feel less comfortable and confident when writing and communicating in English. In fact, Student Two and Student Three, who have already spent several educational years in the United States, remark that becoming comfortable in expressing themselves in English took some time—until the end of their primary education years:

> Student Two: [. . .] I think [paraphrasing] happens a lot in eighth grade, well not just in eighth grade, but . . .

> Student Three: [. . .] But just because you paraphrased, doesn't mean you understand [what you're saying].

As in the previous quote from Student Three, Student Two and Student Three are talking about paraphrasing, but the students are also talking through the difficulties of using and understanding vocabulary in a second language. The second language is generally learned and not acquired, thus making it more difficult and inauthentic to write and communicate. It is this layer of difficulty that the student alludes to with this quote: "just because you paraphrased, doesn't mean you understand [what you're saying]." Not only is the language of the original text complicated and unnatural for the student, but attempting to paraphrase the material in the second language feels inauthentic.

Both a second language and plagiarism are more likely to be learned and not acquired. A writer must be taught strict, often academic, rules of sharing, acknowledgement, and usage of another text. Children who play with others understand that stealing a toy from another may

cause the other to cry, wail, and protest the theft. An adult may inter-
vene and instruct the thief to return the toy to its owner or share the
toy. However, in everyday encounters, adults rarely instruct children
not to steal another's words. If a child repeats a phrase she has heard,
adults usually tell the child the repetition is endearing or accepts it
as part of the child's linguistic development. Generally, children are
not instructed to give credit to another's words outside of various academic institutions, such as schools, where children are likely to encounter secondary discourse and formalized learning. As a result, the
notions of plagiarism may seem disingenuous to writers. The concept
of plagiarism is not acquired, but learned. Furthermore, the concept
of plagiarism is introduced through secondary discourse, outside of
the writer's primary community, like their home. If the individual is a
non-native English speaker, the person can feel further removed from
such an academic concept. The further removed someone feels from
a subject, the more an individual may have difficulty understanding
material or the more likely an individual may be to refuse to engage at
all in any attempt to understand the subject.

Both the appropriate use of language and learning language—
discourse, acquisition, learning, and the misuse of discourse, plagiarism—are largely defined by society and culture. As Bakhtin defined
discourse, communication is relative to the community in which it exists because it is "populated—overpopulated—with the intentions of
others" (294); we are what we speak because of the population around
us.

What makes discourse even more complicated is that how we communicate depends on the culture and society in which we live. For
instance, what some Western societies think of as a peace sign, made
by making a "V" with two fingers, is interpreted in other cultures as a
sign of victory or the equivalent of the solitary middle finger. Idioms
or common, figurative phrases are also dependent on culture. Ask a
non-native English speaker to interpret the phrase "it's raining cats
and dogs," and the explanation may be more literal than expected. So
much of how we communicate is based on how a language or dialect
has developed within a culture. When that language's development is
complemented by a user who can also communicate in another language, a writer may have multiple writing identities, bound by different cultural values for each language they speak. Furthermore, as a
case study of a non-native English speaker in South Africa documents,

how we interact with discourse is through "historically constructed investment in prior discourses." In addition, "Multiple and transitional identities may be evident in students' writing and affect their learning of academic or classroom discourses" (Angelil-Carter 282). Both the appropriate and inappropriate use of discourse, and its interpretation, is defined by the culture and society in which people live and interact, as well as who we are declaring ourselves to be through our writing in any given moment.

Consequently, a discussion surrounding plagiarism must also be dependent on culture. Its ethics must also be culturally embedded. Think about how different cultures punish children: In some cultures a spanking is appropriate, and in others, a spanking is completely inappropriate. It's hard to say just where the determination of right and wrong comes from, but it is culturally bound. In fact, just where the negative ethical implications of plagiarism are is difficult to locate for writers. Writers, like the ones who participated in this study, cannot find a particular moment or place when they learned plagiarism is wrong. To them it just "feels" that way:

> Author: How do you know that plagiarism is wrong, or that copying is wrong?
>
> Student Four: I've been through it.
>
> Author: You've been through it, so it feels wrong to you.
>
> (Student Four nods affirmatively.)
>
> Student Four: And I got in trouble for it, so [. . .]

Student Four demonstrates the difficulty of locating the plagiarism's wrongness by first describing it as a feeling, then admitting that it was wrong because there was a negative consequence. Certainly, it could be that this student had yet to learn exactly how poorly plagiarism is viewed in Western culture; but, it could also be that plagiarism has different associations and different connotations in different academic environments and cultures.

Other cultures do not necessarily put the same emphasis on plagiarism because it is not part of their academic culture. Plagiarism is not wrong because the terms and activities associated with it—copying, cutting and pasting, and even paraphrasing—are part of instruction.

It could be that how activities are structured in other cultures does not allow for a moment of weakness. As Student Two describes, the ways independent composition is established in the Philippines does not allow for plagiarism:

> Student Two: [. . .] We were trained [in the Philippines] to do work as perfect as possible. You just can't do plagiarism. It's just not, like, a vocabulary over there. You don't really use that term, like copying. We were all, like, individuals, and we hardly work in groups [. . .]

Student Two highlights two important points in this brief remark. First, there exists a varying cultural emphasis on plagiarism. Plagiarism or avoiding it is not an innate part of writing in other cultures. The academic culture in the Philippines, according to the student, does not really even acknowledge the existence of plagiarism. Secondly, according to the student, the work done in Western classrooms actually enables plagiarism because our culture emphasizes working in groups and communities.

Typically, there is a binary understanding of how Eastern and Western cultures address education and writing. On the one hand, Eastern cultures are seen as having a more collective approach; Western cultures, alternately, are viewed as more individualistic: "In Asian and African cultures, the commitment to serving first the interests of the group can be very different from the Western emphasis on the importance of the individual" (Williams 589). Student Two suggests, however, that plagiarism is more likely to occur in the United States because of the pedagogical emphasis on group work and collective learning. The assumed binary of the collective versus the individual may not be the precise explanation for an ELL's misuse. Perhaps there's an overarching goal of serving an Eastern culture's collective ideology, but it's not present in the daily instruction and writing.

Interestingly, most participants in this study did not differentiate between their previous learning environments and their current writing environments. While this may be an attribute of negotiating a second language and a second culture, it also may be an attribute of conversations about plagiarism and, simply, the difficulties of middle school. When Student Four was asked to detail the differences between her educational experiences in Chile versus those in the United States, she conflated both experiences into one:

> Author: You were going to mention earlier about what, whether or not, plagiarism had come up in Chile.

> Student Four: It was because, um, when I got here, I would be called, like, the smarty pants or the teacher's pet. The teacher would rely on me to do certain things for her, and people would just copy off my work. [. . .] It was like they wanted to learn from it and still wouldn't ask for help.

> Student Three: That's what I did with the math project. Since I'm not used to [this program] and the work. I just wanted to work at this level.

It is as though Student Four left the Chilean ways of learning writing behind, and can only remember the culture shock experience when she arrived and became "teacher's pet." Perhaps the memory is strong because it marks a shift in one style of learning to another. There are a couple of explanations for the apparent assimilation, but, as Student Three admits, it is also difficult for an English Language Learner raised in the United States to transition from one school to another. Despite the students' apparent assimilation, cultural distinctions of writing and plagiarism do frequently occur and affect definitions of plagiarism. First, how we interact in culture and between cultures is as layered and nuanced as theories of composition and communication. Culture—and how cultures interact—"is not a monolithic, fixed, neutral or objective category but rather a dynamic organism that exists in discursive fields" (Kubota 11). Who we are in a learning situation changes and adapts, as much as our writing is dependent on our predecessors.

Non-Western cultures' stress on writing and plagiarism is useful to note because it exemplifies the cultural relevance of discourse and possible misuse. However, in Western cultures, writers rely on citation to show understanding and authority of particular topics. As a result, there exists a tension between producing unique work and demonstrating knowledge in a particular field, as Alastair Pennycook explains:

[I]n the same way that Western literary practices centre around the notion of the individual creator yet
constantly echo the lines of others, academic work
also stresses the individual, creative thinker and writer and yet constantly emphasizes a fixed canon of disciplinary knowledge. This problem is most obvious
for [. . .] students (and especially if they are writing in
a second language) who, while constantly being told
to be original and critical, and to write things in their
'own words,' are nevertheless only too aware that they
are at the same time required to acquire a fixed canon
of knowledge and a fixed canon of terminology to go
with it. (213)

Writers are taught that producing authentic work is the means by
which they are judged; they are "the individual creator." There is also
a pressure, however, to present information based on a "fixed canon of
knowledge," proving that the writer knows all that is possible within a
particular discipline. The pressure to be both unique, as much as one
is able to do given the nature of discourse, and work within a specific
set of rules and information proves to be difficult for students, "especially if they are writing in a second language" (Pennycook 213).

Where authentic writing exists for non-native English language
speakers becomes a particular quagmire. A native speaker of English must guide himself between the discourses he has both acquired
and learned and communicate his knowledge, but a second-language
speaker must also navigate the discourses in another language entirely—and both must demonstrate a conversance with "a fixed canon
of knowledge" in addition to producing work that is authentic and
unique. What is more, since language is a social construct made up
of all those who have communicated before, and since the rules and
guidelines, like plagiarism, are dependent on the particular culture,
a second-language student must negotiate a whole lot more than just
composing a writing assignment.

The tension between creativity and authority for both native and
non-native English speakers also produces a code of ethics upon which
views of plagiarism in Western culture is based. It is this tension that
dictates how to work with overpopulated discourse and still maintain
individuality; plagiarism says that you acknowledge a fixed canon of
information, but you have nothing new to add and you are not unique.

Additionally, plagiarism is a small part of writing, composition, and communication that is given an enormous amount of weight. Writers, academics, and researchers become fixated on a simplistic conception of plagiarism, when its foundation—discourse and language acquisition—is far more nuanced and complicated. The difficulty in studying plagiarism is that it is dependent on discourses, or specific types of communication, that are reliant on preceding discourses, which, in turn, are reliant on preceding discourses and so on. How do writers identify a single, reliable source when all communication is predicated upon a multitude of sources?

Writing and communication—discourse—is essentially like an elaborate game of telephone. One individual's idea is passed to another who interprets it just a bit differently, rewords it slightly, and passes the information along again. The gist of the idea may stay the same, but each individual puts her own take on it. A plagiarist is like the kid who won't follow the basic rules of the game. Instead of waiting for his turn to hear the information and pass it along, the kid runs from each whispering person, yells out the sentence before he can actually hear what was said, and says that he created it. Any participant in this game would accuse the cheating child of being just that—a cheater. Isn't that what we refer to plagiarists as—cheaters? The students in this study certainly think so:

> Student Three: [. . .] Okay, let's say [there's] somebody who is getting copied off and somebody who is copying, and it's bad for both of them. Because, let's say, um, the person who is, the other person who is copying, or getting copied off of, gets yelled at or gets all the blame or the put downs [if work isn't done correctly] [. . .] And the other person, who is copying, if they get caught, then that's their problem [. . .]

> Student B: [. . .] [C]opying notes, um, copying notes from a teacher, like, from the board or, like, somebody's telling it to you, you're copying, like you're gonna reflect on it later on and see, um, you could also use it for many things. But, um, plagiarism can also be a different topic because, um it's a little bit have to do with teaching, but it may have to do with knowing that you are gonna do plagiarism. And you,

> it's like you writing notes, you have [conscience],
> and if you want conscience to guide you on copying
> somebody else's work or using the whole resource as,
> a, as for a work that you really had to put effort on it,
> then that's plagiarism.

Like the child in the imaginary scenario who runs around stealing the sentences in the telephone game, not participating in an act that seems against the rules indicates a level of awareness and "conscience." Even in the discussion groups, when Student Three says that the students in his scenario are copying and it is "bad for both of them," he is showing an engagement in rules or norms of writing in Western discourse, particularly English. Although plagiarism may not be a concept in other countries, like the Philippines, according to the students, even without direct instruction or guidance, writers know that engaging in plagiarism is a kind of theft that goes against the implied rules of the English language. The participants' statements reinforce the position that plagiarism and its ethical underpinnings are culturally bound (Pennycook 211). As much as our language and communication is culturally driven, so are the implied rules and ethics of language.

The complexities of plagiarism are more difficult than evidenced in the simple, imaginary scenario of a telephone game. Because language and discourse is

> [. . .] social, cultural, and ideological [. . .] we need
> to go beyond a view of language as an infinite series
> of decontextualized sentences or as the idiosyncratic
> production of a completely free-willed subject. Second, if it is in fact so hard to pin down the real originator of a quotation, are we perhaps engaged here
> in a false teleology, an impossible search for the first
> speaking or writing of certain words? (Pennycook
> 208–09)

Pennycook's conclusion is important. If others influence our use of language, and it is difficult to find the absolute original source, then perhaps citation and plagiarism are moot points. Perhaps Pennycook's point would be best illustrated by elaborating on the previous telephone game example. Imagine that instead of one game of telephone, there are five simultaneous games in one large auditorium. Each of these five games has a minimum of ten players. Each of the games begins at the same time using the same phrase. After five seconds of game play, an extra individual is added whose purpose it is to figure out who started the game. Does the individual circulating consider only their circle or others? If others are using the same phrase, does each person who started the game in each circle receive credit collectively or individually? Pennycook's argument is that writing is like the many games of telephone and citation is like trying to discover who started the telephone game. The questions that arise because of the telephone game are the same as the "impossible search for the first speaking or writing of certain words" (Pennycook 208–09).

Perhaps, as Pennycook suggests, it's not the rules of the game—like plagiarism—that are the problem, but the game—how we look at language and composition—itself. By focusing simply on plagiarism, or wrongdoing, we, students and teachers, are ignoring the gray and complicated terrain of composition. In only discussing plagiarism, we're ignoring the culturally-specific implications of both ethics and composition. In emphasizing plagiarism over all else, we ignore the deep allusions in our language, and language as a fundamental of identity and development. Perhaps instead of looking for the source of the first line in a game of telephone, authors, researchers, and students should focus on what exactly is being said and how information is being reinterpreted from person to person. Each time we write a word or even compliment one another in a dressing room, we're defining ourselves as authentic individuals, despite the difficulties in locating an original source. After all, when all the specificities are set aside, isn't it about meaning what we say and saying what we mean?

WORKS CITED

Angelil-Carter, Shelley. "Second Language Acquisition of Spoken and Written English: Acquiring the Skeptron." *TESOL Quarterly* 31.2 (1997): 263–87. *JSTOR*. Web. 30 October 2010.

Bakhtin, M.M. *The Dialogic Imagination: Four Essays*. Trans. Caryl Emerson and Michael Holquist. Ed. Michael Holquist. Austin: U of Texas P, 1981. Print.

Dillon, George L. "My Words of an Other." *College English* 50.1 (1988): 63–73. Print.

Evans, Faun Bernbach, and Madeleine Youmans. "ESL Writers Discuss Plagiarism: The Social Construction of Ideologies." *Journal of Education* 182.3 (2000): 49–65. Print.

Gee, James Paul. "What is Literacy?" *Rewriting Literacy: Culture and the Discourse of The Other*. Ed. Candace Mitchell and Kathleen Weiler. New York: Bergen and Garvey, 1991. 3–11. Print.

Kubota, Ryuko. "Japanese Culture Constructed by Discourses: Implications for Applied Linguistics Research and ELT." *TESOL Quarterly* 33.1 (1999): 9–35. *JSTOR*. Web. 30 October 2010.

NYCENET. New York City Public Schools. Web. 15 October 2005.

Pennycook, Alastair. "Borrowing Others' Words: Text, Ownership, Memory and Plagiarism." *TESOL Quarterly* 30.2 (1996): 201–30. Print.

Pincus, Holly Seirup, and Liora Pedhazur Schmelkin. "Faculty Perceptions of Academic Dishonesty: A Multidimensional Scaling Analysis." *Journal of Higher Education* 74.2 (2003): 196–209. *Wilson Web*. Web. 2 December 2005.

Williams, Bronwyn T. "Speak for Yourself? Power and Hybridity in the Cross-Cultural Classroom." *College Composition and Communication* 54.4 (2003): 586–609. *JSTOR*. Web. 30 October 2010.

QUESTIONS FOR DISCUSSION

1. Rachel Knaizer defines the "very basis of discourse" as "knowing what you want to say, knowing how to say it, and knowing the various meanings, especially of other authors." How does that affect students who are not native speakers of the language in which they are learning? How do definitions of and punishments for plagiarism come into play in these situations?

2. Knaizer concludes with the question: "After all, when all the specificities are set aside, isn't it about meaning what we say and saying what we mean?" Does this conclusion, and the points leading up to it, mean that plagiarism is irrelevant? What would happen if we all did as the author asks; would we be able to "mean what we say and say what we mean" if, in saying, we used the words of others?

11 Plagiarism and Cross-Cultural Mythology

Lise Buranen

Before You Read: *Is academic discourse a 'second language'? If so, how does the learning of academic discourse become more complicated for those whose first language is not English?*

> If it is true that the ability to be puzzled is the beginning of wisdom, then this truth is sad commentary on the wisdom of modern man. Whatever the merits of our high degree of literary and universal education, we have lost the gift for being puzzled. [. . .] In fact, to be puzzled is embarrassing, a sign of intellectual inferiority. [. . .] To have the right answers seems all-important; to ask the right questions is considered insignificant by comparison.
>
> —*Erich Fromm, The Forgotten Language*

> You may associate the word "myth" primarily with the ancient Greeks. [. . .] The stories were not "true" in a literal sense but as reflections of important cultural beliefs. These myths assured the Greeks of the nobility of their origins; [and] they justified inequities in Greek society.
>
> —*Introduction,* Rereading America

169

When I began teaching writing and English as a Second Language (ESL) over twenty years ago, the question of student plagiarism rarely crossed my mind. Of course, the usual prohibitions against plagiarism and the punishments for it were printed in the college catalog, and I knew what plagiarism was (I thought). It lurked in the background as something I was aware of, but like preparing for an earthquake, plagiarism wasn't at the front of my consciousness as I began teaching ESL and first-year writing. Instead, I focused my efforts not on teaching student writers to avoid plagiarism but rather on how to grapple with a topic, to make use of invention strategies to develop an argument, to cultivate a sense of voice and authority, to find and use compelling evidence—in short, not just to remain outsiders to the academic conversation going on around them, but to acquire the tools and the confidence to join in. I didn't actively avoid dealing with plagiarism; at the time, it just didn't seem terribly salient.

Fortunately, no earthquakes, real or metaphorical, drew my attention to plagiarism. In fact, direct experience with student plagiarism itself was not the original catalyst for my growing awareness of the issue. Rather, it was prompted by the concern of the division chair at a community college where I was about to begin a new teaching job. After the chair offered me a job, almost the first thing out of her mouth was the warning, "They cheat."

More than a bit startled by her ominous words, I pondered the reasons, either for the rampant cheating going on at this school or for her excessive concern about it. At this point, I knew not which (if either) was true. I wondered, for example, if she was using the word "cheating" as synonymous with "plagiarism"; to many people they mean the same thing. Or perhaps cheating of some other kind was widespread and hence the chair's alarm was warranted. Mostly I wondered, if her fears were indeed accurate, why so many students felt the "need" to cheat, because I wasn't convinced that students did so out of sheer defiance; such contrariness does exist, but not in great numbers of students. Most students, I've found, are in school (especially in college) to learn something, and while I've gotten used to the fact that first-year composition is not everyone's favorite class, the majority of students really do want to become better writers and readers.

Once in my new teaching job, I soon learned, however, that "they" did in fact "cheat." The "they" in this case was a large and quickly growing Armenian community in the historically conservative white suburb of Los Angeles where the college was located. A couple of "them," Armenian students in my freshman writing classes, provided me with firsthand experiences of their willingness to "cheat," or plagiarize, to get through the class. One student, in fact, did so twice in a semester, submitting first an essay that "borrowed" heavily from our textbook and later one that incorporated long passages from the then-recent report "A Nation at Risk," in both cases with no identification of the original text (and in both cases, the borrowings were easily spotted, though this was long before anyone knew the word Google). Despite the extensive intervention and counseling I conducted, explaining to the student what he had done wrong and why it was not okay, and in the first instance giving him the opportunity to revise the essay, this student ended up earning a report to the Office of Student Affairs and an F for the course. Not surprisingly, he was unhappy about my refusal to cut him some slack, and I was both outraged by his actions and mystified by his blasé expectation that I should look the other way.

A well-meaning friend and colleague, a woman with many more years of teaching under her belt than I, advised me that for Armenian students, or for Middle Eastern students in general, what this student had done was not considered cheating or wrong in any way, that getting this kind of "help," either from another text or from a person, was seen in his community as a cultural value, a mutual, tacitly accepted means of helping someone reach a goal. Similarly, I had heard parallel explanations from other experienced writing teachers about Asian students' alternative ways of understanding plagiarism—that before coming to the U.S. these students had been explicitly taught to copy from other texts without quoting, documenting, or acknowledging their sources in ways American academics understand as "correct." My friend and colleague suggested that because of these culturally divergent characterizations of plagiarism, my anger at this student's actions was misplaced. It made no more sense for me to be upset about his "plagiarizing" than it did about any culturally-specific belief or practice, like whether to have turkey or tamales for Christmas dinner—or indeed, whether to observe Christmas at all.

Seeing myself as tolerant, broad-minded, and inclusive, I tempered my anger and revised my teaching strategies, not with the intention to embrace uncritically these alternative conceptions of plagiarism, nor to accept without comment work from students that would likely get them in trouble in their other classes. Rather, my job was to make students from other countries or cultures aware of the demands and expectations of American universities and the discourse of the American academic community. In fact this was no different from the rest of my work as a writing teacher, in which I had the responsibility to introduce all students to the "second language" of academic discourse, including those for whom English was their first and only language—after all, academic writing is no one's first language. Since teaching students the idiom of this second language was fundamental to my pedagogy, anticipating the difficulties students might have due to differences in cultural expectations and values was as much my duty as understanding the ways the linguistic differences between English and another language might make the use of articles or apostrophes hard to comprehend.

Yet, I was still disturbed not only by the difficulties of identifying and coping with varieties of student "plagiarism" in the classroom but also by the genesis of the explanations I had heard for these "foreign" students' propensity to engage in writing practices categorized in Western academic discourse as wrong or even immoral; I realized that although I'd heard these explanations from many sources, none of them was based on what I would consider evidence. In other words, they had the quality of myth or lore—stories that are believed and passed on (orally) as truth, in this case by apparently knowledgeable and reliable informants (that is, teachers far more experienced than I). Despite the intuitive appeal and seeming ability of these stories to explain a difficult and knotty problem, their origins remained suspicious. I had never read, for instance, a study demonstrating or even an argument positing the veracity of this belief, nor had a student ever reported that this was the reason for her "plagiarizing" another text—that she had been taught to copy without attribution.

To explore the origins of these stories, I decided to conduct my own modest investigation of the issue: I asked students in several of my first-year writing and ESL classes to fill out an anonymous survey describing their own beliefs, attitudes, and definitions of plagiarism, and where these beliefs, attitudes, and definitions had come from, whether from parents, teachers in the U.S. or other countries, or some other source. About 150 students in my classes, from over twenty countries on five continents, responded to my survey.

The results were surprising: Despite the vast array of different cultures and languages represented by the students who took my survey, there was remarkable uniformity in the students' responses. For example, one question I asked was, "In your opinion, are attitudes toward plagiarism or copying different in the U.S. than they are in another country? If so, tell how; if not, how are they the same?" In response, I got a handful of "I don't knows," but those students who did offer an opinion—a strong majority of the respondents—were virtually unanimous in their belief that there was *no basic difference* between what they had been taught in their home country and in the United States. This was true regardless of the students' first language or country of origin.

The questionnaire was anonymous, and in administering it, I endeavored to convince the students that I wanted to find out about people's existing attitudes and beliefs, to hear about what they had been taught and about their own experiences, and I assured them that there were "no right or wrong answers." Despite these disclaimers, however, I was reluctant to accept the results of such a questionnaire at face value: The respondents were, after all, sitting in a college classroom and being asked by their English teacher to write about an issue they probably knew was important in American education, though perhaps not how or why it was so important. Most instructors emphasize or at least mention plagiarism not only in writing classes but also in all disciplines, so students are inevitably exposed to the concept at some point during their time in American schools (I conducted my study in 1993, and while admonitions about plagiarism may be more numerous and more vociferous today, they were not absent then). For example, in ESL classes at one college where I taught, the students were given a brief handout, printed in five languages, which described appropriate classroom behavior, including a caution about avoiding plagiarism. Students who had encountered the word plagiarism clearly had an idea of its gravity, evidenced by the language many of the respondents to my survey used to define it: Several said it was "illegal," and one said the punishment for plagiarizing was jail.

The results of my brief survey left me, ultimately, with more questions than answers. As with any aspect of something as profound and complex as a culture or a language, I believe that there likely are cross-cultural differences in the ways that "ownership" and attribution of text or ideas are defined and regarded; the larger question, though, is whether we, students and teachers, have the ability to identify and tease out such differences, and especially to determine their origins.

Getting at precisely what these complex and subtle cultural differences are needs to be acknowledged as a monumental task, approached with the recognition that one's perception of them is bound to be imperfect and incomplete.

Carolyn Matalene's essay "Contrastive Rhetoric: An American Writing Teacher in China" attempts to address some of these differences between Eastern (specifically Chinese) and Western rhetoric. In her essay, Matalene describes her experiences as a teacher in Shanxi Daxue, China. Though her purpose is not principally to address plagiarism, in her discussion of the role of memorization in Chinese literacy she does talk about some of the difficulties faced by non-Western students in coping with Western conventions of academic discourse, and she argues that some of the imitative practices of Chinese composition can result in what we would call plagiarism. Matalene states:

> Every Chinese schoolchild memorizes the line of the great Du Fu: "If you read ten thousand books until they are well worn, you will be inspired in your writing." When Yang De You explained these lines to me, he wanted me to understand that the important phrase was *well worn*, not *ten thousand*; it's better, he said, to read one book one hundred times than one hundred books once. Surely such study is intended to yield writing that imitates the original. What Chinese students consider perfectly acceptable imitation, however, is often defined by Western teachers as stealing. (803)

In an old *Monty Python* routine, John Cleese sings, "You say to-mah-to, and I say to-mah-to; you say po-tah-to, and I say po-tah-to . . ." Interrupting himself, he looks puzzled and says to the director, "Sorry, I just don't see the conflict here." Likewise, I don't see the conflict Matalene insists on. She seems to misconstrue the word "inspired," jumping to the conclusion that it is synonymous with copying. All writers are "inspired" (influenced, affected, shaped) by their reading; I (and many others) argue that we learn to write primarily by reading, so what she's describing is not all that different from what "we Westerners" do and what we acquire when we read a text. Yet, Matalene states positively that "Western rhetoric is only Western" (790), the implication being that Eastern rhetoric is only Eastern. Well, maybe yes, maybe no. Perhaps the twain can meet. We can choose to look at difference or we can choose to look at similarity (to-may-to, to-mah-to . . .), so the question is more one of focus and emphasis than of difference. Imitation, or observational learning, has an important role not only in Eastern but also in Western rhetorical tradition, not to mention its being a basic element of many other kinds of learning—artists and dancers, for instance, often begin by imitating but then go on to do their own "original" work.

Matalene argues that Chinese rhetoric stresses "repeating set phrases and maxims, following patterns, and imitating texts" (804). However, we might ask how different that is to writing a "thesis-driven argument" in a first-year composition class, with the thesis statement firmly at the end of the first paragraph and a topic sentence starting each subsequent one, or to writing the results of an experiment in psychology using APA format, with its rigid directives about organization and tone, and its typical conclusion calling for the need for more research. What is writing a sonnet or a limerick if not following a rigid pattern? As well, don't politicians and public speakers (not to mention the rest of us) commonly "repeat set phrases and maxims"?

Classical Western rhetoric has a long tradition of focusing on imitation as a method of student learning, and more recently, many other scholars have looked at its role in initiating students into an unfamiliar discourse. One notable example is David Bartholomae. In his essay "Inventing the University," Bartholomae addresses many of the problems students face as "outsiders" in the academic discourse communities in which they are expected to write; as he puts it, "Every time a student sits down to write for [a teacher], he has to invent the university" (589). What he means is that students have to learn not just the "content" of a discipline, whether history or economics or anthropology, but they have to learn to speak, write, and think like historians or economists or anthropologists; they have to learn, among other things, the assumptions and values of a given discourse community as well as its vocabulary. In short, students—like all of us—have to understand the needs and expectations of their audience; but— students must do these things before they are ready to do so because, as Bartholomae says, "speaking and writing will most certainly be required long before the skill is 'learned'" (590). Students need not only attempt to write and speak in a language and a discourse community that is unfamiliar to them, to learn the conventions and formulae taken for granted by the members of that community, but they also need to summon the courage, even the audacity, to do so; they have to crack the code, so to speak, and they have to be bold and daring enough even to take on the challenge.

Learning about audience, for example, is a vital part of a student's task of "inventing the university"; Bartholomae calls the problem of audience one of "power and finesse" (595). Similarly, in their article "On Students' Rights to Their Own Texts: A Model of Teacher Response," Lil Brannon and C. H. Knoblauch argue that the usual relationship between readers and writers is one in which the reader acknowledges a writer's authority and has faith in his or her choices to create a coherent text. We grant this authority to a writer, at least provisionally, and in doing so, we assume that any problems we have in comprehending a text are due to our own shortcomings, not to the writer's deficiencies. Clearly, in the classroom this relationship between reader and writer is inverted: authority resides with the reader, not the writer, and the teacher (reader) rather than the student writer may be the one making decisions about a text (158). Students have to write for an audience (their teachers) who surpass them in both "power and finesse," all the while being judged and evaluated by them not as equals, as colleagues in the academic endeavor, but as novices or even upstarts. As Bartholomae says, "The student has to assume privilege without having any" (598), a daunting prospect, particularly for multilingual students uncertain about their command of English.

Therefore, not surprisingly, imitation and patchwriting become even more important tools for novice writers to employ. According to Bartholomae, students' papers "don't begin with a moment of insight [. . . but] with a moment of appropriation" (600). He tells of his own experience as a graduate student when he would "begin papers by sitting down to write literally in the voice—with the syntax and the key words—of the strongest teacher I had met" (600). The fact that Bartholomae, a white male native English-speaking graduate student, felt the need to appropriate his teacher's prose style demonstrates the way imitation is inherent in the process of entering a new discourse community, even for people well-versed and comfortable in their use of language.

In the academic sphere and elsewhere, the "set phrases, maxims, and patterns" Matalene refers to constitute what Bartholomae calls "acceptable commonplaces." A commonplace is "a culturally or institutionally authorized concept or statement that carries with it its own necessary elaboration" (592). In other words, the concept or statement is "self-explanatory," or at least believed to be understood as self-explanatory within the discourse community in which it is used. In writing classes, for example, teachers may use terms, or commonplaces, like "thesis" or "argument," they assume are understood and shared by their students; they might ask students to "develop" a paragraph or an idea or to "focus" their argument more clearly in the belief that students know what these terms mean, that students understand the perceived problems or weaknesses their teachers are asking them to address, and that they know how to address them. Complicating matters is the fact that students do not always understand these terms in the same ways their teachers do. Furthermore, some of these "commonplaces," notably "argument," are often understood differently among professionals themselves, whether within the larger, cross-disciplinary academic community or in the narrower one of writing teachers. To some, the word argument may denote a very narrow "pro and con" issue or question; to others, it may have the broader meaning of any well-reasoned position. If even "insiders" disagree about the commonplaces (which is all but inevitable), it is not difficult to imagine the problems "outsiders" face in their attempts to negotiate and use those commonplaces.

All discourse communities and languages make use of these idioms or commonplaces; knowing a language, or more exactly becoming a member of a discourse community, involves becoming familiar with the commonplaces, often easily dismissed by outsiders as "jargon." One person's jargon is another person's technical or professional language, however. This is where Bartholomae's concept of "inventing the university" comes into play: Students new to the university learn to mimic their professors.

> They have to appropriate (or be appropriated by) a specialized discourse, and they have to do this as though they were easily and comfortably one with their audience, as though they were members of the academy [. . .] they have to invent the university by assembling and mimicking its language, finding some compromise between idiosyncrasy, a personal history, and the requirements of convention. (590)

The challenge Bartholomae describes is one that all students face, not only those for whom English is a first language but also those for whom it is a second, third, or fourth language. One of these students' tasks is to learn what constitutes a "commonplace," and to do so by "mimicking its language." For instance, the advice of most handbooks about avoiding plagiarism includes the dictum that anything taken from another source must be cited—anything, that is, except "common knowledge." Common to whom, though? In academic writing, what is common to one audience may be completely unfamiliar and impenetrable to another less specialized audience. Knowing what constitutes common knowledge and what therefore does or does not have to be cited thus becomes far more complicated and involved than it would otherwise appear. It requires the time and experience to develop an intimate knowledge of a subject.

The misguided propensity to present students, particularly multilingual students, with these kinds of "clear" and "simple" rules for writing is prompted, no doubt, by good intentions, perhaps the desire to make students' lives easier, or to make writing more comprehensible and less mysterious and frightening for them. Unfortunately, it has, I think, exactly the opposite effect. When teachers or handbooks present neat, easy lists of steps to follow in citing sources and documenting one's findings, the result is that when students struggle with these things—*all* students, first and second language speakers of English alike—they often believe the fault lies in them rather than in the inherent difficulties of the tasks. Students assume the problem is their own lack of intelligence or lack of facility with language, the same syndrome that causes one to believe oneself to be a "bad writer" or just "not good in English."

Similarly, Matalene's purpose in writing her essay is presumably to explain and ameliorate cross-cultural perplexity and the discomfort or even distrust that can arise when people of differing backgrounds meet in the classroom—surely an admirable goal; but when one looks for "evidence" through the kind of essentializing frame that Matalene has constructed, one sees what one wants to see, what one expects to see, and one can't see what one doesn't look for. What results is the essentializing (or stereotyping) of a population, even though it may be for a "positive" reason rather than a "negative" one.

Granted, Matalene was "on the ground" (to use a journalistic set phrase) in China, but her brief and limited experience—teaching fifty English majors for one semester—led her to draw conclusions and make rather broad generalizations about a vast, and vastly disparate, people and culture comprising many different languages and dialects. In his essay "To Capture the Essence of Chinese Rhetoric: An Anatomy of a Paradigm in Comparative Rhetoric," Yameng Liu identifies the "methodological flaws" (323) of Matalene's work and that of other Western scholars who have attempted to define the "essence" of "Asian rhetoric." As he says, "[T]here is a mismatch between the textual/experimental data base and the scope of their generalizations" (323). Beyond his concern with Matalene's use of what might be called a statistically insignificant sample on which to base her conclusions, Liu posits a less benign aspect to her argument than simply overgeneralizing; he finds "[. . .] something not quite plausible in her pairing into neat dichotomies of antinomic concepts such as originality versus conventionality, rationality versus assertive discourse, cogency versus repetitive indirection, with the Chinese rhetoric consistently associated with the negative terms" (319). Matalene's pairs of opposites, in other words, assign the more favorable, flattering qualities to Western rhetoric, and the less favorable ones to Chinese rhetoric.

The attitudes of people who don't anticipate or who refuse to accommodate cultural differences at all concern me; as our world gets smaller, shortsighted and chauvinistic notions about cultural superiority can be not only offensive but also dangerous. I'm equally concerned, however, by the positive pronouncements about the beliefs of another culture voiced by people who may or may not possess sufficient familiarity with it to comprehend the subtleties of its system of values. Confident assertions like "Asian students don't believe such and so," or "Middle Eastern students think this and that" should rightfully arouse our intellectual suspicions, because, although statements like these may have noble intentions meant to foster understanding and tolerance, they are nonetheless misleading and inaccurate, and the effect is ultimately condescending or even demeaning. Such statements reveal an attitude that suggests that other cultures are transparent and simple enough to be easily apprehended and effortlessly summed up in a few words, and they create an "us and them" mindset, putting the complexities of "my culture" against the simplicities of "yours." This kind of mythologizing of students (or of anyone), regardless of intent, is a subtle and pernicious breed of stereotype, and it promotes the same brand of illusory cultural and moral superiority, not to mention intellectual laziness, that most teachers otherwise purport to spend so much time unteaching. The quote by Erich Fromm that opens this chapter suggests that while one ought to be puzzled and ask questions about cultural or linguistic differences, one also should be wary of "the right answers." Too often those answers lead people to conclude, along with the Greeks described in the second quote, that their own nobility is assured, and any social injustices that result may be unfortunate but nonetheless warranted.

Rather than creating and tacitly accepting questionable and condescending narratives about the beliefs or practices of various groups or, at the other extreme, denying any possibility of differences in rhetorical assumptions and the confusion they might create, teachers and students need to meet somewhere in the middle. In particular, teachers need to create a safe haven for students in which to read and write and to learn for themselves how to enter the academic conversation, to use Mike Rose's term. A safe haven is necessary for all student writers, but arguably, it is especially critical for students who don't speak English as a first language. These students are struggling to cope not just with the material covered in a course but also with a new culture and a new language—they must "invent the culture" and the language—even as they "invent the university." To help students in their struggles, teachers need to recognize the complexities and contradictions in the use of citation practices and the resulting confusion for everyone about what plagiarism really is (and isn't); teachers can endeavor to help *all* students grasp this subtle and complicated aspect of learning the "second language" of academic discourse.

In addition to understanding the difficulties with which all writers cope of trying to avoid accusations of plagiarism, teachers have an ethical responsibility to sensitize themselves to the additional problems faced by multilingual students. This doesn't mean that teachers must become experts in every nuance of every rhetorical tradition on the planet, but they can avoid making sweeping generalizations about the beliefs or practices of unfamiliar cultures or discourse communities (including those in neighboring departments on our own campuses). Further, focusing on the similarities of cross-cultural rhetorical conventions rather than their perceived differences could make it easier for students to build on what they know. Teachers can be sensitive to differences, yet still emphasize the aspects of contending with academic discourse that different rhetorical traditions might have in common, and they can endeavor to be aware of the intricacies of the second language of academic discourse for all students (and many teachers, too), anticipating the possibilities of linguistic and cultural differences.

It's a two-way street, though. Like teachers, students have an ethical responsibility to take on the challenges presented in learning the "second language" of academic discourse, regardless of the first language they speak at home. Like any language, academic discourse is comprised of its own idioms, conventions, and vocabulary. Learning the "content" of a discipline is dependent on learning the "accepted commonplaces" of academic discourse—the ways that scholars talk to each other, the assumptions they make, and the often specialized vocabulary and structures they use to convey their messages. In the same way that knowing a language means knowing not just vocabulary and grammar but also the idioms and cultural assumptions that native speakers of a language comprehend intuitively, assimilating academic discourse means knowing not just the punctuation and format of a citation style but also the conventions that govern what to cite and why.

Entering and participating in this ongoing academic conversation is never easy, and the hard work required to gain admission to the academic community is unavoidable. Consequently, teachers have an ethical responsibility to extend the invitation to join the academic community and to ease students' entry by introducing *all* students, first- or second-language speakers of English alike, to the language, assumptions, and secret handshakes of the academic discourse community. Likewise, students have the responsibility to do the hard work of learning to appropriate, ethically and conscientiously, the words and ideas of others.

NOTES

1. I find it necessary to acknowledge that the terms "ESL" and "ESL students" are not without their complications; at this writing, they've been largely replaced by the term "ELL," for English language learner, an acronym I don't like, as I think we're *all* English language learners.

2. For a fuller discussion of this phenomenon, see Alice S. Horning's *Teaching Writing as a Second Language.*

3. For more details and discussion of the survey results, see Lise Buranen's "But I *Wasn't* Cheating: Plagiarism and Cross-Cultural Mythology," in *Perspectives on Plagiarism and Intellectual Property in a Postmodern World.*

Works Cited

Bartholomae, David. "Inventing the University." *Cross-Talk in Comp Theory*. Ed. Victor Villanueva, Jr. Urbana: National Council of Teachers of English, 1997. 589–619. Print.

Brannon, Lil, and C. H. Knoblauch. "On Students' Rights to Their Own Texts: A Model of Teacher Response." *College Composition and Communication* 32 (May 1982): 157–66. Print.

Buranen, Lise. "But I *Wasn't* Cheating: Plagiarism and Cross-Cultural Mythology." *Perspectives on Plagiarism and Intellectual Property in a Postmodern World*. Ed. Lise Buranen and Alice Roy. Albany: SUNY P, 1999. 63–74. Print.

Colombo, Gary, Robert Cullen, and Bonnie Lisle. *Rereading America*. Boston, MA: Bedford/St. Martin's, 2004. Print.

Fromm, Erich. *The Forgotten Language*. New York: Grove Press, 1951. Print.

Horning, Alice S. *Teaching Writing as a Second Language*. Carbondale: Southern Illinois UP, 1987. Print.

Liu, Yameng. "To Capture the Essence of Chinese Rhetoric: An Anatomy of a Paradigm in Comparative Rhetoric." *Rhetoric Review* 14 (Spring 1996): 318–35. Print

Matalene, Carolyn. "Contrastive Rhetoric: An American Writing Teacher in China." *College English* 47 (1985): 789–808. Print.

Rose, Mike. *Lives on the Boundary*. New York: Penguin, 1989. Print.

Questions for Discussion

1. In her discussion of the "fear" of plagiarism that is common to native and ESL or ELL students, Lise Buranen draws a parallel: "Students assume the problem is their own lack of intelligence or lack of facility with language, the same syndrome that causes one to believe oneself to be a 'bad writer' or just 'not good in English.'" In what ways might being a "bad writer" and "not good in English" present very different power struggles?

2. In many universities, ESL or ELL students are placed in separate first-year writing classes so that they can get extra help to, as Buranen states, understand "the 'second language' of academic discourse." What are some of the advantages and disadvantages of separating students in this way, especially in light of helping them understand principles of academic integrity?

12 Thinking Globally about Plagiarism: International Academic Writers' Perspectives

Anne-Marie Pedersen

Before You Read: *In what ways might the privilege of Western culture make avoiding plagiarism easier?*

Although teachers and students alike often assume avoiding plagiarism is as easy as following the rules in writing handbooks, studies of academic writers from around the world suggest otherwise. These studies demonstrate that incorporating words or ideas from other sources (including academic articles, books, and newspaper articles) is a complex and challenging task for people who speak English as a second or foreign language or who live outside the United States. The problems often begin with definitions of plagiarism. What people in the United States call plagiarism might be perfectly acceptable writing to people in other cultures. In addition to competing ideas of appropriate writing, other factors complicate accusations of plagiarism for global writers. The contexts in which writers grow, learn, live, and work affect how they use sources and perceive plagiarism.

In this chapter I offer an overview of scholarship on plagiarism and global English writers, a topic of growing interest as English becomes more widely used in academic writing around the world. I begin with the role of culture in plagiarism, a factor many researchers have held responsible for plagiarism in the writing of non-native English speakers. Recently, however, some researchers have pointed to other important factors, including level of English, resources, and classroom experiences. I explore all these factors, drawing both on other researchers' studies and on my own study of academic writers in the Middle East. I do this to demonstrate that plagiarism, similar to any other issue in writing, is complex and cannot be explained through one simple cause and effect relationship. While the main goal of this chapter is to study plagiarism in a global context, the chapter has implications for understanding writing in the U.S.. By studying why people from outside the U.S. intentionally or unintentionally plagiarize, we learn a great deal about the network of factors that shape all writing situations, including our own.

CULTURAL BELIEFS AND PLAGIARISM

How we conceive of plagiarism stems in part from our culture's beliefs about appropriate ways for writers to interact with the texts that influence their work. The practice in the United States of citing ideas or words to avoid plagiarism occurs within the framework of the Western capitalist economy and of private ownership of property—including intellectual property. In the West, and especially in the U.S., people tend to think of authors as individual owners of the words and ideas in their texts. As owners, writers have the right to receive a reward for their work, whether it's a grade from a teacher or money from people who buy the authored texts. In the case of professors who publish their research, the reward may be promotion—moving from assistant to associate professor, for example.

Although people in the United States often take this understanding of authorship for granted, in other cultures writers work with different notions of text and authorship. Helen Fox argues that the expectations for academic writing in "individualist societies," such as U.S. society, may confuse students who come from "collectivist cultures" (36). Individualist cultures, including the U.S., privilege each person's rights, while collectivist cultures, for example communist China, emphasize the needs and rights of the community. Fan Shen, who moved from China to the United States for college, describes the difficult transition from writing for a collectivist culture to writing for an individualist one. Shen begins by comparing an experience in China to one in the United States, and then explains how this relates to writing:

> One day in June 1975, when I walked into the air-
> craft factory where I was working as an electrician, I
> saw many large-letter posters on the walls and many

> people parading around the workshops shouting slo-
> gans like "Down with the word 'I'!" and "Trust in
> masses and the Party!" I then remembered that a new
> political campaign called "Against Individualism"
> was scheduled to begin that day. Ten years later, I got
> back my first paper at the University of Nebraska-
> Lincoln. The professor's first comments were: "Why
> did you always use 'we' instead of 'I'?" (459)

As a student, Shen quickly noticed the contrasting audience expectations: The ideal perspective in communist China was "we" with
knowledge and experience drawn from the community, while the ideal
one in the United States was "I" with knowledge drawn from personal
experience.

Fox argues that these different cultural expectations can affect plagiarism, and can explain why student writers from collectivist cultures
may not understand the need to document sources:

> In a world where your thoughts, feelings, and experi-
> ences are inextricably connected to those of others,
> why would it be so important to sort out whose idea
> is whose? When the words of others may be so similar
> to your own sometimes that they might be said to *be*
> your own, then isn't it a little exaggerated to say that
> using somebody's particular word choice constitutes
> "theft"? (37)

Fox argues convincingly for the type of logic that may lead some international students to plagiarize unintentionally.

Conflicting ideas about good writing have the potential to cause
serious problems for international students in the United States. Kathryn Valentine offers the case study of Lin, a Chinese PhD student in
the U.S., who didn't understand the need to document sources in a
class presentation. Lin's professor accused him of plagiarism, while Lin
claimed that he had not plagiarized but had simply misinterpreted the
professor's expectations for source documentation. Based on his experiences with constructing an identity as an honest student in China,
Lin assumed that his instructor did not want him to cite sources directly in his presentation: He assumed that the teacher preferred to
infer the citations and believed that the purpose of the assignment was
"to show the professor his familiarity with these sources" (100).

BEYOND CULTURAL DIFFERENCE

Although Valentine focuses on cultural beliefs, other factors likely
came into play in the accusation of plagiarism: Lin's misunderstand-
ing of a new genre (a presentation rather than a written text) and his
unfamiliarity with the higher expectations for PhD students versus
expectations for master's students. It is often difficult to separate student writers' beliefs about classroom expectations from their cultural
beliefs about authorship, as the types of classrooms in which student
writers learn vary depending on the cultural context in which they
grew up. In addition, students often identify with more than one national, ethnic, and linguistic culture. With the advent of a globalized
economy and new communication technologies that allow people all
over the world to exchange information rapidly and constantly, people
rarely live in cultural isolation. Some researchers argue that attributing students' plagiarism to non-Western, or non-American, cultural
backgrounds ignores today's rapid and constant cultural exchange.
Arguments about culturally determined causes of plagiarism also ignore the fact that many academic writers across the globe are familiar
with Western and American ideas about plagiarism and intellectual
property, even if they live outside the West.

   This was certainly the case with the participants in my study of
Arab students and scholars in Jordan. For my study, I interviewed
twenty-seven Arabic speaking graduate students, professors, and researchers about their research writing practices. The study participants
belonged to a variety of disciplines, from education to archaeology,
but all of them researched and wrote primarily in English, a result
of English's dominance in international scholarship. I asked participants about their past and present experiences with academic writing
to learn what conditions might encourage plagiarism in researchers
who live in a non-Western culture and who speak English as second
language. Although these writers worked in a culture that is less individualistic than the United States, the writers often felt at ease with the
expectations of a typical American academic audience. Some writers
had lived in Jordan all their lives, attended only Jordanian schools, but
had studied under so many professors with degrees from the U.S. that
they saw American academic culture as their own culture.

   Joel Bloch has found a similar situation in the work of some Chinese writers. Bloch argues that Chinese researchers are becoming very

aware of American definitions of plagiarism in an effort to compete in the Western science market. Although they understand expectations for Western academic writing, they did not always choose to meet these expectations. Bloch interviewed Chinese graduate students in the applied and social sciences and concluded that rather than lacking appreciation or understanding of intellectual property or private authorship, the Chinese student writers simply had different writing preferences. These students' beliefs about appropriate documentation also varied depending on the genre of writing. In some cases, the students preferred seamless interweaving of words (without interruptions by citation); other times (in an article for publication, for example) they thought it important to pay more attention to giving information about different studies.

POLITICAL AND LINGUISTIC DOMINANCE AND PLAGIARISM

While many Arab and Chinese writers are quite familiar with English and with academic writing in the United States, writers in the U.S. often know little of other countries' languages and indigenous academic cultures. Although we live in a world with unprecedented potential for the transglobal exchange of information, ideas, and goods, in reality the exchange is rarely balanced. Instead, the English language and Western culture exert more than their fair share of power across the globe, which causes some global writers to resent English and Western culture. Some researchers argue that this imbalance of cultural exchange is yet another factor in cases of plagiarism. They argue that students from outside the West may plagiarize in their writing as intentional acts of political resistance against the domination of Western culture and the English language. These students may come from countries with a history of Western colonialism, where English is associated with a violent and oppressive imperialist past. Fox describes how some international students who come to the United States to study resist American ways of writing research papers, including American ways of documentation, in an attempt to counter the pressure to assimilate. These students fear that writing for professors who assume that the American approach to academic writing is the best and only approach may cause the students to forget the communicative styles valued in their home cultures.

Other research suggests that writers may plagiarize to compensate for a lack of English proficiency. Despite poor English skills, these writers feel compelled to write in the dominant global language, English, in order to publish internationally. Spanish scholars in M. St. John's study plagiarized to hide what they perceived as their lack of English proficiency—they copied to ensure that their English was correct. Sharon Myers also argues that English proficiency affects how second-language writers use sources, but unlike St. John, Myers links this to the geopolitics of English. Myers views many of the rules for citation that non-Western scholars must follow in order to publish in prestigious Western English-language journals as ethnocentric, privileging American or Western culture above all others, and discriminatory to writers across the world who learn English as a second language. To prove this point, Myers discusses the case of an Asian scientist accused of plagiarizing the wording of a lab procedure description in a published article, a case that was originally reported by Li Xiguang and Xiong Lei. According to Myers, the writer responded that as a non-native speaker of English, he needed help in phrasing his ideas but that the data and findings in the article were his and were new. Still, he was punished and ridiculed by a scientific community that Myers argues is overly concerned with native-like English and with adhering to Western definitions of plagiarism.

MATERIAL CONDITIONS AS A CAUSE OF PLAGIARISM

Other researchers point to the different living conditions, or material conditions, outside the U.S. to explain why some writers might unintentionally plagiarize. Suresh Canagarajah studies scholars in developing nations, and suggests that the difficult conditions under which these scholars write affect how they use and document sources. For example, in his home university in Jaffna, Sri Lanka, a civil war turned basic tools of scholarship (such as mail service) into precious resources available only irregularly (8–9). According to Canagarajah, scholars in Jaffna often cited key sources incorrectly because they did not have direct access to them or had only limited access to the sources and were unable to view them a second time (130–31). While not citing key sources correctly could be read as plagiarism, working in a war zone is a circumstance that readers should take into account in their judgment of the texts.

In my own study of plagiarism and research writing in Jordan, I found that material conditions had the potential to promote plagiarism. The writers I interviewed described situations in which economic need led to poor quality research—and sometimes to plagiarism. Dr. Hasan, an engineering professor, described how some professors published anything just to receive promotion and economic benefit: "It's hard really for many of the professors, so they try to improve their economic condition, but it's not just the economic condition. It's when they are under the pressure of promotion they just try to produce anything rather than focusing on quality issues or research" (156). Beyond poor quality, research articles by professors under pressure may be wholly plagiarized, as professors sometimes put their names on research articles to which they claim to have contributed, when in reality they played no part in the research or the research writing. Dr. Hasan explained: "Because you are under the pressure, it's common that, okay, you put my name on that article, I will put your name on that article. And so you double or triple or quadruple your publications, and you get promoted easily" (156). A few other participants offered tales in which people plagiarized intentionally in order to advance professionally and felt justified in doing so because the conditions for working as an academic in Jordan are difficult: Professors' salaries and funding for research materials are low and their teaching loads are heavy. In addition, requirements for promotion are relatively high: Professors must publish in competitive international journals and in English, a second language. Participants in my study hypothesized that some professors claimed authorship over texts that they had not written because they saw no other way to meet promotion expectations, and in a country with a high unemployment rate, such as Jordan, losing a job as a professor may mean losing all hope for a living wage.

POOR TEACHING AND PLAGIARISM

Even more than material conditions, poor teaching had an impact on source use and plagiarism in Jordan. The participants often blamed plagiarism on high school and bachelor's degree programs that involved very little writing, other than exams and reports, and thus offered few opportunities to practice proper citation and documentation. Aliyah, a chemical engineering master's student, admitted that she had no practical experience writing from other writers' texts until she began her master's degree program: "I don't have experiences. This is my first time to make a thesis. 'Cause, you know, we have projects in the last year of college [...] we have a project but usually the project is much, much simpler than the thesis. Simpler. And they don't take too much care about the language" (171). When I asked Dr. Sulyman, an architecture professor, if he had learned about plagiarism in his bachelor's degree program, he responded similarly:

> Not at the bachelor, unfortunately, because [. . .] when I studied architecture, there was not so much emphasis on writing. In fact, this is one of the major disadvantages in our universities at the bachelor level. There is no emphasis whatsoever on writing styles, on ethics of writing, and on issues like plagiarism and so on and so forth. (162)

Dr. Hasan also characterized the educational system in Jordan as one that encourages repetition and memorization rather than critical thinking and the synthesis of ideas:

> When you see the way [. . .] education is commenced in Jordan, for example, the teachers are underpaid; many of them are not committed. It's for them like a five hour job. It's not really something that they believe in doing [. . .] And the way they teach is by memorizing. It's not really by encouraging students to [. . .] understand issues and try to imagine [. . .] or find solutions to problems. And this leads to students [. . .] that are like parrots. (162)

Many participants argued that this type of writing instruction encourages students to plagiarize unintentionally because it never teaches students that copying someone else's words without citing them constitutes plagiarism.

Poor teaching is a problem for foreign students globally—even in the United States Pat Currie offers a case study of a native Cantonese-speaking student to prove that culture may not be the main cause of international students' plagiarism. More than cultural norms, some teachers' impossibly high expectations for international students encourage plagiarism. In Currie's example, a teaching assistant gave the students' early assignments, which were not plagiarized and had errors typical of second-language, negative feedback. This same teacher gave later assignments that were partially plagiarized from the course textbook positive feedback—thereby unintentionally encouraging plagiarism. Further to the point that culture may not be the main cause of plagiarism in international students' writing, Lise Buranen conducted a study of ESL students' attitudes toward plagiarism and discovered that across cultures, ESL students condemned plagiarism. She also found that when asked directly, the students in her study did not perceive a difference between what they had learned about plagiarism in their home countries and what they had learned about it in the United States.

CONCLUSION: CULTURE'S COMPLEX ROLE IN CASES OF PLAGIARISM

Although some researchers have argued that differing cultural beliefs about authorship and intellectual property lead students from outside the United States to plagiarize, other research demonstrates that material conditions, language skills, and educational experiences are equally important in deciding how writers use sources. This was certainly the case in my own research. While I went to Jordan assuming that cultural differences would play a large role in cases of plagiarism, I discovered that most of the academic writers to whom I spoke had ideas about authorship and plagiarism that were very similar to those in the U.S. Rather than differing cultural beliefs, lack of resources for researchers and teachers led to an atmosphere where plagiarism was seen as unethical but often necessary for educational and professional survival.

While we, teachers and students, should be aware of the way cultural and material differences across the globe affect writing, we should not assume that people from other cultures are any more likely to plagiarize than native English speakers in the U.S. The writers in my study in Jordan were adamant about preventing plagiarism in their own work and in the work of colleagues and students. Aisha, a master's student in Jordan at the time of my study, is just one example: She felt her education did not prepare her to use sources effectively and ethically, so she sought information on plagiarism and citation practices on her own. She found mentors in her field to advise her and read books on ethics in scientific research. In her interview, she explained how her concern over plagiarism stemmed from a sense of audience expectations. She worried that if she published her thesis, the authors of the sources she used would likely read and evaluate her work: "You have to publish your result(s) to the world and many professors and researchers will take a look." If she weren't careful in her source-use practices, she would make a poor impression on these readers, her colleagues.

As the number of researchers across the globe who write in English and publish for an international audience grows, these writers' impact on expectations for appropriate source use and definitions for plagiarism also grows. Eventually the debate about culture and plagiarism may become moot as expectations for source use become global, unattached to one particular culture or even language. Already international scholars share much in common with U.S. scholars in terms of plagiarism, even as they face unique conditions and restraints in their work. Many of these writers, including Aisha, already view themselves not as outsiders in a U.S.-dominated world of scholarship but as insiders in the world of globally interconnected scholars. Teachers and students should keep this in mind when considering the role culture plays in cases of plagiarism, paying attention not only to cultural contexts but also to cultural exchange.

WORKS CITED

Bloch, Joel. "Plagiarism and the ESL Student: From Printed to Electronic Texts." *Linking Literacies.* Ed. Diane Belcher and Alan Hirvela Belcher. Ann Arbor: U Michigan P, 2001. 209–28. Print.

Buranen, Lise. "'But I Wasn't Cheating': Plagiarism and Cross-Cultural Mythology." *Perspectives on Plagiarism and Intellectual Property in a Postmodern World.* Ed. Lise Buranen and Alice Roy. Albany, NY: SUNY P, 1999. 63–74. Print.

Canagarajah, Suresh. *The Geopolitics of Academic Literacy and Knowledge Production.* Pittsburgh, PA: UP Pittsburgh, 2003. Print.

Currie, Pat. "Staying out of Trouble: Apparent Plagiarism and Academic Survival." *Journal of Second Language Writing* 7.1 (1998): 1–18. Print.

Fox, Helen. *Listening to the World: Cultural Issues in Academic Writing.* Urbana, IL: National Council of Teachers of English, 1994. Print.

Myers, Sharon. "Questioning Author(Ity): ESL/EFL, Science, and Teaching About Plagiarism." *TESL-Electronic Journal* 3.2 (1998). Web. 8 November 2006.

Pedersen, Anne-Marie. "Globalized Research Writing in Jordan: Negotiating English Language and Culture." Diss. University of Louisville, 2007. Print.

Shen, Fan. "The Classroom and the Wider Culture: Identity as a Key to Learning English Composition." *College Composition and Communication* 40.4 (1989): 459–66. Print.

St. John, M. "Writing Processes of Spanish Scientists Publishing in English." *English for Specific Purposes* 6 (1987): 113–20. Print.

Valentine, Kathryn. "Plagiarism as Literacy Practice: Recognizing and Rethinking Ethical Binaries." *College Composition and Communication* 58.1 (2006): 89–109. Print.

Xiguang, Li, and Xiong Lei. "Chinese Researchers Debate Rash of Plagiarism Cases." *Science Magazine* 18 October 1996: 337–38. Print.

QUESTIONS FOR DISCUSSION

1. If, as Anne-Marie Pedersen suggests, "The English language and Western culture exert more than their fair share of power across the globe," will globalization change the ways plagiarism is generally defined across the world? If so, how? If not, why?

2. Consider Pedersen's discussion of "the imbalance of cultural exchange" and plagiarism as an act of political resistance against American culture. How does this resistance complicate composition and rhetoric as a field? What is the role of the field in addressing this resistance?

Part III
Synthesizing What You've Read

1. Rachel Knaizer, Lise Buranen, and Anne-Marie Pedersen all discuss how plagiarism becomes a much more complicated issue for students whose first language is not English, or whose native culture is not American, but Bridget M. Marshall points out that even in American popular culture plagiarism gets misconstrued significantly. What do these cultural misunderstandings suggest about how plagiarism is defined/taught in the academy and how it is translated outside of the academy?

2. Marshall argues that responses to plagiarism are all about the audience; Knaizer notes the importance of context and who *owns* words—our use of language is always tied up with the context in which we learn and hear the words. Buranen and Pedersen introduce the complexities of plagiarism for non-native speakers in a classroom. After reading the essays in this part, consider whether it's really possible to *own* words. Explore the notion of ownership between a culture, its people, and its texts.

IN PRACTICE

1. In Part III, you read about how "outsiders" may interpret American notions of ownership of language and about how Americans interpret the textual practices of non-Americans. Part III also illustrates some of the ways plagiarism is seen as dangerous ground for ESL students or ELLs, and for students whose native culture is non-Western. In her chapter, Buranen argues, "In particular, teachers (and administrators) need to create a safe haven for students in which to read and write and to learn for themselves how to enter the academic conversation." How might a teacher begin to create for ESL students and ELLs the kind

of "safe" atmosphere that Buranen calls for? Working in groups, create a presentation, lesson, or classroom policy statement about plagiarism that addresses the needs of ESL speakers, ELLs, as well as native English speakers. As you work, keep in mind what it means to "create a safe haven" in the classroom.

2. How do postsecondary institutions around the world rhetorically construct their rules around academic integrity? Working with a partner, visit several college/university websites around the world (including the U.S.), and see if you can find their statements on academic integrity. Conduct some rhetorical analysis: Where are the statements located? Who are their authors? How are they worded? What messages are they sending? Next, looking even more closely at the language of these statements, compare/contrast the different statements you've located. You might look for specific similarities in location or wording and "code" them accordingly. What conclusions do you draw about how plagiarism is defined around the world?

About the Editors and Contributors

Lise Buranen is Faculty Director of the University Writing Center at California State University, Los Angeles, where she has taught writing and composition theory since 1988. She has published, with Alice Roy, a book on plagiarism, *Perspectives on Plagiarism and Intellectual Property in a Postmodern World*, and is a contributor (with Denise Stephenson) to *Who Owns This Text?* Her essay, "A Safe Haven: The Role of Librarians and Writing Centers in Addressing Citation Practices and Plagiarism," was the feature article in *Knowledge Quest.*

Dànielle Nicole DeVoss is a professor of professional writing at Michigan State University. Her research interests include computer/technological literacies; feminist interpretations of and interventions in computer technologies; and intellectual property issues in digital space. DeVoss's work has most recently appeared in *Computers and Composition* and *Pedagogy.* DeVoss recently coedited (with Heidi McKee) *Digital Writing Research: Technologies, Methodologies, and Ethical Issues* (Hampton Press, 2007), which won the 2007 Computers and Composition Distinguished Book Award, and coauthored (with the National Writing Project, Elyse Eidman-Aadahl, and Troy Hicks) *Because Digital Writing Matters* (Jossey-Bass, 2011). Martine Courant Rife and DeVoss (along with Shaun Slattery) are the editors of *Copy(write): Intellectual Property in the Composition Classroom* (Parlor Press, 2011), and are currently working on an edited collection titled *Cultures of Copyright.*

Joanna Castner Post is an associate professor of writing and Director of the Writing Center at the University of Central Arkansas, where she teaches courses in composition and professional writing. She has essays in *College Credit for Writing in High School; Small Tech: The Culture of Digital Tools; Technology and English Studies: Innovative Professional Paths;* and *Taking Flight with OWLs.* She has coedited *Compositions in the New Liberal Arts* with James A. Inman.

Michael Donnelly is an assistant professor of English in rhetoric and composition at Ball State University, where he teaches first-year writing, contemporary rhetoric, and composition pedagogy. He served as a writing program administrator for twelve years. His articles have appeared in *PRE/TEXT*; *inventio*; *Reflections*; and the edited collection *Agency in the Margins*.

Deborah Harris-Moore is a lecturer in the Writing Program at University of California, Santa Barbara, where she teaches various writing classes. Her research interests include rhetoric of the body and disability studies, and she has published a related essay in *Rocky Mountain Review*.

Rebecca Ingalls is an assistant professor and Director of the Freshman Writing Program at Drexel University. Her work in composition and cultural rhetoric may be found in *inventio*; *Academe*; *The Review of Education, Pedagogy, and Cultural Studies*; *POROI*; *Harlot*; *Journal of Teaching Writing*; *The Journal of Popular Culture*; and *Writing and Pedagogy* (forthcoming).

Rachel Knaizer is adjunct faculty at University College, University of Denver, where she teaches Graduate Research and Writing. She previously taught courses in Young Adult Literature, Methods of Teaching Writing, and Methods of Teaching Reading at Lehman College.

Bridget M. Marshall is an assistant professor of English at the University of Massachusetts, Lowell, where she teaches courses on the Gothic novel, disability in literature, and American literature. She is the author of *The Transatlantic Gothic Novel and the Law, 1790–1860* (Ashgate, 2011). She is a coeditor, with Monika Elbert, of *Transnational Gothic: Literary and Social Exchanges in the Long Nineteenth Century*, forthcoming from Ashgate, and she is an Assistant Editor for the *Nathaniel Hawthorne Review*.

Phillip Marzluf is an associate professor of English at Kansas State University, where he teaches various courses in composition and rhetoric. His research has appeared in the *Community Literacy Journal*; *Rhetoric Society Quarterly*; *College Composition and Communication*; *Rhetoric Review*; and other journals.

Paul Parker has served in a variety of learning and teaching development roles in higher education over the last twelve years. For nine
of these he taught on and developed resources for academic writing
programs in contexts ranging from university preparation and degree
programs in Australia (undergraduate and postgraduate) to workshops
on English-medium research writing for partner scientists in Vietnam
and Indonesia.

Anne-Marie Pedersen is an assistant professor of English at Chapman
University, where she teaches composition and rhetoric with a focus on
writing centers and writing and identity. Her articles have appeared in
College Composition and Communication; *Writing Center Journal*; and
Across the Disciplines. Her article "Negotiating Cultural Identities
through Language: Academic English in Jordan" won the 2011
Richard Braddock Award.

Martine Courant Rife is a professor of writing at Lansing Community
College where she teaches courses in first-year composition, accelerat-
ed basic writing, technical writing, argumentation, and digital author-
ship. Her research interests include copyright issues as they intersect
with composition studies. Her work has most recently appeared in
Technical Communication. Rife won the 2007 Society for Technical
Communication's (STC) Frank R. Smith Outstanding Journal Article
Award for "Technical Communicators and Digital Writing Risk
Assessment." Rife's forthcoming monograph with Southern Illinois
University Press is *Invention, Copyright, and Digital Writing*.

Esra Mirze Santesso is an assistant professor of English at the
University of Georgia, where she teaches postcolonial literature with
a focus on British imperialism and the South Asian diasporic identity. She has published articles on Turkish literature and film, and her
interview with Orhan Pamuk appeared in *PMLA* (2008). Her current
project, entitled "Disorientations: Muslim Identity in Contemporary
Anglophone Literature," investigates the extent to which the questions
and theories of postcolonial identity can be applied to Muslim subjects
living in the West.

Tracy Ann Morse is an assistant professor in the Department of English
at East Carolina University where she currently serves as the Director

of Writing Foundations. Her work has appeared in *Rhetoric Review*; *Disability Studies*; *inventio*; and *The Journal of Teaching Writing*.

Jessica Reyman is an assistant professor at Northern Illinois University, where she teaches rhetoric and technical communication classes. Her essays have appeared in *College Composition and Communication* and *Technical Communication*, and her book, *The Rhetoric of Intellectual Property: Copyright Law and the Regulation of Digital Culture*, was published by Routledge in 2010.

Richard Schur is the Director of the Law & Society Program and an associate professor of English at Drury University, where he teaches courses on African American literature and American popular culture. He is the author of *Parodies of Ownership: Hip-Hop Aesthetics and Intellectual Property Law* and he coedited *African American Culture and Legal Discourse*.

Anne Meade Stockdell-Giesler is a professional writer and editor as well as former English professor at the University of Tampa and Boston University. She is the editor of *Agency in the Margins: Stories of Outsider Rhetoric* (2010).

Sean Zwagerman is an associate professor of English at Simon Fraser University, where he teaches rhetoric and composition. He has published a book on humor as a rhetorical speech act (*Wit's End: Women's Humor as Rhetorical and Performative Strategy*), and journal articles on humor, plagiarism, and pedagogy.

Index

CPSIA information can be obtained at www.ICGtesting.com
Printed in the USA
BVOW031605051212

307338BV00002B/163/P